普通高等教育车辆工程专业"新工科"建设系列教材

Qiche Zhuanye Yingyu
汽车专业英语

（第 3 版）

黄韶炯　赵建柱　**主　编**
栾志强　李真芳　**副主编**
　　　　王国业　**主　审**

人民交通出版社股份有限公司
北　京

内 容 提 要

本书是"普通高等教育车辆工程专业'新工科'建设系列教材"之一。本书内容以汽车构造为主，并选编了一些有关新能源汽车技术、智能网联汽车技术以及汽车安全新技术等方面的文章。全书共分 20 个单元，每个单元均包括课文、词汇、注释、练习和阅读材料几个部分，叙述通俗易懂、图文并茂。为了便于学习，书中对难词、词组及专业词汇作了注释，各单元后配有练习题，书后附有汽车专业常用英文缩写以及汽车主要零部件词汇表。

本书可作为高等院校汽车类专业的英语课教材，也可供从事汽车工程及相关专业的管理人员和技术人员自学参考。

图书在版编目(CIP)数据

汽车专业英语/黄韶炯,赵建柱主编. —3 版. —北京:人民交通出版社股份有限公司,2022.7
ISBN 978-7-114-18007-1

Ⅰ.①汽… Ⅱ.①黄… ②赵… Ⅲ.①汽车工程—英语—高等学校—教材 Ⅳ.①U46

中国版本图书馆 CIP 数据核字(2022)第 091470 号

书　　名:	汽车专业英语(第 3 版)
著 作 者:	黄韶炯　赵建柱
责任编辑:	钟　伟
责任校对:	孙国靖　魏佳宁
责任印制:	刘高彤
出版发行:	人民交通出版社股份有限公司
地　　址:	(100011)北京市朝阳区安定门外外馆斜街 3 号
网　　址:	http://www.ccpcl.com.cn
销售电话:	(010)59757973
总 经 销:	人民交通出版社股份有限公司发行部
经　　销:	各地新华书店
印　　刷:	北京市密东印刷有限公司
开　　本:	787×1092　1/16
印　　张:	12.75
字　　数:	300 千
版　　次:	2005 年 2 月　第 1 版 2013 年 4 月　第 2 版 2022 年 7 月　第 3 版
印　　次:	2022 年 7 月　第 3 版　第 1 次印刷　总第 15 次印刷
书　　号:	ISBN 978-7-114-18007-1
定　　价:	38.00 元

(有印刷、装订质量问题的图书由本公司负责调换)

普通高等教育车辆工程专业"新工科"建设系列教材

编 委 会

主 任

赵祥模(长安大学)

副主任(按姓名拼音顺序)

陈　南(东南大学)　　　　高振海(吉林大学)　　　　郭应时(长安大学)
黄　彪(北京理工大学)　　刘　杰(湖南大学)　　　　吴光强(同济大学)

委　员(按姓名拼音顺序)

曹立波(湖南大学)　　　　冯崇毅(东南大学)　　　　龚金科(湖南大学)
郭伟伟(北方工业大学)　　韩英淳(吉林大学)　　　　胡兴军(吉林大学)
黄　江(重庆理工大学)　　黄韶炯(中国农业大学)　　李　凡(湖南大学)
李志恒(清华大学)　　　　刘晶郁(长安大学)　　　　鲁植雄(南京农业大学)
栾志强(中国农业大学)　　史文库(吉林大学)　　　　谭继锦(合肥工业大学)
谭堑元(北方工业大学)　　汪贵平(长安大学)　　　　王　方(长沙理工大学)
吴志成(北京理工大学)　　谢小平(湖南大学)　　　　杨　林(北京理工大学)
姚为民(吉林大学)　　　　于海洋(北京航空航天大学)　张　凯(清华大学)
张志沛(长沙理工大学)　　周淑渊(泛亚汽车技术中心)　左曙光(同济大学)

第3版前言
Preface to the third edition

　　为主动应对新一轮科技革命与产业变革,支撑服务创新驱动发展、"中国制造2025"等一系列国家战略,自2017年2月以来,教育部积极推进"新工科"建设,先后形成了"复旦共识""天大行动"和"北京指南",全力探索形成领跑全球工程教育的中国模式、中国经验,助力高等教育强国建设。为顺应"新工科"建设的发展需求,人民交通出版社股份有限公司针对高等院校车辆工程专业课程开设情况进行了充分的调研,并在此基础上,围绕着工程教育改革的新理念、新结构、新模式、新质量、新体系,对原有的车辆工程专业教材进行了全面的调整、修订和增补等,形成了全新的"普通高等教育车辆工程专业'新工科'建设系列教材"。

　　本书于2005年2月首次出版,2013年4月出版第2版,期间多次重印,一直作为汽车类专业的英语课教材。本次修订,除保持第2版的基本结构和基本内容外,主要对以下几个方面进行了补充和调整:

　　(1)针对目前新能源汽车技术、智能网联汽车技术迅猛发展的趋势,本书中增加了混合动力电动汽车、氢动力汽车、智能驾驶辅助系统和网联汽车等内容,可为以后更方便地学习相关新技术提供有益的帮助;

　　(2)增加了自动紧急制动(AEB)和盲点检测(BSD)等汽车新技术的相关内容;

　　(3)受篇幅所限,本次修订删减了汽车纵向动力性、制动性和操纵稳定性的有关内容。

　　第3版由中国农业大学车辆工程系黄韶炯、赵建柱任主编,栾志强、李真芳任副主编。具体分工如下:第8~11单元由栾志强编写,第4~7单元由李真芳编写,第15~18单元由赵建柱编写,其他部分由黄韶炯编写。全书由黄韶炯统稿,由中国农业大学车辆工程系王国业教授主审。此外,本书在编写中得到了曹正清教授、江发潮教授的许多帮助,以及人民交通出版社股份有限公司的大力支持,在此一并表示感谢。

　　最后,殷切希望广大读者对书中的误漏之处,予以批评指正。

编　者

2022年2月

目录 Contents

UNIT 1　AUTOMOTIVE BASICS　1
　Reading Material: Layout of an Automobile　7
UNIT 2　AUTOMOTIVE ENGINE　10
　Reading Material: Valve System　16
UNIT 3　AUTOMOTIVE LUBRICATION SYSTEM　19
　Reading Material: Changing the Oil and the Oil Filter　24
UNIT 4　THE COOLING SYSTEM　26
　Reading Material: Cooling System Maintenance　31
UNIT 5　FUEL INJECTION SYSTEM　34
　Reading Material: Robert Bosch Type VE Diesel Injection Pump　38
UNIT 6　EXHAUST SYSTEM　42
　Reading Material: Emission Control Systems　45
UNIT 7　THE IGNITION SYSTEM　50
　Reading Material: Basics of Engine Management　55
UNIT 8　CLUTCH　60
　Reading Material: Torque Converter　65
UNIT 9　AUTOMATIC TRANSMISSION　69
　Reading Material: The Future of Automotive Transmissions　77
UNIT 10　THE DIFFERENTIAL　81
　Reading Material: The Final Drive　86
UNIT 11　BRAKE SYSTEM　88
　Reading Material: Disk Brake　94
UNIT 12　STEERING SYSTEM　97
　Reading Material: Wheel Alignment　103
UNIT 13　SUSPENSION SYSTEM　106
　Reading Material: An Introduction to Active Suspension Systems　112
UNIT 14　ABS AND TCS　115
　Reading Material: Components of ABS/TCS Units　120
UNIT 15　ADAPTIVE CRUISE CONTROL SYSTEM　123
　Reading Material: Air Bags　130

UNIT 16	ELECTRIC CARS	133
	Reading Material: The Tesla Roadster	139
UNIT 17	HYBRID ELECTRIC VEHICLES	142
	Reading Material: Automatic Emergency Braking (AEB) Systems	147
UNIT 18	FUEL CELL	151
	Reading Material: Hydrogen Cars	156
UNIT 19	ADVANCED DRIVER-ASSISTANCE SYSTEMS	160
	Reading Material: Blind Spot Detection (BSD) System	167
UNIT 20	CONNECTED VEHICLES	171
	Reading Material: Vehicle to Infrastructure Communications	176
APPENDIX A	ABBREVIATIONS OF AUTOMOTIVE ENGLISH	180
APPENDIX B	MAIN CONSTANT AUTOMOBILE PARTS	192
REFERENCES		197

UNIT 1　AUTOMOTIVE BASICS

　　Automobiles, trucks, and buses are essential forms of transportation. They are complex machines made up of many parts. These parts can be grouped into a number of systems. An understanding of how the systems work will help you understand how the automobile works.

　　An automobile can be divided into two basic parts—a body and a chassis(Figure 1-1). The body is the enclosure that houses the engine, passengers, and cargo. It is the part of the automobile that you see. The chassis is that part of the automobile beneath the body.

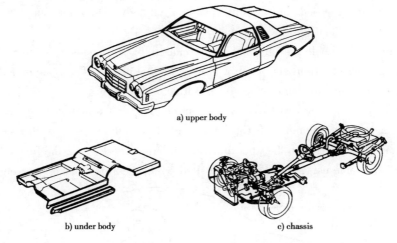

Figure 1-1　*The part of the automobile*

1. The Body

　　An automobile body is a sheet metal shell with windows, doors, a hood, and a trunk deck built into it. It provides a protective covering for the engine, passengers and cargo. The body is designed to keep passengers safe and comfortable. For example, insulation in the body reduces noise and protects against heat and cold. The body styling provides an attractive, colorful, modern appearance for the vehicle. It is streamlined to lessen wind resistance and to keep the car from swaying at driving speeds.

　　The automobile body has two basic parts—the upper body and the under body.

2. The Chassis

　　The chassis is an assembly of those systems that are the major operating parts of a vehicle. The chassis includes everything except the body. The three important parts of the chassis are the frame, the engine, and the power train (also called the drive train). Each of these three parts is made up of a number of systems. A system is a mechanical or electrical unit that performs a specific function. Thus, each system (such as steering, brake, or fuel) has a certain job to do in running a vehicle. We shall look at each of these parts and systems to see how they fit together to form the automobile chassis.

2.1 The Frame

The first major part of the chassis is the frame. It is made from tough steel sections welded, riveted, or bolted together. The frame looks like a steel ladder, though it sometimes has an X shape for extra strength. It forms a foundation for the car body and the parts of the several systems. The body is joined to the frame with bolts. Rubber shock mounts or washers are used at each joint. These reduce vibration and road noise. In most modern cars the frame is built into the body. A car with the frame built into the body has a unitized body or unibody. The frame supports the suspension system, steering system, and braking system.

The front and rear wheels are attached to the chassis by a suspension system. This system is made up of springs, shock absorbers, control arms, and stabilizers. These support the vehicle and cushion it from road bumps for better ride and handling.

The steering system, shown as Figure 1-2, controls the car's direction of travel. It includes a steering wheel, a steering column, steering gears, rods, and linkages. As the steering wheel is turned, its motion is transferred to the idler arm and tie rods. These cause the front wheels to turn to the right or left. On some cars, a power unit (called power steering) makes steering easier.

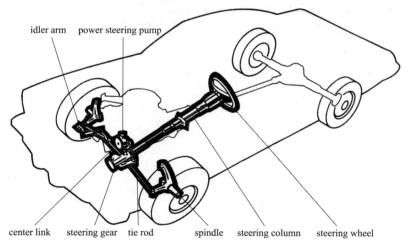

Figure 1-2　The steering system

The brake system gives the automobile stopping power, shown as Figure 1-3. Hydraulic brakes are found on all modern cars. As the brake pedal is pushed with the foot, brake fluid is forced through brake lines into cylinders that press the brake shoes against a drum. This stops the motion of the car. Power units (power brakes) are used to make braking easier. Most modern cars have disc brakes on the front wheels. (Some have them on both the front and rear wheels.) Disc brakes work like a pair of pliers squeezing a rotating disc. Drum brakes are also used.

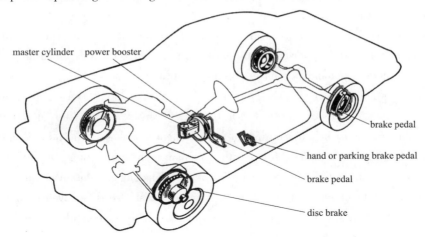

Figure 1-3 The brake system

2.2 The Engine

The engine provides power to move the automobile. The most common type of automotive engine is the gasoline-burning piston engine. It is found in most automobiles. Diesel-fuel burning engines are also used in modern passenger cars, as well as in large trucks. All engines have fuel, exhaust, cooling, and lubrication systems. Gasoline engines also have an ignition system.

The ignition system supplies the electric spark needed to ignite the air-fuel mixture in the cylinders. When the ignition switch is turned on, current flows from the 12-volt storage battery to the ignition coil. The coil boosts the voltage to produce the strong spark of 20,000 V needed to ignite the engine fuel. The distributor directs the electrical current to the right spark plug at the right time. Diesel engines use the heat caused by engine compression to ignite the fuel charge. These engines are called compression ignition engines.

The automobile supplies all the electricity it needs through its electrical system. For example, the electrical system supplies electricity for the ignition, horn, lights, heater, and starter. The electricity level is maintained by a charging circuit. This circuit consists of the battery, alternator (or generator), and the regulator. The battery stores electricity. The alternator changes the engine's mechanical energy into electrical energy and recharges the battery. The regulator prevents damage to the system by regulating the maximum voltage in the circuit.

The fuel system stores liquid fuel and delivers it to the engine. The fuel is stored in the tank, which is connected to a fuel pump by a fuel line. The fuel is pumped from the fuel tank through the fuel lines. It is forced through a filter (which removes moisture and dirt) into the carburetor, where it is mixed with air, or into the fuel injection system. The fuel is mixed with air to form a combustible mixture in the carburetor, the manifold, or the cylinders themselves.

The exhaust system has four jobs:
(a) To collect burned gases from the engine.
(b) To remove dangerous emissions that pollutes the air.

(c) To reduce exhaust noises.

(d) To get rid of the exhaust gases.

Exhaust gases contain carbon monoxide, unburned hydrocarbons, and oxides of nitrogen. Since all of these are harmful, the exhaust system is designed to reduce them as much as possible. In the United States all modern automobiles have emission control systems.

The cooling system removes excessive heat from the engine. The temperature in engine combustion chambers is about 2,000 °F (1,094 °C). Since steel melts at around 2,500 °F (1,354 °C), this heat must be carried away to prevent engine damage. Air and a coolant are used to carry away the heat. The radiator is filled with a coolant. The water pump circulates this coolant through the hollow walls of the engine block and head. Constant circulation of the coolant through the engine and the radiator removes heat from the engine. Heat also is removed by the radiator fan, which draws air through the narrow fins of the radiator. This system also supplies heat to the passenger compartment and the window defrosters.

The lubrication system is important in keeping the engine running smoothly. Motor oil is the lubricant used in the system. The lubrication system has four functions:

(a) It cuts down friction by coating moving parts with oil.

(b) It produces a seal between the piston rings and the cylinder walls.

(c) It carries away sludge, dirt, and acids.

(d) It cools the engine by circulating the motor oil.

To keep this system working efficiently, oil filters and motor oil must be changed regularly. All other moving parts in an automobile must also be lubricated. These include the transmission, differential, wheel bearings, and steering linkage.

2.3 *The Power Train*

The power train, or drive system, delivers power from the engine to the wheels, shown as Figure 1-4. The power from the engine moves through the transmission. Transmissions are either standard, with a manual shift lever and foot clutch, or automatic.

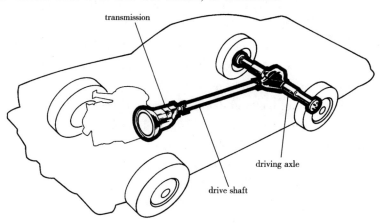

Figure 1-4 *The power train(drive system)*

UNIT 1 AUTOMOTIVE BASICS

  The transmission has gears that control the amount of power delivered to the wheels. The transmission increases the power (torque) to start the car moving. This torque is reduced when the transmission changes gears at higher speeds. The transmission also contains a set of gears that can reverse the direction of the wheels. The transmission delivers the power to the differential. A drive (or propeller) shaft with universal joints at either end of the drive shaft allows axle movement on front-engine, rear-wheel drive cars. These flexible universal joints prevent the drive shaft from breaking. The differential delivers power to the wheels through the axle. Certain gears allow one wheel to turn faster than the other wheel when the vehicle is turning a corner.

  These are the basic systems of the automobile. Each of the systems is designed for a specific job.

NEW WORDS

1.	body	['bɔdi]	n. 车身
2.	chassis	['ʃæsiː, 'tʃæsiː]	n. 底盘
3.	enclosure	[in'kləuʒə]	n. 外壳, 盒子, 套
4.	hood	[hud]	n. 发动机舱盖, 车篷, 车顶
5.	sway	[swei]	v. 摇摆, 摇动
6.	frame	[freim]	n. 车架
7.	steering	['stiəriŋ]	n. 转向, 操纵
8.	brake	[breik]	n. 制动
9.	weld	[weld]	vt. 焊接; n. 焊缝, 焊接
10.	rivet	['rivit]	n. 铆钉; v. 用铆钉铆接
11.	bolt	[bəult]	n. 螺栓, 螺钉; v. 用螺栓连接
12.	washer	['wɔʃə, 'wɔːʃə]	n. 垫圈
13.	vibration	[vai'breiʃən]	n. 振动, 颤动
14.	stabilizer	['steibə,laizə]	n. 稳定器, 稳定杆
15.	ride	[raid]	n. 乘坐舒适性
16.	handling	['hændliŋ]	n. 操纵稳定性
17.	linkages	['liŋkidʒz]	n. 转向传动机构
18.	plier	['plaiə]	n. 钳子
19.	distributor	[di'stribjutə]	n. 分电器
20.	alternator	['ɔːltə(ː)neitə]	n. 交流发电机
21.	regulator	['reɡjuleitə]	n. (发电机)调节器
22.	carburetor	['kɑːbjuretə]	n. 汽化器, 化油器
23.	radiator	['reidiː,eitə]	n. 散热器, 水箱
24.	defroster	[,diː'frɔstə]	n. 除冰(或霜)装置, 防结冰(或霜)装置
25.	sludge	[slʌdʒ]	n. 金属碎屑
26.	transmission	[trænz'miʃən]	n. 变速器
27.	differential	[,difə'renʃəl]	n. 差速器

PHRASES AND EXPRESSIONS

1. power train   传动系统
2. unitized body (or unibody) 承载式车身,无大梁车身
3. suspension system   悬架系统
4. steering system   转向系统
5. brake system   制动系统
6. shock absorbers   减振器
7. control arms   控制臂
8. steering wheel   转向盘
9. steering column   转向轴
10. steering gears   转向器
11. tie rod   横拉杆
12. idler arm   转向臂
13. brake shoe   制动蹄(片)
14. disc brake   盘式制动器
15. drum brakes   鼓式制动器
16. ignition system   点火系统
17. exhaust system   排气系统
18. lubrication system   润滑系统
19. oil filters   机油滤清器
20. drive (or propeller) shaft 传动轴
21. universal joints   万向节

NOTES TO THE TEXT

1. An understanding of how the systems work will help you understand how the automobile works.
了解各个系统如何工作有助于理解汽车是如何工作的。

2. An automobile body is a sheet metal shell with windows, doors, a hood, and a trunk deck built into it.
车身是一个钣金件壳体,它上面有车窗、车门、发动机舱盖和行李舱盖等部件。

3. These support the vehicle and cushion it from road bumps for better ride and handling.
它们(悬架)支撑着车身,并减缓由于路面不平引起的颠簸,以获得更好的乘坐舒适性和操纵稳定性。

EXERCISES

Ⅰ. Answer following questions

1. What is the purpose of the rubber body mounts?
2. Why are car bodies streamlined?
3. List the main parts of the electrical system.

4. List the major functions of the exhaust system.

Ⅱ. **Translate the following passage into Chinese**

1. The automobile's further development will be determined by already existing and steadily increasing requirements, by additional further requirements and by the technical possibilities for meeting these requirements. The following focal points for development and research efforts can be discerned.

2. Further improvements of the automobile through product innovation in all classic functions, i. e., performance, fuel economy, environmental impact, safety, comfort, and reliability.

3. Further development of new technologies such as electrics, alternative materials, new test and production methods.

4. Long-range solutions for traffic problems such as highway congestion, smog in cities and carbon dioxide enrichment of our atmosphere.

Reading Material: Layout of an Automobile

The layout of different types of vehicles is different. A private car which is to carry up to eight persons is generally four-seater.

A car consists of engine located at the front of the vehicle, followed by a clutch, gear box, propeller shaft, universal joint, differential, back axle, etc. The radiator is located in front of the engine. Various other parts of the vehicle shown in the layout are dynamo, horn, steering box, fan, timing gear, carburetor, air filter, gear control, steering wheel, cylinder, petrol tank, rear axle. The drive from the gear box is conveyed through a short shaft to the front universal joint of the propeller shaft. From the propeller shaft it is conveyed to the rear universal joint through a sliding splined type of joint. The bevel gear of the short shaft is driven by the rear universal joint. This bevel gear meshes with a larger bevel gear which drives the two rear axle shafts through a differential gear.

The layout also consists of independent front-wheel springing with quarter-elliptic leaf springs, steering column bevel-gear control and hydraulic braking system.

The wheels which are four in number are fitted below the car chassis to support the load of the vehicle and passengers as well as to run the car. They are fitted with hollow rubber tyres filled with air in rubber tubes under sufficient pressure necessary for carrying the load. The shocks caused by road irregularities are absorbed by them. By fitting springs between the wheels and the vehicle allowing the vertical movement of wheels in relation to vehicle, greater part of unevenness of road surfaces is taken care of.

Front axle is used for steering front wheels carried on stub axles swivelling upon king pins at the axle extremities.

Steering arms and a track rod link the two stub axles together for swivelling them by a steering wheel about the king pins. The steering wheel linked to one of the stub axles by a shaft, a gear box and a suitable linkage is operated by the driver's hand wheel. Previously the axle—a one-piece beam was used to support the vehicle through springs. An arrangement known as independent front suspension has replaced the axle and spring arrangement. Under the control of springs, the wheels are free to rise and fall vertically independently of each other.

For fixing rear wheels, a tube like shaft enclosing driving shafts with suitable bearings for rotating the wheels is used. It is enlarged at the center for enclosing the final-drive gears used for providing main speed reduction between the engine and the driving wheels. The change of direction of the drive from the fore and aft line of the propeller shaft to the transverse line of the axle shafts is also provided by this tube known as rear axle.

When going round a curve, the inner wheel has to travel a smaller distance in comparison to the outer wheel. But both the rear wheels would rotate at the same speed if they are connected by a shaft. This rotation of both the wheels would result in slipping of one or both of them on the road surface causing excessive tyre wear as well as severe twisting loads on the shaft. Moreover, the two wheels of the exactly similar diameter (which is not usually so) can only turn at the same speed without slip on the straight road. Tyres fitted on the opposite sides may be of different states of wear and even tyre of same nominal diameter made by different or same manufacturer may differ in actual dimensions or may not be exactly similar. Due to change of rolling radius (the distance from the wheel center to the ground) the effective size of the tyre may be altered by different inflation pressure also.

Each wheel is provided with its own separate half shaft connected by a differential gear and meeting at about the center of the axle. The wheels are free to rotate at different speeds although they are provided with equal drive by the differential gear.

For preventing the transmission of shock from uneven road surfaces to the vehicle, springs are used to support the vehicle on the axle.

In order to allow for the vertical movements of the wheels relative to the frame as well as to allow the parts of the shaft to operate at different angle, another increasingly used arrangement is used. It consists of mounting the final-drive gears and the differential gear in a casing attached to the frame with independently sprung wheels attached to them by means of shafts through devices called universal joints.

Power unit consists of an internal combustion engine. It is usually mounted at the point end of the car. The clutch and the gear box are placed immediately behind it. The three components, engine, clutch and gear box are assembled into a single unit.

For connecting the output shaft of the gear box to the rear axle, a long shaft known as propeller shaft is used. This shaft is either enclosed in a tubular casing or kept exposed or opened with a universal joint fitted at each end for allowing the changes in the shaft alignment with the rise and fall of the rear axle due to road surface variations. Universal joints cannot be eliminated even if the final drive gears are fixed to the frame with the wheel springing independently. Neither the misalignment resulting from the flexing of the vehicle structure over bumpy road surfaces can be avoided nor the precise alignment of shaft can be ensured without them.

For controlling the movement of the vehicles or to stop them, efficient braking system is a necessity for a vehicle. Brakes attached to each of the four wheels are of two types. In the initial type, a pair of shoes carried on a stationary plate is expanded in contact with a rotating drum mounted on the wheels to arrest the motion of the drum. In the modern type of brakes, one or more pairs of pads are carried in a caliper attached to the axle or wheel supporting linkage. The sides of the disk mounted on the wheel are griped by these pads. By applying pressure on a pedal, the brakes are applied. A hand lever acting through a separate linkage and locked in the on position is used.

For operating the brake, either mechanical or hydraulic system is used. Mechanical system requiring gearing system for mechanical and hydraulic fluid for the hydraulic brakes are used.

NEW WORDS

1. dynamo ['dainə,məʊ] n. 发电机
2. horn [hɔːn] n. 喇叭
3. swivel ['swivəl] v. 旋转

PHRASES AND EXPRESSIONS

1. steering box   转向器
2. timing gear   正时齿轮
3. bevel gear   锥齿轮,伞齿轮
4. mesh with   与……啮合
5. leaf springs   钢板弹簧
6. stub axle   转向节

NOTES

1. They are fitted with hollow rubber tyres filled with air in rubber tubes under sufficient pressure necessary for carrying the load.

它们(车轮)安装有中空的橡胶轮胎(外胎),轮胎中装有充气的内胎,内胎的充气压力应足以承载车辆的载荷。

2. Front axle is used for steering front wheels carried on stub axles swivelling upon king pins at the axle extremities.

前桥用来安装前转向轮,该车轮装在转向节上,可绕主销转动,而该转向节则位于前桥的外端。

3. For operating the brake, either mechanical or hydraulic system is used. Mechanical system requiring gearing system for mechanical and hydraulic fluid for the hydraulic brakes are used.

对于制动器的操纵,机械或液压操纵系统均有使用。它们分别是纯机械传动或者带有液压传动的机械操纵系统。

UNIT 2　AUTOMOTIVE ENGINE

1. Purpose and Locations of Engines

The purpose of an automotive engine is to supply the power needed to move the vehicle. The engine produces this power by burning fuel inside it. Because the engine burns fuel inside, or internally, the engine is known as an internal combustion engine (ICE).

Engines may be fueled by gasoline, propane (LPG-liquefied petroleum gas), or diesel fuel. Compressed natural gas (CNG) may also be used in some vehicles.

Most automotive engines are located at the front of the vehicle. Many engines drive the rear wheels. This requires a long drive shaft extending from the front wheels to the rear wheels. Other engines drive the front wheels. In the rear-wheel-drive arrangement, the engine sits longitudinally. Its long dimension is from front to back.

In the front-wheel-drive arrangement, the engine sits crosswise, transversely. With either arrangement, the power is carried to the drive wheels (rear or front) by gears and shafts.

Some cars have the engine mounted in back of the front seat. This is called a mid-engine arrangement. Other cars have been built with the engine mounted at the rear, in back of rear seat. The Volkswagen "beetle" is an example of rear.

2. Engine Types

Various kinds of engines are used in automotive vehicles. The two major types are:

(a) The piston engine in which pistons move up and down, or reciprocate, in the engine cylinders. This is the engine used in all cars today, except for some models of Mazda.

(b) The Wankel rotary engine in which rotors rotate, or spin. The Mazda Motor Corporation of Japan is the major manufacturer of this engine.

There are two types of piston engines spark-ignition (SI) and compression ignition (CI). Spark-ignition engines use an electric ignition system with spark plugs. Electric sparks at the spark plugs ignite, or set fire, the fuel in the engine cylinders. The combustion of the fuel makes the engine run and produce power. This is the type of engine used in most automotive vehicles.

The compression-ignition engine, the diesel, uses the heat of compression to ignite the fuel. When air is compressed, it gets very hot. In the diesel engine, the air is compressed so much that its temperature goes up to 1,000 degrees Fahrenheit (538 degrees Celsius) or higher. The diesel fuel is sprayed into this very hot air and is ignited by the heat. Some automobiles have diesel engines. Many heavy-duty trucks and buses are powered by diesel engines.

There are other engines still in the experimental stage that might someday become important. These include gas-turbine engines, steam engines, Stirling engines, and electric motors.

3. Basic Engine Systems

A spark-ignition engine requires four basic systems to run. Diesel engines require three of these systems. They are fuel system, ignition system (except diesel), lubricating system and cooling system. Each performs a basic job in making the engine run. These are described briefly below.

3.1 *Fuel System*

The fuel system supplies gasoline or diesel fuel to the engine. This fuel is mixed with air to make a combustible mixture (a mixture that will burn). Each cylinder is repeatedly filled with the mixture. Then, the mixture is ignited and burned, producing high pressure. The high pressure makes the pistons move (or rotors spin). This turns shafts that rotate the wheels, causing the vehicle to move.

3.2 *Ignition System*

Every time the fuel system delivers air/fuel mixture to a cylinder, the ignition system follows up by delivering an electric spark. This ignites the mixture which creates the high pressure that moves the pistons and turns the car wheels. The action is repeated many times each second while the engine is running.

The ignition system takes the low voltage of the battery and builds it up to a very high voltage: as high as 47,000 volts in some systems. This high voltage jumps the gaps in the spark plugs, producing the sparks that ignite the air/fuel mixture in the engine cylinders.

3.3 *Lubricating System*

The engine has many moving metal parts. If metal parts rub against each other, they will wear rapidly. To prevent this, engines have lubricating oil. The oil gets between the metal parts so they slide on the oil, and not on each other.

The lubricating system has an oil pan at the bottom of the engine which holds several quarts [liters] of oil. An oil pump, driven by the engine, sends oil from this reservoir through the engine. After circulating through the engine, the oil drops back down into the oil pan. The oil pump continues to circulate the oil as long as the engine is running.

3.4 *Cooling System*

Where there is fire (combustion), there is heat. Burning of the air/fuel mixture raises the temperature inside the engine cylinders several thousand degrees. Some of this heat produces the high pressure that moves the pistons to produce power. Some of the heat leaves the cylinders with the exhaust gas. The exhaust gas is what is left after the air/fuel mixture burns. It is cleared out of the cylinders after combustion is complete.

Some of the heat is removed by the circulating oil. After the hot oil drops down into the oil pan, the oil gives up some of this heat to the air passing under the oil pan. The rest of the heat is removed by the cooling system.

3.5 Other Engine Systems

An engine will run with the four basic systems described above—fuel, ignition, lubricating, and cooling. However, three other related systems are also necessary. These are the exhaust system, the emission-control system, and the starting system.

The exhaust system reduces the noise of the burned gases leaving the engine cylinders and carries these exhaust gases safely away from the people in the car. The emission-control system is required by law to reduce the air pollution the engine could produce. The starting system is needed to crank the engine. A battery provides the electric power to operate the starting motor and the ignition system during cranking.

4. Energy Conversion

The internal combustion engine is a device used to convert the chemical energy of the fuel (gasoline or diesel fuel) into heat energy, and then to convert this heat energy into usable mechanical energy. This is achieved by combining the appropriate amounts of air and fuel, and burning the mixture in an enclosed cylinder at a controlled rate. A movable piston in the cylinder is forced down by the expanding gases of combustion.

An average air/fuel ratio for good combustion is about 15 parts of air to 1 part of fuel by weight. This means that for every gallon of gasoline burned, the oxygen is about 9,000 to 10,000 gallons of air is required. Air is about 21% oxygen and 78% nitrogen.

Diesel engines operate on a much wider air/fuel ratio, since air intake is not regulated on most diesels. Ratios may range from about 20:1 to about 100:1. The fact, plus the high compression of the diesel, makes it a very fuel efficient engine.

The movable piston in the cylinder is connected to the top of a connecting rod. The bottom of the connecting rod is attached to the offset portion of a crankshaft. As the piston is force down, this force is transferred to the crankshaft, causing the crankshaft to rotate. The reciprocating (back and forth or up and down) movement of the piston is converted to rotary (turning) motion of the crankshaft, which supplies the power to drive the vehicle.

The efficiency of the internal combustion, reciprocating piston engine in converting the potential energy in fuel into mechanical energy is only about 33%. Of the available heat energy in the fuel, about one-third is lost through the exhaust system and one-third is absorbed and dissipated by the cooling system. Of the remaining one-third, about one-half is lost through friction in the engine and drive train parts. The leaves only about 15% of the energy in the fuel is available at the vehicle's drive wheels.

The overall efficiency of the diesel engine is considerably higher than that of the gasoline engine. The reasons for this are: the higher compression ratio, the higher air/fuel ratio, and the higher heat value of the fuel. The useful power developed at the drive wheels by a diesel engine is about 25% as compared to 15% by a gasoline engine.

5. Four-Stroke-Cycle Gasoline Engine Operation

The movement of the piston from its uppermost position (TDC, top dead center) to its lowest position (BDC, bottom dead center) is called a stroke. Most automobile engines operate on the four stroke-cycle principle. A series of events involving four strokes of the piston completes one cycle, shown as Figure 2-1. These events are the intake stroke, the compression stroke, the power stroke, and the exhaust stroke. Two revolutions of the crankshaft and one revolution of the camshaft are required to complete one cycle.

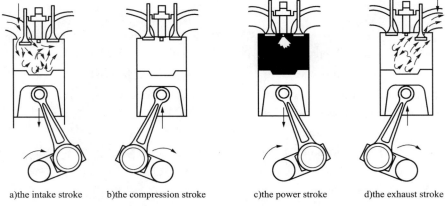

a) the intake stroke   b) the compression stroke   c) the power stroke   d) the exhaust stroke

Figure 2-1 Four-stroke-cycle gasoline engine

On the intake stroke the piston is pulled down in the cylinder by the crankshaft and connecting rod. During this time the intake valve is held open by the camshaft. Since the piston has moved down in the cylinder, creating a low-pressure area (vacuum), atmospheric pressure forces a mixture of air and fuel past the intake valve into the cylinder. Atmospheric pressure is approximately 14.7 pounds per square inch (about 101.35 kilopascals) at sea level. Pressure in the cylinder during the intake stroke is considerably less than this. The pressure difference is the force that causes the air/fuel mixture to flow into the cylinder, since a liquid or a gas (vapor) will always flow from a high-pressure to a low-pressure area.

As the piston is moved up by the crankshaft from BDC, the intake valve closes. The air/fuel mixture is trapped in the cylinder above the piston. Further piston travel compresses the air/fuel mixture to approximately one-eighth of its original volume (approximately 8∶1 compression ratio) when the piston has reached TDC. This completes the compression stroke.

When the piston is at or near TDC, the air/fuel mixture is ignited. The burning of the air/fuel mixture (combustion) takes place at a controlled rate. Expansion of the burning mixture causes a rapid rise in pressure. This increased pressure forces the piston down on the power stroke, causing the crankshaft to rotate.

At the end of the power stroke the camshaft opens the exhaust valve, and the exhaust stroke begins. Remaining pressure in the cylinder, and upward movement of piston, force the exhaust gases out of the cylinder. At the end of the exhaust stroke, the exhaust valve closes and the intake valve opens, repeating the entire cycle of events over and over again.

To start the engine, some method of cranking the engine is required to turn the crankshaft and cause piston movement. This is done by the starter motor when the ignition key is in the start position. When sufficient air/fuel mixture has entered the cylinders and is ignited, the power strokes create enough energy to continue crankshaft rotation. At the point, the ignition key is released to the run position and the starter is disengaged.

Sufficient energy is stored in the flywheel and other rotating parts on the power stroke to move the piston and related parts through the other three strokes (exhaust, intake, and compression). The amount of air/fuel mixture allowed to enter the cylinder determines the power and speed developed by the engine.

NEW WORDS

1. longitudinal [lɔndʒi'tjuːdinl] adj. 纵向的,经度的
2. transverse [træns'vəːs, trænz-] adj. 横向的,横断的
3. reciprocate [ri'siprə‚keit] vt. & vi. 往复,来回
4. spin [spin] v. 旋转; n. 旋转
5. piston ['pistən] n. 活塞
6. ignite [ig'nait] n. 点火,点燃
7. rub [rʌb] v. 摩擦,擦
8. quart [kwɔːt] n. 夸脱(容量单位)
9. reservoir ['rezəvwɑː] n. 油箱
10. mechanical [mi'kænikəl] adj. 机械的,机械制的,呆板的
11. enclosed [in'kləuzd] adj. 被附上的
12. gallon ['gælən] n. 加仑
13. stroke [strəuk] n. 冲程,行程
14. camshaft ['kæmʃɑːft] n. 凸轮轴
15. combustion [kəm'bʌstʃən] n. 燃烧,着火
16. disengaged [‚disin'geidʒd] adj. 脱开的,脱离啮合的
17. flywheel ['flaiwiːl] n. 飞轮,惯性轮,储能轮

PHRASES AND EXPRESSIONS

1. internal-combustion engine 内燃机
2. diesel-fuel 柴油机燃料,柴油
3. LPG 液化石油气体
4. CNG 压缩天然气
5. spark ignition 火花点火
6. compression ignition 压缩点火
7. spark plug 火花塞
8. gas-turbine engine 燃气涡轮发动机

9. steam engine	蒸汽机
10. Stirling engine	斯特灵发动机
11. lubricating system	润滑系统
12. oil pan	油底壳
13. oil pump	机油泵
14. exhaust system	排气系统
15. emission-control system	排放控制系统
16. energy conversion	能量转换
17. air/fuel ratio	空燃比
18. connecting rod	连杆
19. TDC	上止点
20. BDC	下止点
21. intake stroke	进气行程
22. compression stroke	压缩行程
23. power stroke	做功行程
24. exhaust stroke	排气行程
25. compression ratio	压缩率,压缩比

NOTES TO THE TEXT

1. The purpose of an automotive engine is to supply the power needed to move the vehicle.

汽车发动机的功用是提供汽车行驶所需的动力。

2. This high voltage jumps the gaps in the spark plugs, producing the sparks that ignite the air/fuel mixture in the engine cylinders.

高压击穿火花塞间隙,产生电火花,点燃发动机汽缸内的可燃混合气。

3. The internal combustion engine is a device used to convert the chemical energy of the fuel (gasoline or diesel fuel) into heat energy, and then to convert this heat energy into usable mechanical energy.

内燃机是一个将燃料(汽油或柴油)的化学能转化成热能,再把热能转化成可利用的机械能的装置。

4. An average air/fuel ratio for good combustion is about 15 parts of air to 1 part of fuel by weight.

利于燃烧的理想空燃比,按质量大约是15:1。

5. The amount of air/fuel mixture allowed to enter the cylinder determines the power and speed developed by the engine.

进入汽缸的可燃混合气数量,决定了该发动机的功率和转速。

EXERCISES

Ⅰ. Answer following questions

1. What is the purpose of an automotive engine?
2. What is the difference between a gasoline engine and a diesel engine?

3. What are the basic systems to run a spark-ignition engine required?

4. List the strokes of a four-stroke-cycle gasoline engine operation.

5. What is the function of the flywheel?

II. Translate the following passage into Chinese

1. A car usually has a piston engine. It consists of several moving parts: pistons, connecting rods, crankshaft, camshaft, valve lifters, intake valves and exhaust valves. The cast iron or aluminum engine block holds the moving parts. The engine block has a series of holes which are called cylinders. The cylinders can be arranged in line or in a V-shape and in the upper part of the block. Each cylinder holds a piston and connecting rod. A circular ring is used to seal the small gap between the piston and the cylinder wall. The lower part of the block is called crankcase which holds the crankshaft with bearing mounts. Pistons are connected to the crankshaft by connecting rods.

2. The cylinder heads are the top covers of the cylinders which are tightly bolted to the top of the block. The cylinder heads contain combustion chambers. Each combustion chamber contains at least one intake and exhaust valve and one spark plug per cylinder. The valves are opened and closed in a specific sequence with valve lifters controlled by the camshaft. The camshaft is connected to the crankshaft through a time belt.

Reading Material: Valve System

The valve operating assembly includes the lifters or cam followers, pushrods, rocker arms and shafts or pivot, valve, springs, retainers, rotators, seals, and locks, the purpose of this to open and close the intake and exhaust ports that lead to the combustion chambers as required.

Valve Lifter (Tappet)

The valve lifter is the unit that makes contact with the valve stem and the camshaft. It rides on the camshaft. When the cam lobes push it upwards, it opens the valve. The engine oil comes into the lifter body under pressure. It passes through a little opening at the bottom of an inner piston to a cavity underneath the piston. The oil forces the piston upward until it contacts the push rod. When the cam raises the valve lifter, the pressure is placed on the inner piston which tries to push the oil back through the little opening. It can't do this, because the opening is sealed by a small check valve.

When the cam goes upward, the lifter solidifies and lifts the valve. Then, when the cam goes down, the lifter is pushed down by the push rod. It adjusts automatically to remove clearances.

Valve Cover

The valve cover covers the valve train. The valve train consists of rocker arms, valve springs, push rods, lifters and cam (in an overhead cam engine). The valve cover can be removed to adjust the valves. Oil is pumped up through the pushrods and dispersed underneath the valve cover, which keeps the rocker arms lubricated. Holes are located in various places in the engine head so that the oil recirculates back down to the oil pan. For this reason, the valve cover must be oil-tight; it is often the source of oil leaks. The valve cover is often distorted on older cars; because at some point the valve cover screws were over-tightened, bending the valve cover. This happens because the valve cover is made of very thin sheet metal and cannot withstand the force of an over-tightened bolt.

One way to determine if the valve cover is bent is to remove the gasket and put the valve cover back on to the cylinder head. When the valve cover and cylinder head come into contact, the cover should sit flat. If it rocks, it is bent. Cast aluminum valve covers cannot be straightened, they need to be replaced. Sheet metal valve covers can be straightened.

A symptom of a bent or leaking valve cover is a pinching of the valve cover gasket. This means that the gasket is sealing one area and not sealing another area. This condition produces a leak; oil could be leaking down the side of the engine. Some valve covers are hard to access, because they are covered with other engine parts.

Chronic valve cover leakage can sometimes be fixed by using two gaskets glued together instead of using just one.

Valve Ports

Valve ports are openings in the cylinder head. Intake ports let the fuel mixture into the cylinder head, and exhaust ports let the exhaust out.

Valves

The valve's job is to open and close the valve ports. If the ports were always open, the fuel exploded in the combustion chamber would leave through the ports. The explosion has to be kept in the combustion chamber to push the piston down. The valves are set up to open and close at exactly the right moment. One lets the fuel mixture in and closes. After the fuel explodes and pushes the piston down, the other valve lets the exhaust out.

Valve Guides

The valves are usually held in an upright position by the valve stem. The valve stem is the long straight side of the valve, like the stem of a flower. Holes are bored in the cylinder head for the valve stems. Worn valve guides allow oil to enter the combustion chamber and cause blue smoke in the exhaust.

Valve Springs

The valve springs keep the valves closed tightly against their seats until the valve is opened by the cam. After the cam turns (releasing pressure), the valve springs close the valves.

Valve Seals

The valve seal is a unit that goes over the end of the valve stem. It keeps excess oil from getting between the valve guide and the valve stem.

Camshaft

The camshaft is a round shaft with "lobes" (specially formed bumps) which is driven by the timing belt or timing chain. It, directly or through "lifters" and "pushrods" opens and closes the fuel and exhaust valves. The camshaft turns at one-half of the crankshaft speed. It is supported by bearings located in the front and rear of the crankcase.

Rocker Arms

Rocker arms are used to transmit force from cam to valve. Riding on a cam on the camshaft, rocker arms direct the upward motion of the lobe of the cam into an opening motion of the valve stem.

Pushrods

Pushrods attach the valve lifter to the rocker arm. Through their centers, oil is pumped to lubricate the valves and rocker arms.

NEW WORDS

1. lifter   [ˈliftə]   n. 挺柱
2. rocker   [ˈrɔkə]   n. 摇臂
3. retainer   [riˈteinə]   n. 保持器,止动器,弹簧座
4. seal   [si:l]   n. 密封件
5. tappet   [ˈtæpit]   n. 挺柱,推杆
6. lobe   [ləub]   n. 凸起,凸角[齿]
7. gasket   [ˈɡæskit]   n. 密封垫片,垫圈,接合垫

PHRASES AND EXPRESSIONS

1. valve train   配气机构
2. cam follower   凸轮随动杆,气门挺柱[摇臂]
3. rocker arm   摇臂
4. combustion chamber   燃烧室
5. intake valve   进气阀
6. exhaust valve   排气阀
7. valve stem   气门杆
8. valve cover   气门室盖(罩)
9. valve port   阀口,进(排)气口
10. valve guide   气门导管

NOTES

1. The valve operating assembly includes the lifters or cam followers, pushrods, rocker arms and shafts or pivot, valve, springs, retainers, rotators, seals, and locks, the purpose of this to open and close the intake and exhaust ports that lead to the combustion chambers as required.

气门机构总成包括气门挺柱或凸轮随动杆、推杆、摇臂、摇臂轴、气门、气门弹簧、弹簧座、转阀器、油封和锁止夹;其功用是根据需要打开和关闭通到燃烧室的进气口和排气口。

2. One way to determine if your valve cover is bent is to remove the gasket and put the valve cover back on to the cylinder head.

判断气门室盖翘曲变形的一种方法是移去其衬垫,然后把气门室盖放回到汽缸盖上。(根据它们之间的缝隙判断)

3. The valve springs keep the valves closed tightly against their seats until the valve is opened by the cam.

在气门被凸轮打开之前,气门弹簧把气门紧紧地压靠在气门座上。

UNIT 3   AUTOMOTIVE LUBRICATION SYSTEM

1. Lubrication Principles

Reducing friction to minimize wear and loss of power is the primary job a lubrication system must perform. Residual oil on engine parts also provides lubrication for engine start-up.

The engine oil forms a seal between the pistons, rings, and cylinders. It also helps to cool engine parts. Without the cleaning action of the lubricating system, carbon and varnish buildup would be excessive. The engine oil also absorbs the shock and dampens the noise of moving parts.

How successful the lubrication system is in performing all these functions depends on a number of factors and conditions. There must be an adequate supply of good-quality lubricant delivered to all moving engine parts under sufficient pressure to provide hydrodynamic lubrication for rotating parts and oil adhesion to surface subject to sliding friction.

2. Parts of the Pressure-Lubrication System

2.1   *Oil Pan*

The oil pan bolts under the engine block, where it seals off the bottom of engine. Shaped like a trough, this sheet-metal pan serves as the reservoir for about 5 quarts of oil. As oil flows from the engine, it drains downward into the oil pan. The oil pump sucks oil from the lowest part of the oil pan, the oil sump. Many oil pans have baffles, which are thin metal partitions. These keep the oil in the sump when the car corners hard or brakes suddenly. A drain plug at the bottom of the sump allows oil to be drained from the engine. The oil-pan gasket fits between the oil pan and the bottom of the engine block.

In most engines, the oil circulates in the engine, and then returns to the pan. It stays in the pan until drawn back into the engine by the oil pump. During operation, the sump usually holds 2 to 3 quarts of oil. The rest of the oil moves through the passageways of the lubrication system. With the engine off, the pan holds about 4 quarts of oil. The fifth quart is in the oil filter. Because a pool of oil always rests in the sump, the type of lubrication system is called a wet-sump oiling system.

A dry-sump oil system is used in many racing engines. This system has a separate storage tank for the oil. A second oil pump draws oil from the oil pan as soon as the oil drains from the engine. As a result, a dry-sump system can circulate more oil through the engine than a wet-sump system.

2.2 Oil Pump

In most cars, the oil pump is in the crankcase above the sump. It draws oil through a tube that extends downward into the sump. This tube, called the oil-pump pickup tube, has a filter screen over its bottom end. The screen keeps large pieces of sludge and dirt from being drawn into the pump. The tube may be hinged on the pump end so that it can move up and down as the oil level changes in the sump. Thus, the pump always draws oil from the top of the sump, not from the bottom where the dirt and sludge tend to settle. Modern cars use one of two common types of oil pumps--the gear-type and the rotor-type.

2.3 Oil Filters

A modern engine uses a full-flow filtering system (Figure 3-1). In this system, the output of the oil pump flows through the oil filter before moving through the engine. In other words, the oil is filtered and cleaned before each trip through the engine. When an engine runs at 3,000 r/min, its entire five quarts of oil pass through the filter at least once every minute. Thus the oil filter ensures that only clean oil enters the engine.

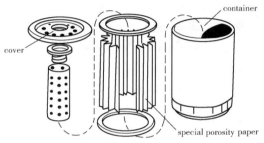

Figure 3-1   Oil filter

Modern engines use replaceable oil filters. When dirty, such a screw-on filter is replaced with a new one. Inside the steel outer casing of the unit, a special paper acts as a filter. Folded and tightly packed, this paper has just the right porosity. These tiny holes in the paper allow oil to pass through, but filter out dirt and sludge. The paper is treated to protect it from acid or water in the oil.

Normally, oil enters the oil filter from the outside. Oil enters the filter around the outer edge of the base. The oil flows through the paper to the center of the container. It then flows out to the engine. Most filters also have a pressure-relief valve, or bypass valve. Such a valve allows oil to flow to the engine without going through the filter. This is necessary when the filter becomes too clogged for oil to pass through it. Thus, a plugged filter allows dirty oil to circulate through the engine. To prevent this, the oil and oil filter should be changed regularly.

2.4 Engine Lubrication

An internal combustion engine would not run for even a few minutes if the moving parts were allowed to make metal-to-metal contact. The heat generated due to the tremendous amounts of friction would melt the metals, leading to the destruction of the engine. To prevent this, all moving parts ride on a thin film of oil that is pumped between all the moving parts of the engine. Once between the moving parts, the oil serves two purposes. One purpose is to lubricate the bearing surfaces. The other purpose is to cool the bearings by absorbing the friction-generated heat. The flow of oil to the moving parts is accomplished by the engine's internal lubricating system. Figure 3-2 shows a engine's lube oil circuit schematic.

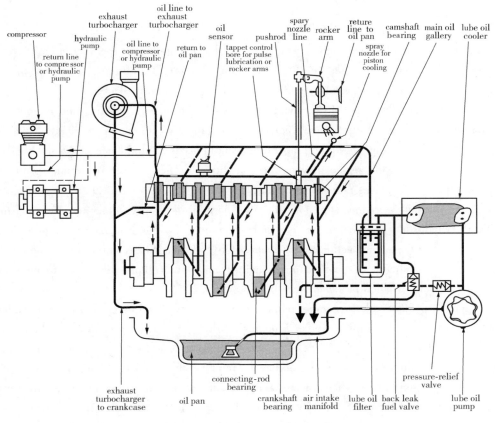

Figure 3-2 Lube oil circuit schematic

The oil pump is of the rotor type, consisting essentially of a driving rotor and a driven rotor in mesh. It is housed in the sump, being driven by a shaft and skew gearing from the camshaft.

Oil from the sump is delivered at full pressure to all main bearings and camshaft bearings through gallery pipes and drillings in the cylinder block. The big-end bearings are fed from the main bearings via passages in the crankshaft.

Lubrication for the timing chain is supplied at two points; by a feed from the front camshaft bearing into the periphery of the camshaft chain wheel and also by oil fed through the hollow shaft on which the timing chain jockey pulley is mounted arid thence through holes in the circumference of the jockey pulley.

The inlet (upper) and exhaust (lower) rocker shafts are hollow, the inlet shaft being fed with oil from the rear end of the main gallery pipe via an external pipeline, whilst that for the exhaust rockers and inlet followers is supplied via drillings from the center camshaft bearings. Each rocker and follower receives its oil through small holes drilled in the rocker shafts and in turn they are themselves also drilled, so that the oil finds its way through them and thence out again to lubricate the points of contact with the valves, push-rods and camshaft. The distributor drive shaft is lubricated with oil fed from the exhaust rocker shaft via a hollow bolt.

Surplus oil from the inlet valve gear returns through the cylinder casting and that from the exhaust valve gear direct to the sump.

2.5 *Lubrication Oils*

Motor oils for automobile engines fall into two basic categories: petroleum-based oils and synthetic oils. Petroleum-based oils, however, contain a variety of additives; so in fact they, too, are partly synthetic. Some of the major additives include those described here.

Antiscuff additives help to polish moving parts, including cams, pistons, and cylinder walls. This is particularly important during new engine break-in and after an engine overhaul. Since heat is the prime enemy of antiscuff additives, operating conditions that produce excessively high engine temperatures reduce the life expectancy of these additives. This type of operation requires more frequent oil changes than does normal operation.

Corrosion inhibitors reduce the formation of harmful acids by attacking the acid-forming ingredients. Combustion produces a number of by-products, including acids and water. Corrosion inhibitors neutralize these combustion by-products before they can do any harm to the engine. A cold engine, rich fuel mixtures, a poorly tuned engine; and much short trip, cold-weather driving increases the amount of acids produced.

Detergent-dispersants clean engine parts during operation and keep these contaminants in suspension in the oil. As the oil is force through the filter, the majority of these contaminants are trapped by the filter.

Viscosity index improvers tend to stabilize or improve the viscosity of engine oils at various temperatures. They tend to give the oil more body when the oil is cold. In other words, they improve the body and fluidity of the oil. The ability of the oil to carry a load at high temperature is improved by this additive, and the ability of the oil to flow when cold is also improved.

Foam inhibitors reduce the tendency of oil to foam. Heat and agitation mix the oil with air to create foam. Oil foam reduces the lubricating ability of the oil and causes oil starvation and failure of engine parts. Loss of oil pressure due to foaming increases this problem.

NEW WORDS

1. residual [ri'zidjuːəl] *adj.* 剩余的,残留的
2. varnish ['vɑːniʃ] *n.* 清漆,积炭
3. buildup [bildʌp] *n.* 组合,集结,累积,形成
4. adhesion [æd'hiːʒən] *n.* 黏着,附着,黏结
5. cleanser ['klenzə] *n.* 清洁剂
6. sludge [slʌdʒ] *n.* 油泥
7. grime [graim] *n.* 污垢,尘垢,烟灰
8. clog [klɔg] *vt. & vi.* 填塞,塞满
9. gum [gʌm] *vt.* 黏合
10. trough [trɔːf, trɔf] *n.* 槽,水槽,木盆,任何槽形物
11. baffle ['bæfl] *n.* 阻板,隔板
12. sump [sʌmp] *n.* 油底壳

UNIT 3 AUTOMOTIVE LUBRICATION SYSTEM

13. crankcase	[ˈkræŋkkeis]	n. 曲轴箱
14. porosity	[pɔːˈrɔsiti]	n. 多孔性,有孔性
15. periphery	[pəˈrifəriː]	n. 外围
16. synthetic	[sinˈθetik]	adj. 合成的,人造的,综合的
17. additive	[ˈæditiv]	n. 添加剂; adj. 添加的,加法的
18. antiscuff	[ˈæntiskʌf]	n. 抗磨损
19. overhaul	[ˌəuvəˈhɔːl, ˈəuvəˌhɔːl]	vt. 彻底检查,大修
20. neutralize	[ˈnuːtrəˌlaiz, ˈnjuː-]	vt. 使无效,抵消,使中和
21. agitation	[ˌædʒiˈteiʃən]	n. 激动,兴奋,煽动,搅动

PHRASES AND EXPRESSIONS

1. start-up   起动
2. engine block   发动机汽缸体
3. dry-sump   干油底壳
4. wet-sump   湿油底壳
5. pickup tube   机油吸油管
6. filter screen   滤网
7. full-flow filtering system   全流式滤清器
8. pressure-relief valve   安全阀,卸压阀
9. bypass valve   旁通阀
10. gear type oil pump   齿轮式机油泵,齿轮泵
11. jockey pulley   张紧轮,导向轮
12. corrosion inhibitor   阻蚀剂,腐蚀抑制剂
13. detergent-dispersant   清洁剂,分散剂
14. viscosity index   黏度指数
15. foam inhibitor   泡沫抑制剂

NOTES TO THE TEXT

1. Reducing friction to minimize wear and loss of power is the primary job a lubrication system must perform.

减少摩擦、降低磨损和动力损失是润滑系统必须完成的主要工作。

2. Each rocker and follower receives its oil through small holes drilled in the rocker shafts and in turn they are themselves also drilled, so that the oil finds its way through them and thence out again to lubricate the points of contact with the valves, push-rods and camshaft.

每个摇臂和挺杆从摇臂轴上的小孔中得到润滑油,然后润滑油进入它们本身带有的孔道;通过这些孔道出来后,再去润滑与之相连的气门、推杆和凸轮轴。

EXERCISES

I. Answer following questions

1. What is the purpose of automobile lubrication system?

2. How does internal engine leakage affect oil pressure?

3. Explain what the function of oil is.

4. Name at least three common additives used in compounding motor oils.

5. Describe how oil pumps and engine lubrication work.

6. Explain how oil reduces friction.

7. Define the word viscosity.

8. What is detergent oil?

9. What is the difference between the full flow filter system and the bypass filter system?

Ⅱ. Translate the following passage into Chinese

1. The purpose of the lubrication system is to circulate oil through the engine. Many parts inside the engine, such as the camshaft, crankshaft, connecting rods, and pistons are connected to other metal parts. When parts rub together, friction is created. Friction produces heat. Although two metal surfaces may appear smooth to the naked eye, they may look rough when seen through a microscope.

2. An engine must have a good lubrication system. Without it, the friction heat from the contact of the moving parts would wear the parts and cause power loss. Oil, when placed between two moving parts, separates them with a film. This oil film prevents the parts from rubbing against each other. This oil film also cushions the parts, giving quieter and smoother engine operation.

Reading Material: Changing the Oil and the Oil Filter

Changing the oil is an easy way to keep an engine working well. Putting a good grade of clean oil into the engine every 4,000 to 6,000 miles will give the engine longer life. Automobile makers set the oil-change intervals for their cars. Automobile users should follow their recommendations. Recently, the interval between oil changes has been lengthened. With better oil and better engines, the oil can be used longer without damaging the engine. Also, unleaded fuels do not dirty oil the way leaded gasoline does.

Remember, oil filters hold 1 quart of oil at all times. So if you drain the oil but leave in the old filter, you are mixing four quarts of fresh oil with one quart of dirty oil. For this reason it is a good idea to change the filter every time you change the oil.

Changing the oil and replacing the filter are easy. Put the car on a hoist or lift. Or, drive the car onto a portable car ramp, and block the wheels. Place a pan under the drain plug in the bottom of the oil pan. Remove the plug to drain the dirty oil into the pan.

Warm the engine before changing the oil. Warm oil flows more freely and carries more dirt with it. Be careful when working on an engine that has been running for a long time. Oil gets quite hot. You could burn yourself in changing the oil on a hot engine.

Once you have drained the oil, clean the drain plug and replace it in the pan. Do not over-tighten the plug. Otherwise, may damage the oil pan.

Remove the oil filter. Some filters are removed from underneath the car, and others from above. Unscrew the filter with an oil-filter wrench.

UNIT 3 AUTOMOTIVE LUBRICATION SYSTEM

Before installing a new filter, make sure the oil-filter mounting pad is clean. Wipe it with a soft dry rag. Next, to assure a proper seal, coat the rubber seal with a light coating of oil. Be sure that the new filter is the same size and type as the old one. If the oil filter fits onto the engine with the mounting surface up, you can fill the filter with as much oil as it can hold. This keeps the engine from being "starved" for oil when it first starts. Tighten the new filter by hand. Do not use the oil-filter wrench.

The oil and filter change intervals should be followed as outlined in the vehicle owner's manual or shop service manual. The SAE rating (viscosity) and the service rating of the oil used, should comply with the vehicle manufacturer's recommendations.

The frequency of oil and filter changes may vary depending on the type of service the vehicle is required to provide. Under severe operating conditions, such as driving in dusty conditions, trailer towing, extensive idling, frequent short trips (especially in cold weather), and sustained high-speed driving (especially in hot weather), more frequent oil changes are required.

In some cases, manufacturers may recommend a special antiscuff additive be used with the engine oil after an engine overhaul or after severe service. Special conditions may have to be observed to use such additives. The manufacturer's recommendations should be followed in every case.

NEW WORDS

1. drain   [drein]   vt. & vi. 排出,流掉
2. ramp   [ræmp]   n. 斜坡,坡道
3. underneath   [ˌʌndə'niːθ]   prep. 在……的下面
4. wrench   [rentʃ]   n. 扳钳,扳手

PHRASES AND EXPRESSIONS

1. unleaded fuel   无铅汽油
2. over-tighten   过紧
3. SAE = Society of Automotive Engineers   汽车工程师学会[美]
4. comply with   遵照

NOTES

1. Also, unleaded fuels do not dirty oil the way leaded gasoline does.
另外,无铅汽油不像含铅汽油那样污染汽油。

2. Most carmakers suggest you changer the oil filter with every other oil change, rather than every oil change.
多数汽车制造商建议每换两次机油换一次机油滤器,而不是每次换机油都一起更换。

UNIT 4　　THE COOLING SYSTEM

　　The purpose of the engine's cooling system is to remove excess heat from the engine, to keep the engine operating at its most efficient temperature, and to get the engine up to the correct temperature as soon as possible after starting. Ideally, the cooling system keeps the engine running at its most efficient temperature no matter what the operating conditions are.

　　Fuel burning engines produce enormous amounts of heat; temperatures can reach up to 4,000°F when the air-fuel mixture burns. However, normal operating temperature is about 2,000°F.

　　The exhaust system takes away much of the heat, but parts of the engine, such as the cylinder walls, pistons, and cylinder head, absorb large amounts of the heat. If a part of the engine gets too hot, the oil film fails to protect it. This lack of lubrication can ruin the engine.

　　On the other hand, if an engine runs at too low a temperature, it is inefficient, the oil gets dirty (adding wear and subtracting horsepower), deposits form, and fuel mileage is poor—not to mention exhaust emissions! For these reasons, the cooling system is designed to stay out of the action until the engine is warmed up.

　　There are two types of cooling systems; liquid cooling and air cooling. Most auto engines are cooled by the liquid type; air cooling is used more frequently for airplanes, motorcycles and lawnmowers.

　　The cooling system of a water-cooled engine consists of the engine's water jacket, a thermostat, a water pump, a radiator and radiator cap, a cooling fan (electric or belt-driven), hoses, and usually an expansion (overflow) tank (Figure 4-1).

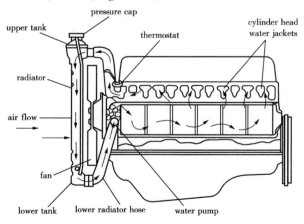

Figure 4-1　The cooling system of a water-cooled engine

　　The pump sends the fluid into the engine block, where it makes its way through passages in the engine around the cylinders. Then it returns through the cylinder head of the engine. The thermostat

UNIT 4 THE COOLING SYSTEM

is located where the fluid leaves the engine. The plumbing around the thermostat sends the fluid back to the pump directly if the thermostat is closed. If it is open, the fluid goes through the radiator first and then back to the pump.

1. Water Pump

The water pump is a simple centrifugal pump driven by a belt connected to the crankshaft of the engine. The pump circulates fluid whenever the engine is running.

The water pump uses centrifugal force to send fluid to the outside while it spins, causing fluid to be drawn from the center continuously. The inlet to the pump is located near the center so that fluid returning from the radiator hits the pump vanes. The pump vanes fling the fluid to the outside of the pump, where it can enter the engine.

2. Water Jacket

The water jacket is a collection of passages within the block and head. These passages let the coolant circulate around the "hot spots" (valve seats and guides, cylinder walls, combustion chamber, etc.) in order to cool them off.

Temperatures in the combustion chamber of the engine can reach 4,500°F (2,500°C), so cooling the area around the cylinders is critical. Areas around the exhaust valves are especially crucial, and almost all of the space inside the cylinder head around the valves that is not needed for structure is filled with coolant. If the engine goes without cooling for very long, it can seize. When this happens, the metal has actually gotten hot enough for the piston to weld itself to the cylinder. This usually means the complete destruction of the engine.

One interesting way to reduce the demands on the cooling system is to reduce the amount of heat that is transferred from the combustion chamber to the metal parts of the engine. Some engines do this by coating the inside of the top of the cylinder head with a thin layer of ceramic. Ceramic is a poor conductor of heat, so less heat is conducted through to the metal and more passes out of the exhaust.

3. Radiator

A radiator is a type of heat exchanger. It is designed to transfer heat from the hot coolant that flows through it to the air blown through it by the fan.

Most modern cars use aluminum radiators. These radiators are made by brazing thin aluminum fins to flattened aluminum tubes. The coolant flows from the inlet to the outlet through many tubes mounted in a parallel arrangement. The fins conduct the heat from the tubes and transfer it to the air flowing through the radiator.

The tubes sometimes have a type of fin inserted into them called a turbulator, which increases the turbulence of the fluid flowing through the tubes. If the fluid flowed very smoothly through the tubes, only the fluid actually touching the tubes would be cooled directly. The amount of heat transferred to the tubes from the fluid running through them depends on the difference in temperature between the tube and the fluid touching it. So if the fluid that is in contact with the tube cools down quickly, less heat will be transferred. By creating turbulence inside the tube, all of the fluid mixes together, keeping the temperature of the fluid touching the tubes up so that more heat can be extracted, and all of the fluid inside the tube is used effectively.

4. Pressure Cap

The radiator cap actually increases the boiling point of your coolant by about 45 °F (25 °C). How does this simple cap do this? The same way a pressure cooker increases the boiling temperature of water. The cap is actually a pressure release valve, and on cars it is usually set to 15 psi. The boiling point of water increases when the water is placed under pressure.

When the fluid in the cooling system heats up, it expands, causing the pressure to build up. The cap is the only place where this pressure can escape, so the setting of the spring on the cap determines the maximum pressure in the cooling system. When the pressure reaches 15 psi, the pressure pushes the valve open, allowing coolant to escape from the cooling system. This coolant flows through the overflow tube into the bottom of the overflow tank. This arrangement keeps air out of the system. When the radiator cools back down, a vacuum is created in the cooling system that pulls open another spring loaded valve, sucking water back in from the bottom of the overflow tank to replace the water that was expelled.

5. Thermostat

Any liquid-cooled car engine has a small device called the thermostat that sits between the engine and the radiator. The thermostat's main job is to allow the engine to heat up quickly, and then to keep the engine at a constant temperature. It does this by regulating the amount of water that goes through the radiator. At low temperatures, the outlet to the radiator is completely blocked—all of the coolant is re-circulated back through the engine.

Once the temperature of the coolant rises to between 180 °F and 195 °F (82 °C to 91 °C), the thermostat starts to open, allowing fluid to flow through the radiator. By the time the coolant reaches 200 °F to 218 °F (93 °C to 103 °C), the thermostat is open all the way (Figure 4-2).

The secret of the thermostat lies in the small cylinder located on the engine-side of the device. This cylinder is filled with a wax that begins to melt at around 180 °F (different thermostats open at different temperatures, but 180 °F is a common one). A rod connected to the valve presses into this wax. When the wax melts, it expands significantly, pushing the rod out of the cylinder and opening the valve. By letting the engine warm up as quickly as possible, the thermostat reduces engine wear, deposits and emissions.

UNIT 4　THE COOLING SYSTEM

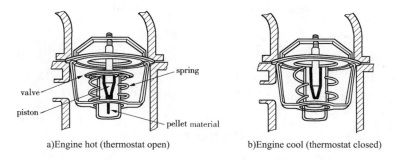

a) Engine hot (thermostat open)　　　b) Engine cool (thermostat closed)

Figure 4-2　*The open and closed positions of a thermostat*

6. Fan

Like the thermostat, the cooling fan has to be controlled so that it allows the engine to maintain a constant temperature.

Front-wheel drive cars have electric fans because the engine is usually mounted transversely, meaning the output of the engine points toward the side of the car. The fans are controlled either with a thermostatic switch or by the engine computer, and they turn on when the temperature of the coolant goes above a set point. They turn back off when the temperature drops below that point.

Rear-wheel drive cars with longitudinal engines usually have engine-driven cooling fans. These fans have a thermostatically controlled viscous clutch. This clutch is positioned at the hub of the fan, in the airflow coming through the radiator.

NEW WORDS

1. water jacket　　['wɔːtəˌdʒækit, 'wɔtə-]　　*n.* 水套
2. thermostat　　['θəːməˌstæt]　　*n.* 节温器,恒温器
3. radiator　　['reidiːˌeitə]　　*n.* 散热器
4. subtract　　[səb'trækt]　　*v.* 减
5. deposits　　[di'pɔzit]　　*n.* 沉积物
6. lawnmower　　[lɔːn'məʊə]　　*n.* 割草机
7. passageway　　['pæsidʒˌwei]　　*n.* 通道,过道
8. braze　　[breiz]　　*v.* 焊(接),铜焊
9. transmission　　[trænz'miʃən]　　*n.* 变速器
10. transversely　　[træns'vəːs, trænz]　　*adv.* 横着,横切地,横断地
11. longitudinal　　[ˌlɔndʒi'tjuːdinl]　　*adj.* 纵向的

PHRASES AND EXPRESSIONS

1. expansion (overflow) tank　　　　膨胀箱,溢流箱
2. on the other hand　　　　另一方面
3. not to mention　　　　更不用说
4. out of the action　　　　不起作用,停止使用

5. water jacket　　　　　　　　　　　　水套
6. combustion chamber　　　　　　　　燃烧室
7. pressure cooker　　　　　　　　　　高压锅
8. be designed to　　　　　　　　　　　目的是,用来
9. psi = pound per square inch　　　　磅数/平方英寸

NOTES TO THE TEXT

1. Areas around the exhaust valves are especially crucial, and almost all of the space inside the cylinder head around the valves that is not needed for structure is filled with coolant.

尤其排气门周围的区域是至关重要的,因此,在满足结构强度的要求下,缸盖内排气门周围几乎所有的空间内都充满了冷却剂。

介词短语 around the exhaust valves 作 Areas 的后置定语,定语从句 that is not needed for structure 的先行词是 space。

2. It is designed to transfer heat from the hot coolant that flows through it to the air blown through it by the fan.

散热器的作用是当空气在风扇的作用下流过散热器时,将在散热器内流动的高温冷却剂的热量带走。transfer… from… to…将……从……传递到……

3. The amount of heat transferred to the tubes from the fluid running through them depends on the difference in temperature between the tube and the fluid touching it.

冷却剂流过散热器芯管时,冷却剂传给散热器芯管的热量取决于芯管以及与芯管接触的液体两者之间的温差。

transferred to the tubes from the fluid 修饰 amount of heat,running through them 修饰 the fluid。

4. The tubes sometimes have a type of fin inserted into them called a turbulator, which increases the turbulence of the fluid flowing through the tubes.

有时,在散热管内插入一种称为湍流器的片状物。当液体流过散热管时,这种湍流器能够增加液体的湍流现象。

过去分词短语 called a turbulator 作 fin 后置定语,非限制性定语从句 which increases the turbulence of the fluid flowing through the tubes 的先行词为 turbulator。

5. When the radiator cools back down, a vacuum is created in the cooling system that pulls open another spring loaded valve, sucking water back in from the bottom of the overflow tank to replace the water that was expelled.

当散热器降回到原来的温度时,散热器内产生真空,此真空吸力克服另一个阀的弹簧力作用后将阀打开,溢流罐内的水就从罐底部被吸入散热器,吸水量与刚溢出的水量相等。

定语从句 that pulls open … 的先行词为 vacuum,sucking …现在分词作伴随状语。

EXERCISES

Ⅰ. Answer following questions

1. What is the function of the cooling system?
2. What are the most common causes of engine overheating?

UNIT 4　THE COOLING SYSTEM

3. Will installing a lower temperature thermostat help the engine run cooler and prevent it from overheating?

4. Why are liquid-cooling systems pressurized?

II. Translate the following into Chinese

1. The fan's activity is not always necessary, and it takes power from the engine to spin. For this reason a thermostatic control, or fan clutch, is often used to reduce drive torque when it isn't needed (variable-speed fan).

2. A different type of fan uses centrifugal force to move its flexible plastic blades, by flattening them when the engine rpm is high (flexible-blade fan). The less angle the blades have, the less power they use. The idea of these units is to save horsepower and reduce the noise the fan makes.

3. A fan can have from four to six blades to suck the air through the radiator. Often the radiator has a shroud for the fan to keep it from re-circulating the same hot air that has collected behind the radiator. Many fans have irregularly spaced blades to reduce resonant noise.

4. Another function of the expansion tank is to remove air bubbles from the cooling system. Coolant without air-bubbles is much more efficient than coolant with air bubbles, because it absorbs heat much faster. The advantage of the expansion tank is that while the level of coolant contained in it rises and falls, the radiator is always full.

Reading Material: Cooling System Maintenance

At least once a year on glycol-based coolants, the engine cooling system should be inspected, flushed, and refilled with fresh coolant. If the coolant is left in the system too long, it loses its ability to prevent rust and corrosion. If the coolant has too much water, it won't protect against freezing.

Silicate free coolants such as DEX-COOL ® can go for 100,000 miles (160,000 km) or 5 years, whichever comes first. However, if you add a silicate coolant to the system (even in small amounts), premature engine, heater core or radiator corrosion may result. In addition, the coolant will have to be changed sooner (12,000 miles (19,300 km) or every year, just like other vehicles not using DEX-COOL ® or other Silicate-free coolant).

The pressure cap should be checked for signs of age or deterioration. The fan belt and other drive belts should be inspected and adjusted to the proper tension. If a belt is cracked, frayed along the edges, or shows signs of peeling, it should be replaced before it fails and causes problems that are more serious.

Leaves, dead insects, and other debris should be removed from the surfaces of the radiator and the air conditioning condenser so air can get through. Hose clamps should be tightened, and soft or cracked hoses replaced. Damp spots or accumulations of rust or dye near hoses, water pump, or other areas indicate possible leakage, which must be corrected before filling the system with fresh coolant.

Checking Coolant Level

Once a month or every 1,000 miles (1,600 km), whichever comes first, check the level of the coolant in the radiator. If you do a lot of hard driving or trailer pulling, check more often.

On vehicles without a coolant overflow system, the coolant level should be checked on a cold engine. If there is a chance the engine is hot, cover the radiator cap with a heavy cloth. Turn the radiator cap to the first stop and let the pressure release. The pressure is gone when the hissing stops. Push down on the cap and turn it all the way around to remove it.

Most late-model vehicles come equipped with a coolant recovery system. Radiator caps for these systems are not interchangeable. Replace only with the proper cap for the system.

On vehicles without coolant recovery systems, keep the coolant level 1 to 2 inches (25 to 50mm) below the filler neck on a cold engine. On vehicles equipped with a coolant recovery system, simply check the level in the plastic tank, located near the radiator. On these types, top off the coolant in the plastic tank, not the radiator. Only when doing a complete refill should you add to the radiator, then the overflow tank.

If the coolant level is constantly low, check for leaks.

Checking the Radiator Cap

While you are checking the coolant level, check the radiator cap for a worn or cracked gasket. If the cap doesn't seal properly, fluid will be lost and the engine will overheat. A worn cap should be replaced with a new one.

Cleaning Radiator of Debris

Periodically clean any debris-leaves, paper, insects, etc. from the radiator fins. Pick the large pieces off by hand. The smaller pieces can be washed away with water pressure from a hose.

Carefully straighten any bent radiator fins. Be careful, the fins are very soft.

V-belts Inspection

Many vehicles utilize one or more V-belts to drive engine accessories (such as the alternator, water pump, power steering pump or A/C compressor off the crankshaft).

V-belts should be checked every 3,000 miles (4,800 km) or 3 months for evidence of wear such as cracking, fraying and incorrect tension. Determine the belt tension at a point halfway between the pulleys by pressing on the belt with moderate thumb pressure. The belt should deflect about 1/4 inch (6 mm) over a 7 to 10 inch (178 to 254 mm) span, or 1/2 inch (13 mm) over a 13 to 16 inch (330 to 406 mm) span. If the deflection is found too much or too little, perform the tension adjustments.

Radiator Hoses Inspection

Upper and lower radiator hoses, along with the heater hoses, should be checked for deterioration, leaks and loose hose clamps at every 1,000 miles (1,600 km) or one month. A quick visual inspection could discover a weakened hose that might have left you stranded if it had remained unrepaired.

Whenever you are checking the hoses, make sure the engine and cooling system are cold. Visually inspect for cracking, rotting or collapsed hoses, and replace as necessary. Run your hand along the length of the hose. If a weak or swollen spot is noted when squeezing the hose wall, the hose should be replaced.

NEW WORDS

1. glycol ['glaikɔl] n. 乙二醇

UNIT 4　THE COOLING SYSTEM

2. flush　　　　　　　［flʌʃ］　　　　　　　　v. 冲洗,清除
3. silicate　　　　　　［'silikit］　　　　　　　n. ［化］硅酸盐
4. deterioration　　　　［di,tiriə'reiʃən］　　　　n. 变质
5. fray　　　　　　　　［frei］　　　　　　　　v. 磨损
6. peeling　　　　　　［'piːliŋ］　　　　　　　n. 鳞剥,剥皮
7. age　　　　　　　　［eidʒ］　　　　　　　　n. 老化
8. deterioration　　　　［di,tiriə'reiʃən］　　　　n. 损坏,变质
9. clamp　　　　　　　［klæmp］　　　　　　　n. 管夹
10. filler　　　　　　　［'filə］　　　　　　　　n. 注入口,加水口,加油口
11. deflect　　　　　　［di'flekt］　　　　　　　n. & v. 变形,下垂
12. span　　　　　　　［spæn］　　　　　　　　n. 跨度

PHRASES AND EXPRESSIONS

1. pick…off　　　　　　　　　　　　　　摘去,拾取
2. air conditioning condenser　　　　　　　空调冷凝器
3. top off　　　　　　　　　　　　　　　终止,完成,结束

NOTES

1. Silicate free coolants such as DEX-COOL ® can go for 100,000 miles (160,000 km) or 5 years, whichever comes first.

诸如 DEX-COOL ® 等不含硅酸盐的冷却剂可以运行100,000 英里(160,000 km)或者5年,到底能运行多久,要看两个条件中的哪个条件先达到。非限制性定语从句 whichever comes first 的先行词是 100,000 miles or 5 years。

2. Damp spots or accumulations of rust or dye near hoses, water pump, or other areas indicate possible leakage, which must be corrected before filling the system with fresh coolant.

在软管,水泵或者其他地方,若发现有潮湿,生锈或者局部颜色发生变化等现象,则说明这些地方很可能有渗漏。在向冷却系统内加注新鲜冷却剂之前,必须要先对这些地方进行修理。which must be corrected…. 先行词为前面整句话。

3. Only when doing a complete refill should you add to the radiator, then the overflow tank.

仅仅当冷却剂被完全更换时,才需要先向散热器内添加冷却剂,然后再向溢流罐内添加冷却剂。

UNIT 5　FUEL INJECTION SYSTEM

Fuel injection systems have been used on vehicles for many years. The earliest ones were purely mechanical. As technology advanced, electronic fuel injection systems became more popular. Early mechanical and electronic fuel injection systems did not use feedback controls. As emissions became more of a concern, feedback controls were adapted to both types of fuel injection systems.

Both mechanical and electronic fuel injection systems can be found on gasoline engines. Diesel engines are most commonly found with mechanical type systems, although the newest generations of these engines have been using electronic fuel injection(EFI).

1. Basic Theory

EFI uses solenoid valves called injectors to meter fuel delivery. Most vehicles today use 1 injector per cylinder. When the solenoid is energized, fuel sprays out into the valve port. Fuel is delivered to the injector by a high-pressure electric pump at around 40 psi. Fuel delivery is controlled by the injectors which are cycled by the computer. The computer produces a signal to open the injectors for a certain length of time depending on engine conditions relayed by sensors. The longer that the injector is open, the more fuel is injected. As engine load and rpm are increased, the injector open times are increased to match increasing airflow. This computer output signal is called the injector pulse width. The longer the pulse width, the more fuel is injected.

2. Engine Requirements

Standard spark ignited, 4 stroke engines require that the correct proportion of fuel be mixed with the incoming air for efficient operation. This proportion is in the range of 13 parts air to 1 part fuel for best power, 15 to 1 for best emissions and 17 to 1 for best economy. Most modern engines aim for a ratio of around 14.7 to 1 for the majority of cruising and medium power conditions. This is the chemically correct ratio which results in the lowest average emissions and reasonable power. A rich condition is characterized by an excess of fuel, and a lean condition is characterized by an excess of air or lack of fuel.

As rpm is increased, up to a point, airflow also increases and fuel flow must increase to match it. As the throttle is opened at a given rpm, airflow increases to a certain point and again, fuel flow must follow airflow.

3. Fuel System

EFI fuel systems consist of a tank, pump, fuel rail, regulator, injectors and return line. Fuel is drawn from the tank by the pump which steps up pressure to around 40 psi. Fuel pressure is controlled by the fuel pressure regulator located on one end of the fuel rail by bleeding fuel back to the tank through the return line. The pump always puts out an excess of fuel so large quantities are returned back to the tank during idle and low speed conditions and less as engine demand increases. The fuel rail is essentially a tubular fuel manifold designed to carry fuel to the injectors as well as hold them in place on the intake manifold. The injectors are usually sealed with O-rings on each end. One end has the fuel entering from the rail and the other end spigots into the manifold. The injector has an 2 pin electrical plug to carry switching current to the solenoid windings. When energized, the solenoid core is pulled back which pulls back a sealing pintle, disc or ball, allowing fuel to spray out in a fine, conical pattern.

4. Air Metering and Measurement

The amount of air entering the engine is controlled by a conventional butterfly valve on most engines located in a throttle body assembly.

Airflow measurement is by one of two basic methods: Mass Airflow and Speed Density. The mass airflow method uses either a spring loaded flap attached to a potentiometer or a heated wire mounted in front of the throttle body to sense actual airflow. The position of the flap or amount of current required to keep the wire heated to a certain temperature is relayed to the computer as a voltage signal. A certain voltage equals a certain airflow rate.

The speed density system uses a solid state pressure transducer to measure the pressure in the intake manifold combined with rpm and air temperature to indirectly determine airflow. Again, a certain pressure relates to a certain voltage which is relayed to the computer.

5. Sensor Inputs

Most EFI systems measure the same basic 6 inputs as follows.

5.1 *Rpm*

Most systems measure rpm off of the ignition coil tachometer pulse or crank triggered magnetic/Hall effect sensors. Rpm is considered a primary input signal on all EFI systems. Most systems generate an injection pulse for every tach pulse so as rpm is increased, the frequency of injection pulses is also increased.

5.2 *Airflow*

On mass airflow type systems, this input is also considered a primary input signal. X amount of air requires Y amount of fuel. As rpm and throttle opening is increased, airflow increases to a point.

5.3 *Manifold Pressure*

On speed density type systems, this input is essential when combined with the rpm signal to calculate airflow. As the throttle is opened, the manifold pressure increases which will require more fuel.

5.4 Throttle Position

This input is a secondary input on most systems. It is required mainly for acceleration enrichment when the throttle is rapidly opened. By looking at the rate of change of throttle blade angle, the computer can determine how quickly the throttle is being opened and can supply the extra fuel required momentarily to alleviate the lean condition. Throttle position is measured by a potentiometer attached to the throttle shaft.

5.5 Water Temperature

Water temperature is a secondary input required mainly to ensure proper starting and warm-up of the engine. When the engine is cold, the air to fuel ratio must be very rich to enable enough fuel to vaporize for proper starting. The computer increases the injector pulse width to supply extra fuel when cold and tapers this fuel off as the water temperature increases. Once the water warms past 120℃ or so, the computer does not need to add any extra fuel.

5.6 Air Temperature

This is a secondary input required especially on speed density systems. The sensor is usually mounted in the intake manifold or air filter area. As the air temperature drops, its density increases. Denser air requires more fuel. As the temperature of the inducted air increases, the computer reduces the pulse width to compensate for lower density. Mass airflow systems are not critically affected by operation without an air temperature sensor because the airflow meter is already measuring the air mass entering the engine.

6. Oxygen Sensor

This sensor is employed in closed loop systems to modify the basic pulse width after the fact. It is mounted into the exhaust manifold area. By looking at the oxygen content of the exhaust gasses after combustion, the computer can determine if the air/fuel ratio is too rich or too lean for optimum combustion and adjust the next few injections accordingly. This sensor is primarily employed for emission control and to a lesser degree, fuel economy. For the lowest average emissions, the air/fuel ratio must be kept around 14.7 to 1.

Under full throttle conditions, this sensor input is ignored by the computer so that the engine can produce more power. This is called open loop mode and the computer is supplying the injector pulse width from tables based on all of the other sensor inputs. Once throttle opening and rpm are reduced to cruising conditions, most systems will jump back into the closed loop mode where they will stay for a large portion of the time on most street driven applications.

7. Basic Operation

As explained in the Basic Theory section, the computer processes all of the voltage signals from

UNIT 5　FUEL INJECTION SYSTEM

the various sensors to determine the engine operating conditions at the moment and delivers the appropriate pulse width to the injectors. If engine airflow increases by 10%, the pulse width is also increased by about 10% to keep the air/fuel ratio constant. If the rpm is doubled from 2,000 to 4,000 r/min, the number of injections are also doubled to double the fuel flow.

The computer looks at the changes in sensor inputs every few milliseconds in order to be ready to modify the pulse width if any parameter changes.

NEW WORDS

1. feedback　　　　　　['fiːdbæk]　　　　　　*n.* 反馈
2. injector　　　　　　[in'dʒektə]　　　　　　*n.* 喷油器
3. sensor　　　　　　　['sensə]　　　　　　　*n.* 传感器
4. given　　　　　　　['givən]　　　　　　　*adj.* 给定的
5. bleed　　　　　　　[bliːd]　　　　　　　　*v.* 放油
6. spigot　　　　　　　['spigət]　　　　　　　*v.* 连接管,接合,安装
7. alleviate　　　　　　[ə'liːvieit]　　　　　　*v.* 易于忍受
8. momentarily　　　　[ˌməumən'tərəliː]　　　*adv.* 瞬时地

PHRASES AND EXPRESSIONS

1. electric pump　　　　　　　　　电动燃油泵
2. pulse width　　　　　　　　　　脉冲宽度
3. fuel rail　　　　　　　　　　　　油轨
4. return line　　　　　　　　　　　回油管路
5. fuel pressure regulator　　　　　燃油压力调节器
6. throttle body assembly　　　　　节气门体总成
7. solid state pressure transducer　　晶体管压力传感器
8. measure off　　　　　　　　　　量出
9. hall effect sensor　　　　　　　　霍尔效应传感器
10. taper off　　　　　　　　　　　逐渐减少

NOTES TO THE TEXT

1. Fuel delivery is controlled by the injectors which are cycled by the computer. The computer produces a signal to open the injectors for a certain length of time depending on engine conditions relayed by sensors.

喷油量是由喷油器控制的,而喷油器的开启和关闭又是被计算机控制的。计算机根据传感器发送来的工况信号,向喷油器发送开启以及开启持续时间的信号。Which 的先行词为 injector。

2. As rpm is increased, up to a point, airflow also increases and fuel flow must increase to match it.

在转速小于某个值时,随着转速的增加,空气流量也会增加,因而燃油流量必须随之增加。

3. This sensor is employed in closed loop systems to modify the basic pulse width after the fact.

这种传感器被用于闭环控制系统中,以便对根据发动机实际工作情况得到的基本脉冲宽度进行修改。

4. Once throttle opening and rpm are reduced to cruising conditions, most systems will jump back into the closed loop mode where they will stay for a large portion of the time on most street driven applications.

一旦节气门开度和转速下降到经济工况下的值时,大多数系统都会跳回闭环控制模式,车辆在街上行驶的大部分时间都处于这种模式。

EXERCISES

Ⅰ. Answer following questions

1. Which sensors are used for fuel injection system?
2. What determine the amount of fuel injected to each cylinder?
3. How a fuel injection system works?

Ⅱ. Translate the following passage into Chinese

1. The injection pump in the jerk pump system is used to time, meter and pressurize the fuel. This is the most common and utilized system. The plungers are driven by a camshaft that is designed to control the injection characteristics of the engine.

2. Compared to gasoline engines, diesels have a number of important advantages. One is fuel economy. Diesel engines are unthrottled, so pumping losses are reduced. This improves breathing efficiency for more fuel-efficient operation. Diesel engines also run much leaner air/fuel ratios than their gasoline counterparts, and have much higher compression ratios which improves thermal efficiency and helps squeeze even more power out of every drop of fuel.

3. The injection system that delivers fuel to a diesel engine operates at much higher pressure than a gasoline: as much as 17,400 psi for traditional pump, line and injector systems and up to 23,500 psi for common rail systems, compared to 35 to 90 psi for most gasoline EFI systems. The fuel is also sprayed directly into the combustion chamber rather than into the intake port.

4. Diesel engines have no ignition system, so there are no spark plugs, plug wires or distributor to cause problems. The fuel is ignited by the heat of compression and is controlled by injector timing. For cold starting, diesels use a glow plug system as an additional heat source to aid in the combustion process until the engine is running and generating its own heat.

5. The HEUI System develops injection pressures as high as 18,000 to 24,000 psi by applying high-pressure oil to the top of an intensifier piston. By varying the oil pressure, injection rate can be controlled independently of the crank or cam. Thus injection timing, rates, and pressures are no longer dependent on camshaft position, speed or cam ramp velocity. This is all controlled by a solenoid-actuated valve that determines when high-pressure oil is applied to the piston.

Reading Material: Robert Bosch Type VE Diesel Injection Pump

The purpose of the fuel injection pump is to deliver an exact metered amount of fuel, under high pressure, at the right time to the injector. The injector, unlike in a gasoline engine, injects the

UNIT 5 FUEL INJECTION SYSTEM

fuel directly into the cylinder or a pre-chamber connected to the cylinder.

The VE in the name of the Bosch pump used in the VW diesels and many other small diesel engines stands for "Verteiler", which is German for distributor or divider. The other common kind of injection pump is the inline pump. The difference between them is that the VE pump has one fuel metering plunger, and a mechanism (the "Verteiler"/distributor) to send the fuel to the right cylinder. The inline pump has one plunger for each cylinder.

The Bosch VE has comparatively few moving parts, but what does move does so in a complex way. On the leftmost end in the picture (Figure 5-1) is the fuel feed pump. This is a vane pump. Its purpose is to suck fuel from the tank and deliver it to the metering pump. All the things shown on the right in the Figure 5-1 have to do with the metering, timing and distribution of fuel delivery.

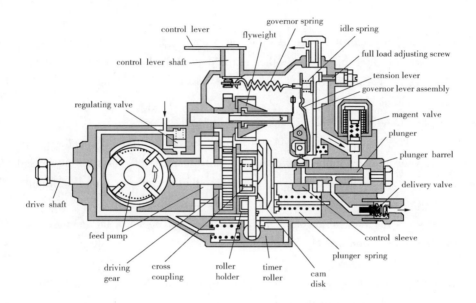

Figure 5-1 Robert Bosch type VE Diesel injection pump

The plunger (right middle in the Figure 5-1) in the VE pump both rotates along its axis and performs a reciprocating translation in and out. It is the translation that performs the high pressure pumping, while the rotation is responsible for metering and sending the fuel to the correct cylinder.

The cam disk is rigidly attached to the plunger. The drive shaft rotates the cam disk. The cam disk rides on four rollers (only one shown in this picture), and has four lobes. Thus for each revolution the plunger will pump four times. Note that with this arrangement the plunger stroke is constant. The metering (regulation of how much fuel is delivered) is done not by changing the mechanical stroke, but by spilling some of the fuel through spill ports, and thus changing the effective stroke. This is done by uncovering a spill port under the control sleeve at a particular angle of rotation. The other purpose of the rotation is to deliver the fuel to the correct cylinder. This is done by four delivery valves (only one shown in the Figure 5-1), one for every 90° of rotation. During a full revolution the plunger makes four strokes, one at 0°, 90°, 180° and 270°. During each stroke the delivery port in the middle of the plunger is connected to a particular delivery valve.

To understand the function in some detail lets consider one stroke. During the backward motion of the plunger, the rotation uncovers a fill port (to the right in the Figure 5-1, just below the magnet valve (solenoid)), and the plunger barrel is loaded with fuel. At bottom dead center the fill port is closed. On the forward pressure stroke fuel is pressurized (to over 120 bar). At this time the plunger barrel is connected to a particular delivery valve through the channel in the center of the plunger, and a port in the side. When pressure builds up to the delivery valve opening pressure, the valve will open and deliver high-pressure fuel to the injector.

When the desired amount of fuel has been injected the spill port opens (located under the control sleeve in the Figure 5-1), and the pressure quickly drops. This causes the delivery valve to close. During the rest of the stroke fuel is "spilled" through the spill port instead of being injected into the cylinder.

The position of the control sleeve controls at what angle the spill port opens, and thus determines the amount of fuel injected, in other words it controls the metering. The control sleeve is moved in response to a combination of accelerator position and engine speed. The latter is determined by a mechanical governor.

Some other functions of the fuel injection pump are:

(1) Timing. The timing is adjusted in response to engine rpm. At higher rpm, the fuel pressure from the vane transfer pump is higher. Pressure changes effects a spring loaded plunger, and the resulting movement will move the cam rollers to either advance or retard the timing. There is also a cold start device, which advances the idle timing manually.

(2) Governor. A mechanical governor limits the maximum speed of the engine to 4,800 r/min in the bus/vanagon application and 5,350 r/min in newer passenger cars. It can be seen just above the cam disk in the middle figure.

(3) Stop. A magnet valve or solenoid (shown in the Figures) opens and shuts off the fuel channel between the feed pump and the metering pump.

(4) Aneroid. An air inlet pressure sensor is used to determine maximum amount of fuel delivered on injection pumps for turbo engines.

NEW WORDS

1. injector [in'dʒektə] n. 喷油器
2. pre-chamber [priː'tʃæmbə] n. 预燃室
3. meter ['miːtə] v. 计量, 测流; n. 仪表, 米
4. leftmost ['leftməust] adj. 最左边的
5. translation [træns'leiʃən] n. 移动, 位移
6. solenoid ['səulinɔid] n. 电磁线圈
7. manually ['mænjuəli] adv. 手动地, 人工地
8. governor ['gʌvənə] n. 调速器
9. aneroid ['ænərɔid] n. 空盒气压表

UNIT 5 FUEL INJECTION SYSTEM

PHRASES AND EXPRESSIONS

1. stand for   代表
2. inline pump   直列式(喷油)泵
3. fuel feed pump   输油泵
4. vane pump   叶片式泵
5. cam disk   平面凸轮
6. drive shaft   传动轴
7. be attached to   固定在,连到……上,附属于
8. spill port   溢流口
9. effective stroke   有效(供油)行程
10. plunger barrel   柱塞套
11. build up   积累,增加
12. control sleeve   控制套筒
13. delivery valve   出油阀
14. in detail   详细地

NOTES

1. The Bosch VE has comparatively few moving parts, but what does move does so in a complex way.

博世 VE 泵的运动零部件相当少,但是这些在内部运动的零部件的运动方式确实很复杂。what does move does so 中,第一个 does 为强调助动词,第二个 does 为代动词。

2. The plunger (right middle in the Figure 5-1) in the VE pump both rotates along its axis and performs a reciprocating translation in and out. It is the translation that performs the high pressure pumping, while the rotation is responsible for metering and sending the fuel to the correct cylinder.

VE 泵中的柱塞(图 5-1 中右侧中间部分)既绕其轴线作旋转运动,也沿其轴线作往复直线运动。就是这种往复直线运动完成了高压泵油工作,而旋转运动则计量燃油并向正确的汽缸输送燃油。

It is…that…为强调句,while 在此为转折连词,含义是"而,却"。

3. During a full revolution the plunger makes four strokes, one at 0°, 90°, 180° and 270°.

柱塞旋转一周,移动四个行程(左右移动四次),分别是在 0°、90°、180°和 270°时。

UNIT 6   EXHAUST SYSTEM

The exhaust system carries exhaust gases from the engine's combustion chamber to the atmosphere and reduces, or muffles, engine noise. Exhaust gases leave the engine in a pipe, traveling through a catalytic converter and a muffler before exiting through the tailpipe.

1. The Tailpipe

The tailpipe is a long metal tube attached to the muffler. It sticks out from under the body of a car, at the rear, in order to discharge the exhaust gases from the muffler of the engine into the air outside the car.

2. The Muffler

Exhaust gases leave the engine under extremely high pressure. If these gases escaped directly from the engine, the noise would be tremendous. For this reason, the exhaust manifold sends the gases to a muffler where they go through metal plates, or tubes, with a series of holes. The pressure of the gases is reduced when they pass through the muffler, so they go out of the tailpipe quietly.

The muffler is made of metal and is located underneath the body of a car. It's connected between the tailpipe and the catalytic converter.

There are two types of muffler design. One type uses several baffled chambers to reduce noise. The other type sends the gases straight through perforated pipe wrapped in metal or fiberglass. This type of muffler is designed for the purpose of reducing backpressure and, consequently, makes slightly more noise.

The muffler quiets the noise of the exhaust by "muffling" the sound waves created by the opening and closing of the exhaust valves. When an exhaust valve opens, it discharges the burned gases at high pressures into the exhaust pipe, which is at low pressure. This type of action creates sound waves that travel through the flowing gas, moving much faster than the gas itself (up to 1,400 mile/h) that the muffler must silence. It generally does this by converting the sound wave energy into heat by passing the exhaust gas and through perforated chambers of varied sizes. Passing into the perforations and reflectors within the chamber forces the sound waves to dissipate their energy.

Car manufacturers are experimenting with an electronic muffler, which uses sensors to monitor the sound waves of the exhaust noise. The sound wave data are sent to a computer that controls speakers near the tailpipe. The system generates sound waves 180 degrees out of phase with the engine noise. The sound waves from the electronic muffler collide with the exhaust sound waves and they cancel each other out, leaving only low-level heat to emerge from the tailpipe.

3. The Exhaust Manifold and Header

The exhaust manifold, usually constructed of cast iron, is a pipe that conducts the exhaust gases from the combustion chambers to the exhaust pipe. It has smooth curves in it for improving the flow of exhaust. The exhaust manifold is bolted to the cylinder head, and has entrances for the air that is injected into it. It is usually located under the intake manifold. A header is a different type of manifold; it is made of separate equal-length tubes.

4. Manifold to Exhaust Pipe Gaskets

There are several types of gaskets that connect the exhaust pipe to the manifold. One is a flat surface gasket. Another type uses a ball and socket with springs to maintain pressure. This type allows some flexibility without breakage of the seal or the manifold. A third type is the full ball connector type, which also allows a little flexibility.

5. Exhaust Pipe Hangers

Hangers hold the exhaust system in place. They give the system flexibility and reduce the noise level. The hanger system consists of rubber rings, tubes and clamps.

6. Exhaust Pipe

The exhaust pipe is the bent-up or convoluted pipes underneath a car. Some are shaped to go over the rear axle, allowing the rear axle to move up and down without bumping into the exhaust pipe; some are shaped to bend around under the floor of the car, connecting the catalytic converter with the muffler. Exhaust pipes are usually made out of stainless steel, since the high heat conditions involved with the muffler system will cause rust.

7. Dual Exhaust System

The advantage of a dual exhaust system is that the engine exhausts more freely, thereby lowering the backpressure, which is inherent in an exhaust system. With a dual exhaust system, a sizable increase in engine horsepower can be obtained because the "breathing" capacity of the engine is improved, leaving less exhaust gases in the engine at the end of each exhaust stroke. This, in turn, leaves more room for an extra intake of the air-fuel mixture.

NEW WORDS

1. tremendous   [tri'mendəs]   adj. 巨大的,极大的
2. perforated   ['pɜːfə,reitid]   adj. 多孔的
3. muffler   ['mʌflə]   n. 消声器
4. tailpipe   ['teilpaip]   n. 尾气管
5. hanger   ['hænə]   n. 吊耳,吊钩
6. manifold   ['mænə,fəuld]   n. 歧管
7. fiberglass   ['faibəglɑːs]   n. 玻璃纤维,玻璃丝
8. speaker   ['spiːkə]   n. 扬声器
9. header   ['hedə]   n. 集气管
10. baffled   ['bæfld]   adj. 用挡板隔开的,阻挡的
11. convoluted   ['kɔnvə,luːtid]   adj. 回旋状的,盘旋的
12. flat   [flæt]   n. 平面; adj. 平坦的
13. socket   ['sɔkit]   n. 插座
14. sizable   ['saizəbəl]   adj. 相当大的,大小相当的
15. room   [ruːm]   n. 空间
16. bump   [bʌmp]   v. 碰撞,冲击

PHRASES AND EXPRESSIONS

1. stick out   伸出,显眼,触目
2. the body of a car   车身
3. cast iron   铸铁
4. catalytic converter   催化转换器
5. out of phase with   与……反相
6. collide with   与……相撞
7. cancel out   取消
8. backpressure   背压

NOTES TO THE TEXT

1. Passing into the perforations and reflectors within the chamber forces the sound waves to dissipate their energy.

使声波穿过消声器室内的很多小孔,并经多次反射,这样就能够消耗掉声波的能量。

2. This type of action creates sound waves that travel through the flowing gas, moving much faster than the gas itself (up to 1,400 mile/h) that the muffler must silence.

以这种方式(从排气门)排出的废气就会在废气流中产生声波,这种声波在废气流中的传播速度比气体本身的流动速度要快得多(高达1400英里/小时),因此,必须使用消声器来净化这种噪声。

句中 that travel through… 和 that the muffler… 都是定语从句,先行词都是 sound waves, silence 是及物动词,"抑制,遏止,净化"。

EXERCISES

Ⅰ. Answer following questions

1. Describe the functions of the exhaust system.
2. Name the main components of the exhaust system.
3. Describe the types of the muffler.
4. Describe the operation of an electronic muffler.

Ⅱ. Translate the following into Chinese

1. Carbon monoxide (CO) also increases the rate at which the photochemical smog is formed by speeding up the conversion of nitric oxide (NO) to nitrogen dioxide.

2. Oxides of sulfur were initially ignored in the exhaust system emissions, since the sulfur content of gasoline as a fuel is less than 1/10 of 1 percent. Because of this small amount, it was felt that it contributed very little to the overall pollution problem. However, the automobile exhaust system, when equipped with a catalytic converter, changes the sulfur dioxide into sulfur trioxide. When this combines with water vapors, a sulfuric acid mist is formed and is a very difficult pollutant to handle since it is extremely corrosive.

3. By visually inspecting the tailpipe emissions, a determination can be made as to where an engine defect may exist. An engine with light gray or blue smoke emitting from the tailpipe normally indicates an increase in the oil consumption through burning due to internal engine wear. Black smoke would indicate a defective fuel delivery system, causing the engine to operate in a rich mode.

Reading Material: Emission Control Systems

The purpose of the emission control system is just that it controls the emissions and exhaust from a vehicle. The idea is to turn the harmful gases a car manufactures into harmless ones that don't ruin the environment, or persons. Some of the problem gases are: hydrocarbons (unburned), carbon monoxide, carbon dioxide, nitrogen oxides, sulfur dioxide, phosphorus, lead and other metals.

There are five popular systems used to reduce emissions: the crankcase ventilation system, the evaporative emission control system, the Exhaust Gas Recirculation (EGR) system, the air injection system and the catalytic converter system. In addition to these emission systems, some vehicles incorporate an electronically controlled fuel system (feedback system), which further reduces emissions.

Note: Not all vehicles are equipped with these emission systems.

Crankcase Ventilation Systems

Since the early 1960s, all cars have been equipped with crankcase ventilation systems.

When the engine is running, a small portion of the gases which are formed in the combustion chamber leak past the piston rings and enter the crankcase. Since these gases are under pressure, they tend to escape from the crankcase and enter the atmosphere. If these gases are allowed to remain in the crankcase for any length of time, they contaminate the engine oil and cause sludge to build up in the crankcase. If the gases are allowed to escape to the atmosphere, they pollute the air with unburned hydrocarbons. The job of the crankcase ventilation system is to recycle these gases back into the engine combustion chamber where they are re-burned.

The crankcase (blow-by) gases are recycled as the engine is running by drawing clean filtered air through the air filter and into the crankcase. As the air passes through the crankcase, it picks up the combustion gases and carries them out of the crankcase, through the oil separator, through the PCV valve or orifice, and into the induction system. As they enter the intake manifold, they are drawn into the combustion chamber where they are re-burned.

The most critical component in the system is the PCV valve that controls the amount of gases that are recycled. At low engine speeds, the valve is partially closed, limiting the flow of gases. As engine speed increases, the valve opens to admit greater quantities of air to the intake manifold. Some systems do not use a PCV valve. They simply use a restrictor or orifice in the ventilation hose to meter the crankcase gases.

If the PCV valve/orifice becomes blocked or plugged, the gases cannot be vented from the crankcase. Since they are under pressure, they will find their own way out of the crankcase. This alternate route is usually a weak oil seal or gasket in the engine. As the gas escapes by the gasket, it usually creates an oil leak. Besides causing oil leaks, a clogged PCV valve also allows these gases to remain in the crankcase for an extended period, promoting the formation of sludge in the engine.

Evaporative Emission Control System

The evaporative emission control system is designed to prevent fuel tank and carburetor bowl (if equipped) vapors from being emitted into the atmosphere. Fuel vapors are absorbed and stored by a fuel vapor charcoal canister. The canister stores them until certain engine conditions are met and the vapors can be purged and burned by the engine.

The charcoal canister purge cycle is controlled different ways: either by a thermostatic vacuum switch, a solenoid or by a timed vacuum source. The thermostatic switch is installed in the coolant passage and prevents canister purge when the engine is below a certain temperature. The solenoid is usually controlled by a computer and is used on feedback controlled fuel systems. The computer determines when canister purge is appropriate. Depending on the system, this can be engine operating temperature, engine speed, evaporative system pressure or any combination of these. The timed vacuum source uses a manifold vacuum controlled diaphragm to control canister purge. When the engine is running, full manifold vacuum is applied to the top tube of the purge valve which lifts the valve diaphragm and opens the valve.

A vent located in the fuel tank, allows fuel vapors to flow to the charcoal canister. A tank pressure control valve, used on some high altitude applications, prevents canister purge when the engine is not running. The fuel tank cap does not normally vent to the atmosphere, but is designed to provide both vacuum and pressure relief.

Air Injection System

Introducing a controlled amount of air into the exhaust stream promotes further oxidation of the gases. This in turn reduces the amount of carbon monoxide and hydrocarbons. The carbon monoxide and hydrocarbons are converted to carbon dioxide and water, the harmless by-products of combustion. Some systems use an air pump, while other use negative exhaust pulses to draw air (pulse air).

The air pump, usually driven by a belt, simply pumps air under a pressure of only a few pounds into each exhaust port. Between the nozzles and the pump is a check valve to keep the hot exhaust gases from flowing back into the pump and hoses thereby destroying them. Most pumps also utilize a gulp valve or a diverter valve. Early systems used a gulp valve, while later systems use diverter valves. They both operate on the same principle. During deceleration, as the throttle is closed, the fuel mixture tends to get too rich. If the air continued to be pumped during deceleration, an explosion in the exhaust system could occur that could blow the muffler apart. During deceleration, the air is either diverted into the atmosphere or into the intake system.

On pulse air systems, clean air (from the air cleaner) is drawn through a silencer, the check valve(s) and then into the exhaust ports. The negative exhaust pulses opens the reed valve in the check valve assembly, allowing air to flow into the exhaust port.

Some feedback-controlled vehicles utilize an oxidizing catalytic converter. Under certain operating conditions, the air is diverted into the catalytic converter to help oxidize the exhaust gases.

Exhaust Gas Re-Circulation (EGR) Systems

The EGR system's purpose is to control oxides of nitrogen (NO_x) which are formed during the combustion process. NO_x emissions at low combustion temperatures are not severe, but when the combustion temperatures go over $2,500°F$ ($1,371°C$), the production of NO_x in the combustion chambers shoots way up. The end products of combustion are relatively inert gases derived from the exhaust gases. These are redirected (under certain conditions) through the EGR valve and back into the combustion chamber. These inert gases displace a certain amount of oxygen in the chamber. Since not as much oxygen is present, the explosion is not as hot. This helps lower peak combustion temperatures.

The EGR valve can either be actuated by a vacuum diaphragm, a solenoid or a stepper motor. On feedback controlled vehicles, the EGR system is controlled by the computer.

Catalytic Converter

The catalytic converter is a muffler-like container built into the exhaust system to aid in the reduction of exhaust emissions. The catalyst element is coated with a noble metal such as platinum, palladium, rhodium or a combination of them. When the exhaust gases come into contact with the catalyst, a chemical reaction occurs which reduces the pollutants into harmless substances such as water and carbon dioxide. Oxidizing catalysts require the addition of oxygen to spur the catalyst into reducing the engine's HC and CO emissions into H_2O and CO_2.

While catalytic converters are built in a variety of shapes and sizes, they all fall into two general types, the pellet, or bead type and the monolithic type. Construction may differ slightly, but the object is the same-to present the largest possible surface area to passing exhaust gases. Older vehicles use bead/pellet type converters. The exhaust gas must pass through a bed of these pellets. This type of converter is rather restrictive. The cross-section of a monolithic type converter resembles a honeycomb. The exhaust gases are exposed to a greater amount of surface area in these converters; as a result they are more efficient. They also tend to be less restrictive.

NEW WORDS

1. hydrocarbon　　　[ˌhaidrəˈkɑːbən]　　　n. 碳氢化合物
2. phosphorus　　　[ˈfɔsfərəs]　　　n. 磷
3. contaminate　　　[kənˈtæmineit]　　　v. 污染
4. sludge　　　[slʌdʒ]　　　n. 油泥,淤泥
5. byproduct　　　[ˈbaiˌprɔdʌkt]　　　n. 副产品
6. cross-section　　　[ˈkrɔːsˈsekʃən]　　　n. 横截面
7. platinum　　　[ˈplætnəm]　　　n. 铂
8. palladium　　　[pəˈleidiəm]　　　n. 钯
9. rhodium　　　[ˈrəudiəm]　　　n. 铑

PHRASES AND EXPRESSIONS

1. sulfur dioxide　　　二氧化硫
2. carbon monoxide　　　一氧化碳
3. nitrogen oxides　　　氮氧化物
4. Exhaust Gas Re-circulation (EGR)　　　废气再循环
5. tend to　　　必然
6. carburetor bowl　　　化油器浮子室
7. charcoal canister　　　炭罐
8. check valve　　　止回阀
9. gulp valve　　　补气阀
10. diverter valve　　　换向阀,分流阀
11. as a result　　　结果
12. stepper motor　　　步进电动机
13. PCV = positive crankcase ventilation　　　曲轴箱强制通风

NOTES

1. On pulse air systems, clean air (from the air cleaner) is drawn through a silencer, the check valve(s) and then into the exhaust ports. The negative exhaust pulses opens the reed valve in the check valve assembly, allowing air to flow into the exhaust port.

在脉冲空气系统中,来自空气滤清器的清洁空气经过消声器、止回阀后被吸进排气口。排气负脉冲打开止回阀总成中的簧片阀,从而使空气流进排气口。

2. The catalyst element is coated with a noble metal such as platinum, palladium, rhodium or a combination of them.

催化剂单元表面涂以诸如铂、钯、铑或由它们组合而成的贵重金属。

3. NO_x emissions at low combustion temperatures are not severe,…, the production of NO_x in the combustion chambers shoots way up.

在燃烧温度低时,NO_x 的排放量并不多,……,燃烧室内 NO_x 的生成量急剧增加。句中 shoot up 是一个词组,"急升,直升,上涨";way 是副词,"远远,大大,非常"。

4. When the exhaust gases come into contact with the catalyst, a chemical reaction occurs which reduces the pollutants into harmless substances such as water and carbon dioxide.

如果废气与催化剂接触,化学反应就会发生,从而就可以将污染物转化为水和 CO_2 等无害物质。句中,定语从句 which reduces…的先行词为前面整句话;reduce… into…在此处的含意为"转换……为……",另外它还有"还原……为……"的含义。

5. While catalytic converters are built in a variety of shapes and sizes, they all fall into two general types, the pellet, or bead type and the monolithic type.

尽管催化转化器的形状和大小各种各样,但都可以归结为两种基本类型:颗粒型和整体型。句中 While 引导让步状语从句,"尽管,虽然"。

UNIT 7　THE IGNITION SYSTEM

There are many different types of ignition systems. Most of these systems can be placed into one of three distinct groups: the conventional breaker point type ignition systems (in use since the early 1,900s); the electronic ignition systems (popular since the mid 1970s); and the distributorless ignition system (introduced in the mid 1980s).

The automotive ignition system has two basic functions: it must control the spark and timing of the spark plug firing to match varying engine requirements, and it must increase battery voltage to a point where it will overcome the resistance offered by the spark plug gap and fire the plug.

1. Point-Type Ignition System

An automotive ignition system is divided into two electrical circuits—the primary and secondary circuits (Figure 7-1). The primary circuit carries low voltage. This circuit operates only on battery current and is controlled by the breaker points and the ignition switch. The secondary circuit consists of the secondary windings in the coil, the high-tension lead between the distributor and the coil (commonly called the coil wire), the distributor cap, the distributor rotor, the spark plug leads and the spark plugs.

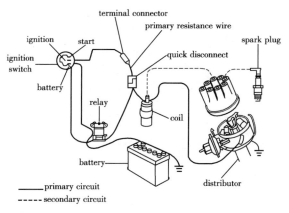

Figure 7-1　A schematic of a typical conventional breaker-point ignition system

The distributor is the controlling element of the system. It switches the primary current on and off and distributes the current to the proper spark plug each time a spark is needed. The distributor is a stationary housing surrounding a rotating shaft. The shaft is driven at one-half engine speed by the engine's camshaft through the distributor drive gears. A cam near the top of the distributor shaft has one lobe for each cylinder of the engine. The cam operates the contact points, which are mounted on a plate within the distributor housing.

A rotor is attached to the top of the distributor shaft. When the distributor cap is in place, a spring-loaded piece of metal in the center of the cap makes contact with a metal strip on top of the rotor. The outer end of the rotor passes very close to the contacts connected to the spark plug leads around the outside of the distributor cap.

The coil (Figure 7-2) is the heart of the ignition system. Essentially, it is nothing more than a transformer which takes the relatively low voltage (12 volts) available from the battery and increases it to a point where it will fire the spark plug as much as 40,000 volts. The term "coil" is perhaps a misnomer since there are actually two coils of wire wound about an iron core. These coils are insulated from each other and the whole assembly is enclosed in an oil-filled case. The primary coil, which consists of relatively few turns of heavy wire, is connected to the two primary terminals located on top of the coil. The secondary coil consists of many turns of fine wire. It is connected to the high-tension connection on top of the coil (the tower into which the coil wire from the distributor is plugged).

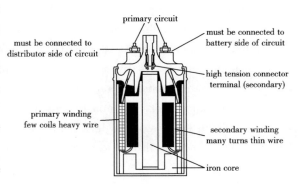

Figure 7-2 Cutaway view of a conventional coil

Under normal operating conditions, power from the battery is fed through a resistor or resistance wire to the primary circuit of the coil and is then grounded through the ignition points in the distributor (the points are closed). Energizing the coil primary circuit with battery voltage produces current flow through the primary windings, which induces a very large, intense magnetic field. This magnetic field remains as long as current flows and the points remain closed.

As the distributor cam rotates, the points are pushed apart, breaking the primary circuit and stopping the flow of current. Interrupting the flow of primary current causes the magnetic field to collapse. Just as current flowing through a wire produces a magnetic field, moving a magnetic field across a wire will produce a current. As the magnetic field collapses, its lines of force cross the secondary windings, inducing a current in them. Since there are many more turns of wire in the secondary windings, the voltage from the primary windings is magnified considerably up to 40,000 volts.

The voltage from the coil secondary windings flows through the coil high-tension lead to the center of the distributor cap, where it is distributed by the rotor to one of the outer terminals in the cap. From there, it flows through the spark plug lead to the spark plug. This process occurs in a split second and is repeated every time the points open and close, which is up to 1,500 times a minute in a 4-cylinder engine at idle.

2. Electronic Ignition Systems

The need for higher mileage, reduced emissions and greater reliability has led to the development of the electronic ignition systems. These systems generate a much stronger spark, which is needed to ignite leaner fuel mixtures. Breaker point systems needed a resistor to reduce the operating voltage of the primary circuit in order to prolong the life of the points. The primary circuit of the electronic ignition systems operates on full battery voltage, which helps to develop a stronger spark. Spark plug gaps have widened due to the ability of the increased voltage to jump the larger gap. Cleaner combustion and less deposit have led to longer spark plug life.

On some systems, the ignition coil has been moved inside the distributor cap. This system is said to have an internal coil as opposed to the conventional external one.

Electronic Ignition systems are not as complicated as they may first appear. In fact, they differ only slightly from conventional point ignition systems. Like conventional ignition systems, electronic systems have two circuits: a primary circuit and a secondary circuit (Figure 7-3). The entire secondary circuit is the same as in a conventional ignition system. In addition, the section of the primary circuit from the battery to the battery terminal at the coil is the same as in a conventional ignition system.

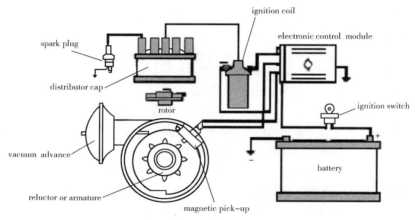

Figure 7-3 Typical electronic ignition system

Electronic ignition systems differ from conventional ignition systems in the distributor component area. Instead of a distributor cam, breaker plate, points, and condenser, an electronic ignition system has an armature (called by various names such as a trigger wheel, reluctor, etc.), a pickup coil (stator, sensor, etc.), and an electronic control module.

3. Distributorless Ignition Systems (DIS)

The third type of ignition system is the distributorless ignition system. The spark plugs are fired directly from the coils. The spark timing is controlled by an Ignition Control Unit (ICU) and the Engine Control Unit (ECU). The distributorless ignition system may have one coil per cylinder, or one coil for each pair of cylinders.

Some popular systems use one ignition coil per two cylinders. This type of system is often known as the waste spark distribution method. In this system, each cylinder is paired with the cylinder opposite it in the firing order (usually 1-4, 2-3 on 4-cylinder engines or 1-4, 2-5, 3-6 on

V6 engines, Figure 7-4). The ends of each coil secondary leads are attached to spark plugs for the paired opposites. These two plugs are on companion cylinders, cylinders that are at Top Dead Center (TDC) at the same time. But, they are paired opposites, because they are always at opposing ends of the 4-stroke engine cycle. When one is at TDC of the compression stroke, the other is at TDC of the exhaust stroke. The one that is on compression is said to be the event cylinder and one on the exhaust stroke, the waste cylinder. When the coil discharges, both plugs fire at the same time to complete the series circuit.

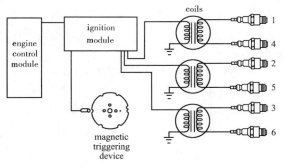

Figure 7-4 Typical distributorless ignition schematics

Since the polarity of the primary and the secondary windings are fixed, one plug always fires in a forward direction and the other in reverse. This is different than a conventional system firing all plugs the same direction each time. Because of the demand for additional energy; the coil design, saturation time and primary current flow are also different. This redesign of the system allows higher energy to be available from the distributorless coils, greater than 40 kilovolts at all rpm ranges.

The distributorless ignition system uses either a magnetic crankshaft sensor, camshaft position sensor, or both, to determine crankshaft position and engine speed. This signal is sent to the ignition control module or engine control module, which then energizes the appropriate coil.

The advantages of no distributor, in theory, are:

(a) No timing adjustments;
(b) No distributor cap and rotor;
(c) No moving parts to wear out;
(d) No distributor to accumulate moisture and cause starting problems;
(e) No distributor to drive thus providing less engine drag.

The major components of a distributorless ignition are:

(a) ECU or Engine Control Unit;
(b) ICU or Ignition Control Unit;
(c) Magnetic Triggering Device such as the Crankshaft Position Sensor and the Camshaft;
(d) Position Sensor;
(e) Coil Pack.

NEW WORDS

1. distributor　　　　[di'stribjətə]　　　　　　n. 分电器

2. condenser   [kən'densə]   n. 电容器
3. wear   [wεə]   v. 磨损
4. saturation   [ˌsætʃə'reiʃn]   n. 磁饱和
5. series   ['siəri:z]   n. 串联
6. wind   [wind]   v. 缠绕
7. coil   [kɔil]   n. (点火)线圈
8. transformer   [træns'fɔ:mə]   n. 变压器
9. turn   [tə:n]   n. 匝数
10. term   [tə:m]   n. 术语,学期,条件

PHRASES AND EXPRESSIONS

1. breaker point type ignition system   触点型点火系统
2. distributorless ignition system   无分电器点火系统
3. primary and secondary circuits   (点火线圈的)初级电路和次级电路
4. magnetic field   磁场
5. high tension lead   高压导线
6. distributor rotor   分火头
7. spark plug   火花塞
8. nothing more than   只不过是,简直是
9. (be) different than   与……不同,不同于

NOTES TO THE TEXT

1. The distributor is the controlling element of the system. …The distributor is a stationary housing surrounding a rotating shaft.

分电器是点火系统的控制元件。…… 配电器是围绕转轴的一个固定壳体。第一个 distributor 指"分电器",第二个 distributor 指"配电器"。

2. The cam operates the contact points, which are mounted on a plate within the distributor housing.

凸轮控制断电器触点的打开和闭合,断电器触点安装在分电器壳体内的一个金属板上。

3. The primary coil, which consists of relatively few turns of heavy wire, is connected to the two primary terminals located on top of the coil.

相对而言,初级绕组匝数很少、导线粗,该绕组两端分别连接到点火线圈上部的两个初级绕组接线柱上。

4. Under normal operating conditions, power from the battery is fed through a resistor or resistance wire to the primary circuit of the coil and is then grounded through the ignition points in the distributor (the points are closed).

在正常工作条件下,蓄电池通过一个电阻器向点火线圈的初级绕组供电,然后,从初级绕组流出的电流又通过断电器触点(位于分电器内部)搭铁(触点闭合时)。

5. Instead of a distributor cam, breaker plate, points, and condenser, an electronic ignition system has an armature (called by various names such as a trigger wheel, reluctor, etc.), a pickup

coil (stator, sensor, etc.), and an electronic control module.

电子点火系统使用电枢,传感线圈(定子、传感器等)以及电子控制模块来代替分电器凸轮、断电器金属板,断电器触点和电容器。电枢有各种各样的名字,比如触发轮、磁组分配头等。

6. Since the polarity of the primary and the secondary windings are fixed, one plug always fires in a forward direction and the other in reverse.

因为初级绕组和次级绕组的极性是固定的,所以一个火花塞总是正向发火,而另一个总是反向发火。(指电流流动方向)

EXERCISES

Ⅰ. Answer following questions

1. Describe the functions of an automobile ignition system.
2. Explain the operation of point-type ignition system.
3. What does the term "waste spark" mean?
4. Explain why a distributorless ignition system has more than one ignition coil.
5. Describe the purpose of the ignition coil.

Ⅱ. Translate the following into Chinese

1. The ignition system provides for the timely burning of the fuel mixture within the engine. Not all engine types need an ignition system, for example, a diesel engine relies on compression-ignition, that is, the rise in temperature that accompanies the rise in pressure within the cylinder is sufficient to ignite the fuel spontaneously. All conventional petrol engines, by contrast, require an ignition system.

2. The time that the fuel takes to burn is roughly constant. But the speed of the pistons increases as the engine speed increases. This means that the faster the engine goes, the earlier the spark has to occur. This is called spark advance: The faster the engine speed, the more advance is required.

3. Ignition timing is the measurement, in degrees of crankshaft rotation, of the point at which the spark plugs fire in each of the cylinders. It is measured in degrees before or after Top Dead Center (TDC) of the compression stroke.

4. Ignition timing on many of today's vehicles is controlled by the engine control computer and is not adjustable. However the timing can be read using a scan tool connected to the data link connector.

Reading Material: Basics of Engine Management

Modern engine management systems (EMS) do a fine job of ensuring that engines run cleanly and efficiently in a wide variety of conditions, they are for the most part reliable and require little or no maintenance. The two basic functions performed by an EMS are as follows:

(a) To meter fuel to the engine in the right quantity;
(b) To provide a spark at the right time.

What is an Engine Management System?

An EMS is a self contained custom built computer which controls the running of an engine by monitoring the engine speed, load and temperature and providing the ignition spark at the right time for the prevailing conditions and metering the fuel to the engine in the exact quantity required.

There are two discrete subsystems in operation within the EMS, the fuel injection system and the ignition system. It is possible to run an engine management system which just provides one of these subsystems, for example just the ignition system. It is much more common to use the mapped ignition within an EMS in isolation than it is to use just the injection.

What is a "Map"?

Most of us have heard the term "Mapped ignition" and programmed or mapped injection but may not understand what this actually is. Whilst the engine is running its requirements for fuel and ignition timing will vary according to certain engine conditions, the main two being engine speed and engine load. A "map" is no more than a lookup table by engine speed and load, which gives the appropriate fuel or timing setting for each possible speed and load condition. There will normally be a map for the injector timings (fuel map) and a separate map for the ignition timing settings (ignition map) within the EMS.

Each map has entries for a pre-determined range of engine speeds (called speed sites) and a predetermined range of engine load conditions (called load sites), which generally indicate how far open the throttle is. The EMS knows the engine speed (derived from the crank sensor or distributor pickup) and the engine load (from the Throttle Position Sensor or airflow meter) and will use these two values to "look-up" the appropriate fuel and timing settings in each map.

If the current engine telemetry falls between the sites in the map then the value is interpolated between the nearest two sites. Normally there will be speed sites every about 500 r/min and 8 to 16 load sites between closed and open throttle. In the example below (Table 7-1) speed sites are spaced every 1,000 r/min and the 8 load sites are numbered 0 to 7.

Simple example of an ignition map   Table 7-1

load sites	speed sites								
	0	1,000	2,000	3,000	4,000	5,000	6,000	7,000	8,000
0	8	25	20	35	38	38	38	40	40
1	8	15	20	32	34	35	35	38	38
2	8	12	20	26	32	33	32	34	36
3	8	12	19	26	30	31	32	32	34
4	8	12	18	25	30	30	30	32	32
5	8	12	18	25	30	30	30	30	31
6	8	12	18	25	30	30	30	30	31
7	8	12	18	25	30	30	30	30	31

In this example the engine load increases as the load site numbers in the left column increase. If the engine were running at 3,000 r/min, load site 3, then the value looked up would be 26, i.e. 26 degrees of advance. If the engine were running at 3,500 r/min, load site 3 then the EMS would interpolate between the value for 3,000 r/min (26) and the value for 4,000 r/min (30) and calculate a value of 28 degrees.

UNIT 7   THE IGNITION SYSTEM

Timing Adjustments

In the normal course of events with the engine operating at the correct temperature in defined conditions, the EMS will use load and engine speed to derive the correct ignition timing from the map, however there are circumstances under which the EMS may need to vary the ignition timing. These normally boil down to four circumstances, engine/coolant temperature, air temperature, knocking and start-up.

Engine Temperature

When the engine temperature is low the burn times within the cylinders are longer than with a fully warmed up engine and the ignition timing will normally need to be advanced a little to adjust. The EMS usually has a small map of ignition timing adjustments graded by engine temperature that are added to the base timing figures. The engine temperature information is relayed to the EMS by an engine temperature sensor attached to the engine.

Air Temperature

When air temperature varies so does burn time of the inducted mixture, again a small map of ignition adjustments graded by air temperature are added to the base timing figures. The engine temperature information is relayed to the EMS by an air temperature sensor located near to the air inlet.

Knock Sensing

There may be times during the operation of the engine, even after adjustments have been applied when the timing calculated does not meet the engines requirements. Sometimes this may result in "pinking" ("knocking" or "pinging") where the mixture burns so fast that it meets the piston just before TDC while it is still on the compression stroke rather than meeting the piston just after TDC on the power stroke. This is very harmful to the engine. Some EMS systems have an acoustic sensor called a "knock sensor" which listens for knocking and will inform the EMS when this occurs. The EMS is then able to make adjustments to the timing to prevent knocking from occurring.

Start-up or Cranking

When starting an engine its effective rpm is quite low, around 200 r/min or so. If the ignition timing used at idle is set to around 25 degrees (which is about average for a mapped engine) the chances are that the piston will hit the ignited mixture while still on the compression stroke. This will have the effect of pushing the piston down against its normal rotation, effectively this is "knocking" at cranking speeds. This is known as "kicking back" and is normally characterized by the starter motor "straining" and slowing right down, this makes the engine difficult to start and can easily destroy a starter motor in short order.

This is a common problem on engines equipped with mechanical ignition systems and more extreme cams since the engine needs plenty of ignition advance at idle to run properly. Unfortunately this extra advance can also cause "kick back" and there is no way with a mechanical system to differentiate the timing between cranking and idle.

EMS based systems solve this problem by having a separate timing value for cranking/start-up which is normally set to around 5 to 8 degrees. This is low enough to prevent kickback but is high enough to start the engine; the moment the engine fires the appropriate ignition setting from the base map is used.

NEW WORDS

1. prevailing   [priˈveiliŋ]   *adj.* 主要的
2. discrete   [disˈkriːt]   *adj.* 独立的,离散的
3. interpolate   [inˈtɜːpə,leit]   *v. & n.* 内插,插入
4. telemetry   [tiˈlemitri]   *n.* 遥测数据,遥测学,遥测技术
5. relay   [ˈriːlei]   *v.* 传递; *n.* 继电器
6. acoustic   [əˈkuːstik]   *adj.* 听觉的,声学的
7. figure   [ˈfigə]   *n.* 图形,数字,人物

PHRASES AND EXPRESSIONS

1. little or no   几乎没有,简直没有
2. as follows   如下
3. according to   根据
4. boil down to   归结起来是
5. listens for   听听(有否……),等着听
6. the moment   一……就,正当……的一刹那

NOTES

1. An EMS is a self contained custom built computer which controls the running of an engine by monitoring the engine speed, load and temperature and providing the ignition spark at the right time for the prevailing conditions and metering the fuel to the engine in the exact quantity required.

发动机电子管理系统是一个定制的嵌入式计算机系统,通过监测发动机的转速、负荷以及温度情况,它能够使运行在各种工况下的发动机都能够在精确的时刻获得火花,并且能够精确地计量发动机所需的燃油量。

2. It is much more common to use the mapped ignition within an EMS in isolation than it is to use just the injection.

在发动机电子管理系统中,单独使用映射式(电子)点火系统的情况比单独使用(电控)喷射系统的情况更多一些。句中 it is to use just the injection 为省略句,应该为 it is common to use just the injection within an EMS。

3. A "map" is no more than a lookup table by engine speed and load.

一个映射就是一个根据发动机速度和负荷进行查找的表。

4. Sometimes this may result in "pinking" ("knocking" or "pinging") where the mixture burns so fast that it meets the piston just before TDC while it is still on the compression stroke rather than meeting the piston just after TDC on the power stroke.

这有时也会导致"轻微爆震"现象出现。出现这种情况时,混合气燃烧得如此之快,以至于燃烧膨胀的混合气体撞向活塞时,活塞还处在上止点前的压缩冲程中,而不是在上止点后的做功冲程中。句中,where 为"在这场合",while 为"然而,却"。

UNIT 7　THE IGNITION SYSTEM

5. This is known as "kicking back" and is normally characterised by the starter motor 'straining' and slowing right down…

这也被称为"逆转现象",其特征通常表现为起动电机的负荷增加,转速明显下降……

6. This will have the effect of pushing the piston down against its normal rotation, effectively this is "knocking" at cranking speeds.

其结果是推动活塞朝着与正常运动方向相反的方向运动,实际上这就是起动时的爆震现象。

7. There may be times during the operation of the engine, even after adjustments have been applied when the timing calculated does not meet the engines requirements.

在发动机运转期间,也许会发生这样的情况:虽然已经修正了点火时刻,但是修正后的点火时刻仍不能满足发动机的要求。

UNIT 8　CLUTCH

The engine produces the power to drive the vehicle. The drive line or drive train transfers the power of the engine to the wheels. The drive train consists of the parts from the back of the flywheel to the wheels. These parts include the clutch, the transmission, the drive shaft, and the final drive assembly (Figure 8-1).

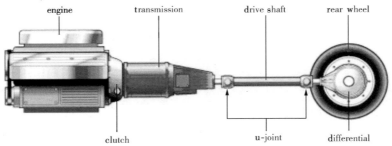

Figure 8-1　*The parts of drive train*

The clutch which includes the flywheel, clutch disc, pressure plate, springs, pressure plate cover and the linkage necessary to operate the clutch is a rotating mechanism between the engine and the transmission (Figure 8-2). It operates through friction which comes from contact between the parts. That is the reason why the clutch is called a friction mechanism. After engagement, the clutch must continue to transmit all the engine torque to the transmission depending on the friction without slippage. The clutch is also used to disengage the engine from the drive train whenever the gears in the transmission are being shifted from one gear ratio to another.

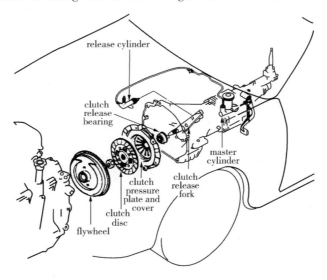

Figure 8-2　*Structure of a clutch*

UNIT 8 CLUTCH

To start the engine or shift the gears, the driver has to depress the clutch pedal with the purpose of disengagement the transmission from the engine. At that time, the driven members connected to the transmission input shaft are either stationary or rotating at a speed that is slower or faster than the driving members connected to the engine crankshaft. There is no spring pressure on the clutch assembly parts. So there is no friction between the driving members and driven members. As the driver lets loose the clutch pedal, spring pressure increases on the clutch parts. Friction between the parts also increases. The pressure exerted by the springs on the driven members is controlled by the driver through the clutch pedal and linkage. The positive engagement of the driving and driven members is made possible by the friction between the surfaces of the members. When full spring pressure is applied, the speed of the driving and driven members should be the same. At the moment, the clutch must act as a solid coupling device and transmit all engine power to the transmission, without slipping.

However, the transmission should be engaged to the engine gradually in order to operate the car smoothly and minimize torsional shock on the drive train because an engine at idle just develops little power. Otherwise, the driving members are connected with the driven members too quickly and the engine would be stalled.

The flywheel is a major part of the clutch. The flywheel mounts to the engine's crankshaft and transmits engine torque to the clutch assembly. The flywheel, when coupled with the clutch disc and pressure plate, makes or breaks the flow of power from the engine to the transmission.

The flywheel provides a mounting location for the clutch assembly as well. When the clutch is applied, the flywheel transfers engine torque to the clutch disc. Because of its weight, the flywheel helps to smooth engine operation. The flywheel also has a large ring gear at its outer edge, which engages with a pinion gear on the starter motor during engine cranking.

The clutch disc fits between the flywheel and the pressure plate. The clutch disc has a splined hub that fits over splines on the transmission input shaft. A splined hub has grooves that match splines on the shaft. These splines fit in the grooves. Thus, the two parts are held together. However, back-and-forth movement of the disc on the shaft is possible. Attached to the input shaft, the disc turns at the speed of the shaft.

The clutch pressure plate is generally made of cast iron. It is round and about the same diameter as the clutch disc. One side of the pressure plate is machined smooth. This side will press the clutch disc facing are against the flywheel. The outer side has various shapes to facilitate attachment of spring and release mechanisms. The two primary types of pressure plate assemblies are coil spring assembly and diaphragm spring (Figure 8-3).

In a coil spring clutch the pressure plate is backed by a number of coil springs and housed with them in a pressed-steel cover bolted to the flywheel. The springs push against the cover. Neither the driven plate nor the pressure plate is connected rigidly to the flywheel and both can move either towards it or away. When the clutch pedal is depressed, a thrust pad riding on a carbon or ball thrust bearing is forced towards the flywheel. Levers pivoted so that they engage with the thrust pad at one end and the pressure plate at the other end pull the pressure plate back against its springs. This releases pressure on the driven plate disconnecting the gearbox from the engine (Figure 8-4).

Diaphragm spring pressure plate assemblies are widely used in most modern cars. The diaphragm spring is a single thin sheet of metal which yields when pressure is applied to it. When pressure is removed the metal springs back to its original shape. The centre portion of the diaphragm spring is slit into numerous fingers that act as release levers. When the clutch assembly rotates with the engine these weights are flung outwards by centrifugal forces and cause the levers to press against the pressure plate. During disengagement of the clutch the fingers are moved forward by the release bearing. The spring pivots over the fulcrum ring and its outer rim moves away from the flywheel. The retracting spring pulls the pressure plate away from the clutch plate thus disengaging the clutch (Figure 8-5).

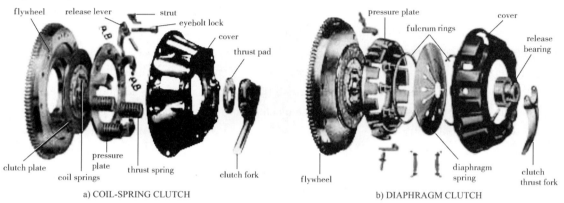

Figure 8-3　*Structure of coil spring clutch and diaphragm clutch*

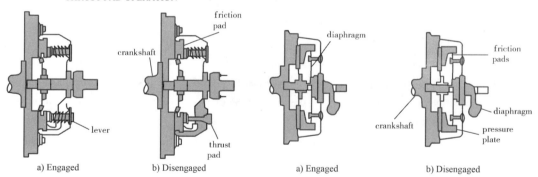

Figure 8-4　*Thrust pad operation*　　　　*Figure* 8-5　*Action of diaphragm*

When engaged the release bearing and the fingers of the diaphragm spring move towards the transmission. As the diaphragm pivots over the pivot ring its outer rim forces the pressure plate against the clutch disc so that the clutch plate is engaged to the flywheel.

The advantages of a diaphragm type pressure plate assembly are its compactness, lower weight, fewer moving parts, less effort to engage, reduces rotational imbalance by providing a balanced force around the pressure plate and less chances of clutch slippage.

The clutch pedal is connected to the disengagement mechanism either by a cable or, more commonly, by a hydraulic system. Either way, pushing the pedal down operates the disengagement mechanism which puts pressure on the fingers of the clutch diaphragm via a release bearing and causes the diaphragm to release the clutch plate. With a hydraulic mechanism, the clutch pedal arm operates a piston in the clutch master cylinder. This forces hydraulic fluid through a pipe to the clutch release cylinder where another piston operates the clutch disengagement mechanism. The alternative is to link the clutch pedal to the disengagement mechanism by a cable.

The other parts including the clutch fork, release bearing, bell-housing, bell housing cover, and pilot bushing are needed to couple and uncouple the transmission. The clutch fork, which connects to the linkage, actually operates the clutch. The release bearing fits between the clutch fork and the pressure plate assembly. The bell housing covers the clutch assembly. The bell housing cover fastens to the bottom of the bell housing. This removable cover allows a mechanic to inspect the clutch without removing the transmission and bell housing. A pilot bushing fits into the back of the crankshaft and holds the transmission input shaft.

NEW WORDS

1. clutch   [klʌtʃ]   n. 离合器,联轴器,接合器
2. flywheel   ['flaiwiːl]   n. 飞轮
3. stationary   ['steiʃənəri]   adj. 静止的,不动的,不变的,固定的
4. torsional   ['tɔːʃənəl]   adj. 扭转的,扭力的
5. crankshaft   ['kræŋkʃɑːft]   n. 曲轴,机轴
6. stall   [stɔːl]   v. 停转,停止,迟延
7. mount   [maunt]   v. 安放,设置,装上
8. groove   [gruːv]   n. (凹)槽,沟
9. lever   ['liːvə]   n. 杆,杠杆,控制杆
10. pivot   ['pivət]   n. 枢轴,支点
11. gearbox   ['giəbɔks]   n. 变速(器)箱
12. retract   [ri'trækt]   v. 缩回,缩进,收回,取消,撤销
13. compactness   [kəm'pæktnis]   n. 紧密,简洁,结构紧凑

PHRASES AND EXPRESSIONS

1. drive train   传动系统
2. drive shaft   驱动轴,传动轴
3. pressure plate   压盘
4. clutch disc   离合器从动盘,离合器摩擦片
5. gear ratio   传动比,齿轮齿数比
6. release bearing   分离轴承
7. release fork   分离拨叉
8. master cylinder   主缸
9. clutch pedal   离合器踏板
10. coupling device   接合装置

11.	at idle	空转，空闲
12.	couple with	与……连接，与……结合
13.	ring gear	环形齿轮，齿圈，冕状齿轮
14.	pinion gear	小齿轮
15.	splined hub	花键毂
16.	cast iron	铸铁，锻铁
17.	diaphragm spring	膜片弹簧
18.	thrust pad	止推(推力)垫
19.	engage with	(齿轮等)与……啮合，接合
20.	centrifugal force	离心力
21.	fulcrum ring	(膜片弹簧)支撑环
22.	pilot bushing	导轴衬，控制轴衬
23.	bell housing	钟形外壳，离合器壳，变矩器外壳

NOTES TO THE TEXT

1. The clutch which includes the flywheel, clutch disc, pressure plate, springs, cover and the linkage necessary to operate the clutch is a rotating mechanism between the engine and the transmission.

离合器是位于发动机和变速器之间的一个旋转装置，它包括飞轮、离合器摩擦片、压盘、压紧弹簧、离合器盖及操作离合器所需的连接杆件等。

Which 引导了一个主语从句，句子真正的谓语是 is。

2. To start the engine or shift the gears, the driver has to depress the clutch pedal with the purpose of disengagement the transmission from the engine. At that time, the driven members connected to the transmission input shaft are either stationary or rotating at a speed that is slower or faster than the driving members connected to the engine crankshaft.

为了起动发动机或换挡，驾驶人必须踩下离合器踏板以便实现变速器和发动机的分离。此时，与变速器输入轴相连的离合器从动件可能处于静止状态，也可能以一定的速度旋转，这一速度可能高于或低于与发动机相连的离合器主动件的旋转速度。

To 引导状语从句，表示主句发起行为的目的。with the purpose of 指"以……为目的"。connected to the transmission input shaft 表示主语 driven members 的状态，句子真正的谓语是 are。that is slower or faster than the driving members connected to the engine crankshaft 是一个修饰 speed 的定语从句。

3. Either way, pushing the pedal down operates the disengagement mechanism which puts pressure on the fingers of the clutch diaphragm via a release bearing and causes the diaphragm to release the clutch plate.

无论采用哪种方式，踩下踏板，操纵分离机构，通过分离轴承对离合器膜片弹簧施加压力，均可解除膜片弹簧对离合器盘的压紧。which puts pressure on the fingers of the clutch diaphragm via a release bearing 是修饰 disengagement mechanism 的定语从句，而整个句子的谓语是 operates 和 causes。

UNIT 8　CLUTCH

EXERCISES

I. Answer following questions

1. What is the function of the power train?

2. What does the power train consist of?

3. What does the clutch consist of?

4. Please explain the advantages of a diaphragm type pressure plate assembly.

5. Please answer how many different states a clutch has? And describe the states respectively.

6. Please describe how a diaphragm type clutch is engaged and disengaged?

7. Please describe the disadvantages of a coil spring type clutch comparing with a diaphragm one.

8. Please list some popular clutch types used today.

II. Translate the following passage into Chinese

1. The clutch assembly is a rotating mechanism between the engine and the transmission.

2. The clutch is usually attached directly to the engine flywheel, and its driven member is in the form of one or more disks faced with material having high frictional properties, pressed into engagement by springs.

3. The material used for facing the clutch disk is similar to that used for lining brakes, being composed of woven asbestos bonded with phenol resin, and sometimes enclosing metal wire mesh to strengthen it.

Reading Material: Torque Converter

The Basics

Just like manual transmission cars, cars with automatic transmissions need a way to let the engine turn while the wheels and gears in the transmission come to a stop. Manual transmission cars use a clutch, which completely disconnects the engine from the transmission. Automatic transmission cars use a torque converter.

A torque converter is a type of fluid coupling, which allows the engine to spin somewhat independently of the transmission. If the engine is turning slowly, such as when the car is idling at a stoplight, the amount of torque passed through the torque converter is very small, so keeping the car still requires only a light pressure on the brake pedal.

If you were to step on the gas pedal while the car is stopped, you would have to press harder on the brake to keep the car from moving. This is because when you step on the gas, the engine speeds up and pumps more fluid into the torque converter, causing more torque to be transmitted to the wheels.

Inside a Torque Converter

There are four components inside the very strong housing of the torque converter, pump, turbine, stator, transmission fluid.

The housing of the torque converter is bolted to the flywheel of the engine, so it turns at whatever speed the engine is running at. The fins that make up the pump of the torque converter are attached to the housing, so they also turn at the same speed as the engine. The cutaway below shows how everything is connected inside the torque converter (Figure 8-6).

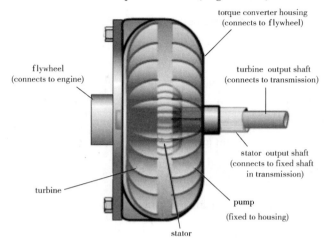

Figure 8-6　*The parts of a torque converter*

　　The pump inside a torque converter is a type of centrifugal pump. As it spins, fluid is flung to the outside, much as the spin cycle of a washing machine flings water and clothes to the outside of the wash tub. As fluid is flung to the outside, a vacuum is created that draws more fluid in at the center.

　　The fluid then enters the blades of the turbine, which is connected to the transmission. The turbine causes the transmission to spin, which basically moves the car. The blades of the turbine are curved. This means that the fluid, which enters the turbine from the outside, has to change direction before it exits the center of the turbine. It is this directional change that causes the turbine to spin.

　　The fluid exits the turbine at the center, moving in a different direction than when it entered. The fluid exits the turbine moving opposite the direction that the pump (and engine) are turning. If the fluid were allowed to hit the pump, it would slow the engine down, wasting power. This is why a torque converter has a stator.

　　The stator resides in the very center of the torque converter. Its job is to redirect the fluid returning from the turbine before it hits the pump again. This dramatically increases the efficiency of the torque converter.

　　The stator has a very aggressive blade design that almost completely reverses the direction of the fluid. A one-way clutch (inside the stator) connects the stator to a fixed shaft in the transmission. Because of this arrangement, the stator can't spin with the fluid—it can spin only in the opposite direction, forcing the fluid to change direction as it hits the stator blades.

　　Something a little bit tricky happens when the car gets moving. There is a point, around 40 mile/h (64 km/h), at which both the pump and the turbine are spinning at almost the same speed (the pump always spins slightly faster). At this point, the fluid returns from the turbine, entering the pump already moving in the same direction as the pump, so the stator is not needed.

　　Even though the turbine changes the direction of the fluid and flings it out the back, the fluid still ends up moving in the direction that the turbine is spinning because the turbine is spinning faster in one direction than the fluid is being pumped in the other direction. If you were standing in the back of a pickup moving at 60 mile/h, and you threw a ball out the back of that pickup at 40 mile/h, the ball would still be going forward at 20 mile/h. This is similar to what happens in the turbine: The fluid is being flung out the back in one direction, but not as fast as it was going to start with in the other direction.

At these speeds, the fluid actually strikes the back sides of the stator blades, causing the stator to freewheel on its one-way clutch so it doesn't hinder the fluid moving through it.

Benefits and Weak Points

In addition to the very important job of allowing a car come to a complete stop without stalling the engine, the torque converter actually gives the car more torque when you accelerate out of a stop. Modern torque converters can multiply the torque of the engine by two to three times. This effect only happens when the engine is turning much faster than the transmission.

At higher speeds, the transmission catches up to the engine, eventually moving at almost the same speed. Ideally, though, the transmission would move at exactly the same speed as the engine, because this difference in speed wastes power. This is part of the reason why cars with automatic transmissions get worse gas mileage than cars with manual transmissions.

To counter this effect, some cars have a torque converter with a lockup clutch. When the two halves of the torque converter get up to speed, this clutch locks them together, eliminating the slippage and improving efficiency.

NEW WORDS

1. pump   [pʌmp]   n. 泵轮
2. turbine   ['tə:bin]   n. 涡轮
3. stator   ['steitə]   n. 导轮
4. redirect   [ˌri:di'rekt]   vt. 使改道,使改变方向
5. tricky   ['triki:]   adj. 棘手的,复杂的
6. hinder   ['hində]   vt. 妨碍,阻碍
7. stall   [stɔ:l]   v. (使)停转,(使)停止,迟延
8. counter   ['kauntə]   vt. 抵消,消除

PHRASES AND EXPRESSIONS

1. torque converter   (液力)变矩器
2. gas pedal   加速踏板
3. one-way clutch   单向离合器,超越离合器
4. gas mileage   加仑英里
5. get up to   达到

NOTES

1. Just like manual transmission cars, cars with automatic transmissions need a way to let the

engine turn while the wheels and gears in the transmission come to a stop.

就像装有手动变速器的汽车(有离合器)一样,装有自动变速器的汽车需要有一个装置,使发动机在车轮和变速器齿轮停止转动时还能继续运转。

2. If the engine is turning slowly, such as when the car is idling at a stoplight, the amount of torque passed through the torque converter is very small, so keeping the car still requires only a light pressure on the brake pedal.

如果发动机转动很慢,例如,在制动灯亮时汽车怠速行驶,通过液力变矩器传递的转矩很小,所以要使汽车停下来,只需要用很小的力踩制动踏板。

3. This is part of the reason why cars with automatic transmissions get worse gas mileage than cars with manual transmissions.

这是为什么装有自动变速器的汽车比装有手动变速器的汽车燃油经济性差的原因之一。

UNIT 9 AUTOMATIC TRANSMISSION

The modern automatic transmission is by far, the most complicated mechanical component in today's automobile. It is a type of transmission that shifts itself. A fluid coupling or torque converter is used instead of a manually operated clutch to connect the transmission to the engine.

There are two basic types of automatic transmissions based on whether the vehicle is rear wheel drive or front wheel drive. On a rear wheel drive car, the transmission is usually mounted to the back of the engine and is located under the hump in the center of the floorboard alongside the gas pedal position. A drive shaft connects the rear of the transmission to the final drive which is located in the rear axle and is used to send power to the rear wheels. Power flow on this system is simple and straight forward going from the engine, through the torque converter, then through the transmission and drive shaft until it reaches the final drive where it is split and sent to the two rear wheels.

On a front wheel drive car, the transmission is usually combined with the final drive to form what is called a transaxle. The engine on a front wheel drive car is usually mounted sideways in the car with the transaxle tucked under it on the side of the engine facing the rear of the car. Front axles are connected directly to the transaxle and provide power to the front wheels. In this example, power flows from the engine, through the torque converter to a large chain that sends the power through a 180 degree turn to the transmission that is along side the engine. From there, the power is routed through the transmission to the final drive where it is split and sent to the two front wheels through the drive axles.

There are a number of other arrangements including front drive vehicles where the engine is mounted front to back instead of sideways and there are other systems that drive all four wheels but the two systems described here are by far the most popular. A much less popular rear drive arrangement has the transmission mounted directly to the final drive at the rear and is connected by a drive shaft to the torque converter which is still mounted on the engine. This system is found on the new Corvette and is used in order to balance the weight evenly between the front and rear wheels for improved performance and handling. Another rear drive system mounts everything, the engine, transmission and final drive in the rear. This rear engine arrangement is popular on the Porsche.

The modern automatic transmission consists of many components and systems that are designed to work together in a symphony of planetary gear sets, the hydraulic system, seals and gaskets, the torque converter, the governor and the modulator or throttle cable and computer controls that has evolved over the years into what many mechanically inclined individuals consider to be an art form. Here try to use simple, generic explanations where possible to describe these systems.

1. Planetary gear sets

Automatic transmissions contain many gears in various combinations. In a manual transmission, gears slide along shafts as you move the shift lever from one position to another, engaging various sized gears as required in order to provide the correct gear ratio. In an automatic transmission, however, the gears are never physically moved and are always engaged to the same gears. This is accomplished through the use of planetary gear sets.

The basic planetary gear set consists of a sun gear, a ring gear and two or more planet gears, all remaining in constant mesh. The planet gears are connected to each other through a common carrier which allows the gears to spin on shafts called "pinions" which are attached to the carrier.

One example of a way that this system can be used is by connecting the ring gear to the input shaft coming from the engine, connecting the planet carrier to the output shaft, and locking the sun gear so that it can't move. In this scenario, when we turn the ring gear, the planets will "walk" along the sun gear (which is held stationary) causing the planet carrier to turn the output shaft in the same direction as the input shaft but at a slower speed causing gear reduction (similar to a car in first gear).

If we unlock the sun gear and lock any two elements together, this will cause all three elements to turn at the same speed so that the output shaft will turn at the same rate of speed as the input shaft. This is like a car that is in third or high gear. Another way that we can use a planetary gear set is by locking the planet carrier from moving, then applying power to the ring gear which will cause the sun gear to turn in the opposite direction giving us reverse gear.

The illustration in Figure 9-1 shows how the simple system described above would look in an actual transmission. The input shaft is connected to the ring gear, the output shaft is connected to the planet carrier which is also connected to a "Multi-disk" clutch pack. The sun gear is connected to a drum which is also connected to the other half of the clutch pack. Surrounding the outside of the drum is a band that can be tightened around the drum when required to prevent the drum with the attached sun gear from turning.

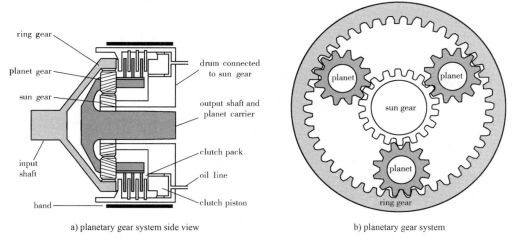

a) planetary gear system side view   b) planetary gear system

Figure 9-1 *Planetary gear system*

UNIT 9　AUTOMATIC TRANSMISSION

The clutch pack is used, in this instance, to lock the planet carrier with the sun gear forcing both to turn at the same speed. If both the clutch pack and the band were released, the system would be in neutral. Turning the input shaft would turn the planet gears against the sun gear, but since nothing is holding the sun gear, it will just spin free and have no effect on the output shaft. To place the unit in first gear, the band is applied to hold the sun gear from moving. To shift from first to high gear, the band is released and the clutch is applied causing the output shaft to turn at the same speed as the input shaft.

Many more combinations are possible using two or more planetary sets connected in various ways to provide the different forward speeds and reverse that are found in modern automatic transmissions.

2. Clutch pack

A clutch pack consists of alternating disks that fit inside a clutch drum. Half of the disks are steel and have splines that fit into grooves on the inside of the drum. The other half have a friction material bonded to their surface and have splines on the inside edge that fit grooves on the outer surface of the adjoining hub. There is a piston inside the drum that is activated by oil pressure at the appropriate time to squeeze the clutch pack together so that the two components become locked and turn as one.

3. One-Way Clutch

A one-way clutch (also known as a "sprag" clutch) is a device that will allow a component such as ring gear to turn freely in one direction but not in the other. This effect is just like that of a bicycle, where the pedals will turn the wheel when pedaling forward, but will spin free when pedaling backward.

A common place where a one-way clutch is used is in the first gear when the shifter is in the Drive position. When you begin to accelerate from a stop, the transmission starts out in the first gear. But have you ever noticed what happens if you release the gas while it is still in the first gear? The vehicle continues to coast as if you were in neutral. Now, shift into Low gear instead of Drive. When you let go of the gas in this case, you will feel the engine slow you down just like a standard shift car. The reason for this is that in Drive, a one-way clutch is used whereas in Low, a clutch pack or a band is used.

4. Bands

A band (Figure 9-2) is a steel strap with friction material bonded to the inside surface. One end of the band is anchored against the transmission case while the other end is connected to a servo. At the appropriate time hydraulic oil is sent to the servo under pressure to tighten the band around the drum to stop the drum from turning.

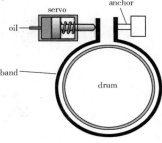

Figure 9-2　Band

5. Torque Converter

On automatic transmissions, the torque converter takes the place of the clutch found on standard shift vehicles. It is there to allow the engine to continue running when the vehicle comes to a stop. The principle behind a torque converter is like taking a fan that is plugged into the wall and blowing air into another fan which is unplugged. If you grab the blade on the unplugged fan, you are able to hold it from turning but as soon as you let go, it will begin to speed up until it comes close to the speed of the powered fan. The difference with a torque converter is that instead of using air, it uses oil or transmission fluid, to be more precise.

A torque converter is a large doughnut shaped device (10 to 15 inches in diameter) that is mounted between the engine and the transmission. It consists of three internal elements that work together to transmit power to the transmission. The three elements of the torque converter are the Pump, the Turbine, and the Stator. The pump is mounted directly to the converter housing which in turn is bolted directly to the engine's crankshaft and turns at engine speed. The turbine is inside the housing and is connected directly to the input shaft of the transmission providing power to move the vehicle. The stator is mounted to a one-way clutch so that it can spin freely in one direction but not in the other. Each of the three elements has fins mounted in them to precisely direct the flow of oil through the converter.

With the engine running, transmission fluid is pulled into the pump section and is pushed outward by centrifugal force until it reaches the turbine section which starts it turning. The fluid continues in a circular motion back towards the center of the turbine where it enters the stator. If the turbine is moving considerably slower than the pump, the fluid will make contact with the front of the stator fins which push the stator into the one way clutch and prevent it from turning. With the stator stopped, the fluid is directed by the stator fins to re-enter the pump at a "helping" angle providing a torque increase. As the speed of the turbine catches up with the pump, the fluid starts hitting the stator blades on the back-side causing the stator to turn in the same direction as the pump and turbine. As the speed increases, all three elements begin to turn at approximately the same speed.

Since the 1980s, in order to improve fuel economy, torque converters have been equipped with a lockup clutch which locks the turbine to the pump as the vehicle speed reaches approximately 45-50 mile/h. This lockup is controlled by computer and usually won't engage unless the transmission is in the 3rd or 4th gear.

6. Hydraulic System

The Hydraulic system is a complex maze of passages and tubes that sends transmission fluid under pressure to all parts of the transmission and torque converter. Transmission fluid serves a number of purposes including: shift control, general lubrication and transmission cooling. Unlike the engine, which uses oil primarily for lubrication, every aspect of a transmission's functions is dependant on a constant supply of fluid under pressure. In order to keep the transmission at normal operating temperature, a portion of the fluid is sent through one of two steel tubes to a special chamber that is submerged in anti-freeze in the radiator. Fluid passing through this chamber is cooled and then returned to the transmission through the other steel tube. A typical transmission has an average of ten quarts of fluid between the transmission, torque converter, and cooler tank. In fact, most of the components of a transmission are constantly submerged in fluid including the clutch packs and bands. The friction surfaces on these parts are designed to operate properly only when they are submerged in oil.

7. Oil Pump

The transmission oil pump (not to be confused with the pump element inside the torque converter) is responsible for producing all the oil pressure that is required in the transmission. The oil pump is mounted to the front of the transmission case and is directly connected to a flange on the torque converter housing. Since the torque converter housing is directly connected to the engine crankshaft, the pump will produce pressure whenever the engine is running as long as there is a sufficient amount of transmission fluid available. The oil enters the pump through a filter that is located at the bottom of the transmission oil pan and travels up a pickup tube directly to the oil pump. The oil is then sent, under pressure to the pressure regulator, the valve body and the rest of the components, as required.

8. Valve Body

The valve body is the control center of the automatic transmission. It contains a maze of channels and passages that direct hydraulic fluid to the numerous valves which then activate the appropriate clutch pack or band servo to smoothly shift to the appropriate gear for each driving situation. Each of the many valves in the valve body has a specific purpose and is named for that function. For example the 2-3 shift valve activates the 2nd gear to 3rd gear up-shift or the 3-2 shift timing valve which determines when a downshift should occur. The most important valve and the one that you have direct control over is the manual valve. The manual valve is directly connected to the gear shift handle and covers and uncovers various passages depending on what position the gear shift is placed in. When you place the gear shift in Drive, for instance, the manual valve directs fluid to the clutch pack(s) that activates the 1st gear. It also sets up to monitor vehicle speed and throttle position so that it can determine the optimal time and the force for the 1-2 shift. On computer controlled transmissions, you will also have electrical solenoids that are mounted in the valve body to direct fluid to the appropriate clutch packs or bands under computer control to more precisely control shift points.

9. Computer Controls

The computer uses sensors on the engine and transmission to detect such things as throttle position, vehicle speed, engine speed, engine load, stop light switch position, etc. to control exact shift points as well as how soft or firm the shift should be. Some computerized transmissions even learn your driving style and constantly adapt to it so that every shift is timed precisely when you would need it.

Because of computer controls, sports models are coming out with the ability to take manual control of the transmission as though it were a stick shift, allowing the driver to select gears manually. This is accomplished on some cars by passing the shift lever through a special gate, then tapping it in one direction or the other in order to up-shift or down-shift at will. The computer monitors this activity to make sure that the driver does not select a gear that could over speed the engine and damage it.

Another advantage to these "smart" transmissions is that they have a self diagnostic mode which can detect a problem early on and warn you with an indicator light on the dash. A technician can then plug test equipment in and retrieve a list of trouble codes that will help pinpoint where the problem is.

10. Governor, Vacuum Modulator, Throttle Cable

These three components are important in the non-computerized transmissions. They provide the inputs that tell the transmission when to shift. The governor is connected to the output shaft and regulates hydraulic pressure based on vehicle speed. It accomplishes this using centrifugal force to spin a pair of hinged weights against pull-back springs. As the weights pull further out against the springs, more oil pressure is allowed past the governor to act on the shift valves that are in the valve body which then signal the appropriate shifts. Of course, vehicle speed is not the only thing that controls when a transmission should shift, the load that the engine is under is also important. The more load you place on the engine, the longer the transmission will hold a gear before shifting to the next one.

There are two types of devices that serve the purpose of monitoring the engine load: the Throttle Cable and the Vacuum Modulator. A transmission will use one or the other but generally not both of these devices. Each works in a different way to monitor engine load. The Throttle Cable simply monitors the position of the gas pedal through a cable that runs from the gas pedal to the throttle valve in the valve body.

The Vacuum Modulator monitors engine vacuum by a rubber vacuum hose which is connected to the engine. Engine vacuum reacts very accurately to engine load with high vacuum produced when the engine is under light load and diminishing down to zero vacuum when the engine is under a heavy load. The modulator is attached to the outside of the transmission case and has a shaft which passes through the case and attaches to the throttle valve in the valve body. When an engine is under a light load or no load, high vacuum acts on the modulator which moves the throttle valve in one direction to allow the transmission to shift early and soft. As the engine load increases, vacuum is diminished which moves the valve in the other direction causing the transmission to shift later and more firmly.

UNIT 9　AUTOMATIC TRANSMISSION

11. Seals and Gaskets

An automatic transmission has many seals and gaskets to control the flow of hydraulic fluid and to keep it from leaking out. There are two main external seals: the front seal and the rear seal. The front seal seals the point where the torque converter mounts to the transmission case. This seal allows fluid to freely move from the converter to the transmission but keeps the fluid from leaking out. The rear seal keeps fluid from leaking past the output shaft.

A seal is usually made of rubber (similar to the rubber in a windshield wiper blade) and is used to keep oil from leaking past a moving part such as a spinning shaft. In some cases, the rubber is assisted by a spring that holds the rubber in close contact with the spinning shaft.

A gasket is a type of seal used to seal two stationary parts that are fastened together. Some common gasket materials are: paper, cork, rubber, silicone and soft metal.

Aside from the main seals, there are also a number of other seals and gaskets that vary from transmission to transmission. A common example is the rubber O-ring that seals the shaft for the shift control lever. This is the shaft that you move when you manipulate the gear shifter. Another example that is common to most transmissions is the oil pan gasket. In fact, seals are required anywhere that a device needs to pass through the transmission case with each one being a potential source for leaks.

NEW WORDS

1. hump   [hʌmp]   n. 圆形隆(凸)起
2. transaxle   [træns'æksl]   n. 变速驱动桥
3. tuck   [tʌk]   n. 缝褶;vt. 把一端塞进,挤进,使隐藏
4. gasket   ['gæskit]   n. 垫圈,衬垫,密封垫
5. governor   ['gʌvənə]   n. (自动变速器)油压调节器,调速器
6. modulator   ['mɔdjuleitə]   n. (自动变速器)调制器
7. spline   [splain]   n. 止转楔,花键;v. 用花键联结,开键槽
8. bond   [bɔnd]   n. 结合,黏结,联结;v. 结合
9. strap   [stræp]   n. 带,传动带;vt. 用带缚住,用带捆扎
10. doughnut   ['dəunʌt]   n. 油炸圈饼;n. 圆环图([美俚]轮胎)
11. stator   ['steitə]   n. 定子,固定片
12. maze   [meiz]   n. 曲径,迷宫
13. submerge   [səb'mə:dʒ]   v. 浸没,淹没
14. quart   [kwɔ:t]   n. 夸脱(容量单位=1/4 加仑,约1.14 升)
15. downshift   ['daun,ʃift]   v. (汽车等)调低速挡,向下换挡
16. optimal   ['ɔptəməl]   adj. 最佳的,最理想的
17. solenoid   ['səulinɔid]   n. 螺线管,电磁线圈
18. retrieve   [ri'tri:v]   v. 重新得到;n. 找回
19. cork   [kɔ:k]   n. 软木塞,软木,(用塞子)塞住

20. manipulate　　　[məˈnipjuleit]　　　vt.(熟练地)操作,使用(机器等),操纵(人或市价、市场),利用

PHRASES AND EXPRESSIONS

1. fluid coupling　　　　　　　液力耦合器
2. torque converter　　　　　　液力变矩[扭]器,转矩变换器
3. planetary gear set　　　　　行星齿轮组
4. throttle cable　　　　　　　节气门拉线[索]
5. ring gear　　　　　　　　　齿圈,环形齿轮,冕状齿轮
6. high gear　　　　　　　　　高速挡
7. reverse gear　　　　　　　　〈汽车〉倒挡
8. sprag clutch　　　　　　　　楔块式超越离合器,楔块式单向离合器
9. centrifugal force　　　　　　离心力
10. gear up　　　　　　　　　　使换快挡,促进,增加
11. stick shift　　　　　　　　顶挡杆,一种具有用手操纵的换挡杠杆的自动换挡装置
12. vacuum hose　　　　　　　　真空软管
13. throttle valve　　　　　　　节流阀
14. leak out　　　　　　　　　　泄漏
15. windshield wiper　　　　　　刮水器,雨雪刷

NOTES TO THE TEXT

1. The modern automatic transmission consists of many components and systems that are designed to work together in a symphony of planetary gear sets, the hydraulic system, seals and gaskets, the torque converter, the governor and the modulator or throttle cable and computer controls that has evolved over the years into what many mechanically inclined individuals consider to be an art form.

自动变速器由许多的部件和系统组成,它们有行星齿轮组、液压系统、密封圈和密封衬垫、变矩器、油压调节器、调制器、节气门拉索、电子控制装置等,经精心设计,运转协调,其中的电子控制装置经历了多年的发展,已经以巧妙的形式融入了许多人性化的设计。

2. In this scenario, when we turn the ring gear, the planets will "walk" along the sun gear (which is held stationary) causing the planet carrier to turn the output shaft in the same direction as the input shaft but at a slower speed causing gear reduction (similar to a car in first gear).

这种情况下,当转动齿圈,行星齿轮将沿着(被固定的)太阳(齿)轮"运行",从而行星齿轮架带动输出轴以与输入轴相同方向转动但速率较小,来实现减速(类似于普通变速器的一挡)。

3. The fluid continues in a circular motion back towards the center of the turbine where it enters the stator. If the turbine is moving considerably slower than the pump, the fluid will make contact with the front of the stator fins which push the stator into the one way clutch and prevent it from turning.

UNIT 9 AUTOMATIC TRANSMISSION

油液继续沿圆周方向运动着,流向涡轮中心,从那里进入导轮。如果涡轮比泵轮转动得慢得多,油液就接触到了导轮叶片的前面,并推动导轮使单向离合器起作用,阻止导轮转动。

EXERCISES

I. Answer following questions

1. Please explain the main components that make up an automatic transmission.
2. Please illustrate the main differences between an automatic transmission and manual transmission.
3. Please describe how to get reverse gear and gear reduction using a planetary gear set.
4. If you are going to buy a car, which transmission type will you choose? Why?
5. Please describe the function of the hydraulic system in an automatic transmission.
6. Please describe the differences of a torque converter and a mechanical clutch in car.

II. Translate the following passage into Chinese

Every self-propelled road-going vehicle needs some form of transmission to take the output from its power unit to the driven wheels. The vast majority of vehicles are powered by internal combustion engines, and a large part of the task of the transmission in these vehicles is to compensate for the inherent drawbacks of the engine—in particular, its need to remain running when the vehicle is stationary, and the limited range of speed within which it develops sufficient torque to drive the wheels. To overcome the first problem, some kind of clutching arrangement is necessary. To overcome the second, the transmission needs to include a gearbox providing a range of different ratios of input to output speed, enabling the engine's speed to be maintained within the useful range of torque output over a more or less wide range of vehicle speeds. So important have these solutions become that "transmission" has in many minds come to mean that part of the system between the engine output and the gearbox output, neglecting the many complexities which exist between the gearbox output and the driven wheels.

Reading Material: The Future of Automotive Transmissions

A flurry of innovations and developments is on the agenda in context of transmission designs of the future. Major manufacturers are constantly striving to improve existing technology as R&D divisions focus on figuring out ways and means to conjure up better and simpler forms of transmission units (even though the physics of it all is highly complex).

Here are some cutting edge transmission systems that are and will be production realities in the cars of the future.

Continuously Variable Transmission(CVT)

A continuously variable transmission(Figure 9-3) is an automatic that can select any desired drive ratio within its operating range. Unlike a traditional three-, four-, or five-speed automatic transmission, the CVT is an "infinite speed" transmission. It continually selects an optimum overall drive ratio between engine and drive wheels for all operating conditions, whether accelerating or cruising. Unlike conventional automatics, there are no perceptible shifts. During maximum acceleration, the drive ratio is adjusted to maintain peak engine horsepower. At a constant vehicle speed, the ratio is set to maintain an optimum balance of fuel economy and driveability. A CVT provides smooth, fast acceleration and high cruising efficiency with the convenience of an automatic transmission.

The Continuously Variable Transmission (CVT) system is slowly finding acceptance with major automobile manufacturers though the technology has been around for some time now employed in two wheelers especially scooters. A typical CVT gearbox (left) uses a toothed V-belt (below) running between two pulleys.

Figure 9-3   Continuously variable transmission (CVT)

The most common CVT design uses a segmented metal V-belt running between two pulleys. Each pulley consists of a pair of cones that can be moved close together or further apart to adjust the diameter at which the belt operates. The pulley ratios are electronically controlled to select the best overall drive ratio based on throttle position, vehicle speed and engine speed. CVT systems are commonly in use in Audi's Multitronic, Honda's MMT and Mitsubishi's INVECS-III CVT among others.

Auto Shift Manual Transmission and Select Shift Manual Transmission

Select Shift Manual (SSM) and Auto Shift Manual (ASM) employ a combination of Auto-Clutch and Shift-By-Wire electronic control system technology to offer the car driver a fun-to-shift experience along with significant improvements in fuel economy over a base manual transmission. The Select Shift Manual mode allows a driver to control gear changes according to his/her personal preference as in a conventional manual transmission. The Auto Shift Manual mode provides automatic gear shifting much like automatic transmission.

Both the Auto-Clutch and Shift-By-Wire sub systems make use of an electro-hydraulic or electro-mechanical actuation system controlled by a stand-alone transmission control module. The driver requests a gear shift by using the appropriate driver interface mechanism (shift lever, push buttons, etc). In place of the usual cable/linkage (which is eliminated), a sensor informs the controller of the requested gear shift. The controller processes the request and commands the actuators to open/close the clutch and disengage/engage the gear sequence with very fast response

UNIT 9 AUTOMATIC TRANSMISSION

times. Engine torque is controlled during the shift either by controlling the throttle directly (Drive-By-Wire) or enabling ignition/fuel injection control to provide smooth shifts.

Adaptive Transmission Control (ATC)

The Adaptive Transmission Control system recognizes individual styles of driving (e.g., aggressive vs. relaxed) and adapts transmission shift parameters accordingly. The two types of ATC are adaptive shift-scheduling and adaptive shift-quality control. Adaptive shift scheduling uses information to assess driving style and decides when to upshift or downshift. It can also identify uphill or downhill gradients and recognize hard cornering. This helps inhibit shifts that could be irritating to the driver or affect vehicle stability. Adaptive shift-quality control uses information about the vehicle or environment, such as changes in the transmission due to wear, to improve the quality of shifts. This system can also adjust shift smoothness to suit driving style (e.g., crisper shifts for aggressive driving or smoother shifts for normal driving).

Adaptive Shift Scheduling uses a microprocessor to read signals from various sensors besides a complex algorithm and ongoing memory to decide when to shift. For example, high lateral acceleration during cornering may prevent shifting even if the accelerator is suddenly depressed or released. This helps avert potential loss of tyre grip due to load reversal. Shift points can be based on calibration curves in memory. Adaptive shift-quality control adjusts parameters that affect the speed and smoothness of the shift by interpreting data, including driveline feedback from various sensors, as well as post shift parameters.

Electronically Controlled Automatic Transmission

An Electronically Controlled Automatic Transmission utilizes an electronic control module to signal when to shift. The module also determines when to lock and unlock the torque converter. By controlling these functions electronically rather than mechanically, the transmission can be tuned for better driveability.

Electronically Controlled Automatic Transmissions use computer-controlled solenoids to control primary functions (internal pressure, converter lock-up, shift and clutch scheduling) through the transmission hydraulic system. Meanwhile, non-electronic transmissions rely on mechanical controls such as centrifugal weights and mechanical valves.

Better control of transmission shifting improves driveability.

NEW WORDS

1. flurry ['flɜːriː, 'flʌriː] n. 阵风，小雪，小雨，飓风，潮流
2. innovation [ˌinəu'veiʃən] n. 改革，创新
3. driveability [ˌdraivə'biləti] n. (汽车的)驾驶性能,操纵性能,操纵灵活性
4. perceptible [pə'septəbəl] adj. 可察觉的，显而易见的，感觉得到的
5. crisp [krisp] adj. 爽快的

PHRASES AND EXPRESSIONS

1. Continuously Variable Transmission (速度)连续可变的变速器,无级变速器
2. drive ratio 传动比

3. metal V-belt　　　　　　　　　　　　　金属 V 形带
4. Select Shift Manual（SSM）　　　　　　手动选挡的机械变速器
5. Auto Shift Manual（ASM）　　　　　　　自动换挡的机械变速器
6. along with　　　　　　　　　　　　　　连同……一起，随同……一起
7. Adaptive Transmission Control（ATC）　（自动变速器）自适应式变速器控制
8. Electronically Controlled Automatic Transmission　电控自动变速器

NOTES

Select Shift Manual (SSM) and Auto Shift Manual (ASM) employ a combination of Auto-Clutch and Shift-By-Wire electronic control system technology to offer the car driver a fun-to-shift experience along with significant improvements in fuel economy over a base manual transmission.

手动选挡和自动换挡的机械变速器是通过结合自动换挡离合器和手动换挡的电控系统技术来为驾驶人提供有趣的换挡经历，同时在手动机械变速器的基础上，大大改善其燃油经济性。

UNIT 10 THE DIFFERENTIAL

Most cars have a standard, or unlimited-slip, differential. (A limited-slip differential costs more and is not necessary in most normal driving conditions.) As mentioned, a differential must split power unequally when a car goes around a corner. Like the transmission, the differential has many gears and parts.

1. The Main Gears

Suppose a shaft spins in one direction. You want that shaft to drive another shaft at an angle of 90° to the first shaft. You can do this by meshing two gears, each having teeth set at a 45° angle. There would be one gear on each shaft. Together, the two gears produce a 90° change in direction shown as Figure 10-1. Gears with teeth at such an angle are called bevel gears because they are beveled, or cut on an angle.

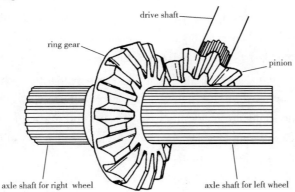

Figure 10-1 Bevel gears turn the flow of power

The bevel gears in Figure 10-1 work well when one shaft must drive another. But in a final drive assembly, two axle shafts must be driven. (One shaft goes to each drive wheel.) Then one of the beveled gears must have a hole in its center through which the shaft extends. The large circular gear on the axle shafts is called the ring gear shown as Figure 10-1.

The final drive assembly also provides gear reduction so that the drive wheels spin more slowly than the drive shaft. The gear reduction varies, depending on engine size and power, engine torque, and vehicle size and weight. In general most final drives produce gear reduction ratios of about 2.50:1 to 3.50:1. Thus, the drive wheels turn at about one-third the speed of the drive shaft. (If the drive shaft spins at 3,000 r/min, the drive wheels turn at about 1,000 r/min.) To give the necessary reduction, the driving gear in the final drive must be smaller than the driven gear, which is the ring gear. Thus, the driving gear must make several turns for every single turn of the ring

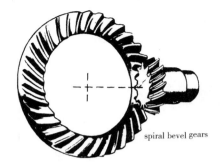

Figure 10-2 *Spiral bevel gears mesh more easily and quietly than bevel gears*

gear. The driving gear is called the pinion gear or pinion. The drive shaft turns the pinion. The pinion rotates the ring gear and axle shafts. If the teeth of the beveled gears are curved, the pinion meshes more easily and quietly with the larger ring gear. Now we can refer to the gears as spiral bevel gears. Figure 10-2 shows a set of spiral bevel gears.

Spiral bevel gears were used for many years. However, another arrangement allows the drive shaft and the floor pan to be lowered. Study Figure 10-2. If the center line of the pinion were extended rearward, it would pass through the center of the ring gear. Half the ring gear would be above the centerline and half below it. The newer system places the pinion at a lower point on the ring gear. Thus, the center lines do not intersect. Since the drive shaft connects directly to the pinion, the drive shaft can be lowered. Front-engine, rear-wheel drive vehicles use this arrangement, which uses hypoid gears.

2. The Differential System

The final drive works fine as long as both drive wheels turn at the same speed. However, this system cannot provide different rates of speed for different wheels. As noted earlier, a differential system is needed to allow for speed differences. This gear system is the heart of the final drive assembly.

The differential system has a differential case. Figure 10-3. This case houses the differential gears. The ring gear bolts to a flange on one side of the case. When the pinion drives the ring gear, the differential case also turns. The case has circular holes through which the axle shafts fit. Thus, the inside ends of the axle shafts are inside the case. On the end of each axle shaft, there is a bevel gear called a side gear or differential gear. In fact, the side gears are splined to the axle shafts. Whenever the side gears turn, the axle shafts turn.

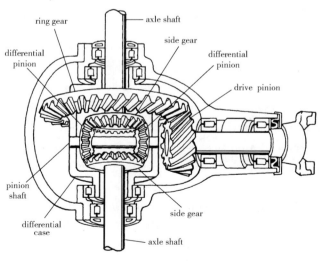

Figure 10-3 *The ring gear fastens to a differential case that has holes. The ends of the axle shafts fit through these holes.*

UNIT 10   THE DIFFERENTIAL

There is a space between the two side gears. A shaft that is perpendicular to the axle shafts fits in this space. This shaft is called the pinion shaft. On each end of the pinion shaft, there is a bevel gear that meshes with both side gears. We call these gears the differential pinions.

Do not confuse the two pinions. As mentioned, the drive shaft rotates the main drive gear. This drive gear is the drive pinion. The other pinions, called the differential pinions, mesh with the two side gears that are splined to the ends of the axle shafts.

Look at the differential system in Figure 10-4. The parts of the differential form a rectangular shape inside the differential case. The side gears are parallel to the drive wheels. The differential pinions are perpendicular to the side gears and drive wheels. Each side gear meshes with both differential pinions. As noted, each side gear is splined to an axle shaft. However, the differential pinions are not splined to the pinion shaft. A pinion shaft lock bolt holds the pinion shaft stationary. The differential pinions are at the ends of the shaft and can either turn or remain stationary.

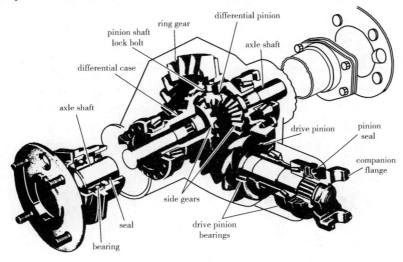

Figure 10-4   *The differential gears form a rectangular shape inside the differential case*

3. How the Differential System Works

Refer to Figure 10-5. In normal, straight-ahead driving, the drive shaft turns the drive pinion, which turns the ring gear. The ring gear turns the entire differential case because it is bolted solidly to the case. Since the pinion shaft is bolted to the case, it revolves with the case. The differential pinions also turn end-over-end with the pinion shaft. The differential pinions press against the side gears, and the side gears rotate. Since the axle shafts are splined to the side gears, the shafts also rotate.

When a car moves straight ahead, the drive wheels have an equal amount of traction. The forces on the differential pinions are equal, and the differential pinions will not turn about the pinion shaft. Instead, the differential pinions act as if they were locked to the pinion shaft. Now both the side gears and axle shafts move at the same speed. Power flows through the drive pinion, ring gear, case, and pinion shaft to the differential pinions. Then power splits equally and goes to the side gears, axle shafts, and drive wheels.

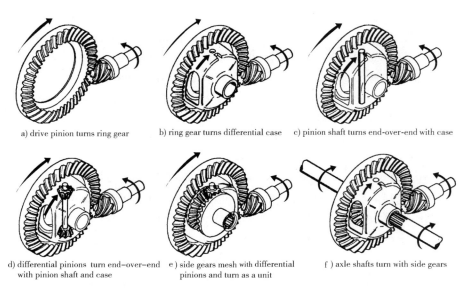

Figure 10-5 How the differential system works

When a car goes around a corner, power can no longer be divided evenly between the two side gears when it reaches the differential pinions. The inside wheel turns more slowly and lowers the speed of the inside axle shaft, shown as Figure 10-6. As a result, the differential pinions begin to rotate about the pinion shaft. The rotation of the differential pinions makes the outside gear speed up. As a result, the outside wheel turns faster than the inside wheel.

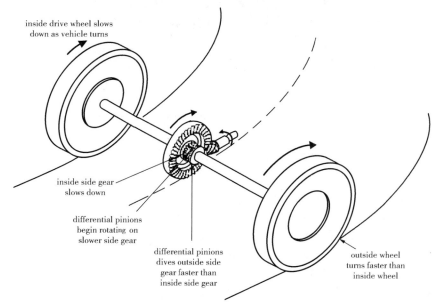

Figure 10-6 When a car turns a corner, the differential pinions turn on the pinion shaft. Now power splits unevenly. The inside drive wheel slows down and the outside drive wheel speeds up.

The differential pinions act as balancing levers. They keep equal tooth loads to both side gears but allow the side gears and axle shafts to turn at different speeds. Of course, the differential case still rotates at the same speed as the ring gear. However, the axle shafts no longer rotate at that speed. For example, when the inside axle shaft slows down, the outside shaft must speed up to allow for the difference. This speeding up and slowing down of the side gears allows differential speeds at the drive wheels.

On a slick surface, one wheel may have no traction and begin to spin. Power, like electricity, will then take the path of least resistance. If one wheel has no traction, power will flow to that wheel and the other wheel will remain stationary. Power will go from the pinion shaft through the differential pinions to only one side gear because the other side gear is stationary. At this point, the differential case will still turn end-over-end and one axle shaft will spin twice as fast as the case, while the other shaft will not turn at all.

NEW WORDS

1. differential [ˌdifəˈrenʃəl] n. 差速器
2. hypoid [ˈhaɪpɔɪd] adj. 准双曲面的
3. intersect [ˌintəˈsekt] vi. 相交，交叉
4. mesh [meʃ] v. 啮合
5. traction [ˈtrækʃən] n. 牵引力
6. stationary [ˈsteɪʃənəri] adj. 静止的，不动的

PHRASES AND EXPRESSIONS

1. limited-slip differential (LSD)　　防滑差速器
2. drive shaft　　传动轴
3. axle shafts　　半轴，驱动轴
4. final drive assembly　　主减速器总成，最终传动装置
5. gear reduction　　齿轮减速
6. gear reduction ratios　　齿轮减速比
7. spiral bevel gear　　螺旋锥齿轮
8. side gear (differential gear)　　半轴齿轮
9. pinion shaft　　行星齿轮轴
10. differential pinion　　行星齿轮
11. drive pinion　　（主减速器）主动小齿轮

NOTES TO THE TEXT

The final drive assembly also provides gear reduction so that the drive wheels spin more slowly than the drive shaft.
主减速器总成具有减速作用，因而驱动轮要比传动轴转得慢。

EXERCISES

I. Answer the following questions

1. What are bevel gears?

2. Which is the driving gear in a differential?

3. How does the differential system work?

4. Why is the position of the drive pinion in the final-drive housing important?

II. Translate the following into Chinese

1. The last component in the drive train is the axle. In a rear wheel drive car the axle is in the rear. Engine power is transmitted from the transmission to the axle via the drive shaft. The drive shaft is basically a metal tube with joints on each end called universal joints. These joints allow the tube to move in relation to the suspension and keep powers flowing to the rear. In front wheel drive cars the axle is integrated into the transmission thus the term transaxle.

2. The drive shaft, or propeller shaft, connects the transmission output shaft to the differential pinion shaft. Since all roads are not perfectly smooth, and the transmission is fixed, the drive shaft has to be flexible to absorb the shock of bumps in the road. Universal, or "U-joints" allow the drive shaft to flex (and stop it from breaking) when the drive angle changes.

3. Drive shafts are usually hollow in order to weigh less, but of a large diameter so that they are strong. High quality steel, and sometimes aluminum are used in the manufacture of the drive shaft. The shaft must be quite straight and balanced to avoid vibrating. Since it usually turns at engine speeds, a lot of damage can be caused if the shaft is unbalanced, or bent. Damage can also be caused if the U-joints are worn out.

Reading Material: The Final Drive

The final drive transfers power from the engine and transmission to the wheels that drive the car, shown as Figure 10-7. The final drive takes power from the spinning drive shaft and transfers it 90° to make the drive wheels turn. The final drive must also divide the power between the two drive wheels. When a vehicle moves straight ahead, the power divides equally so that both wheels receive an equal amount of power and move an equal distance, shown as Figure 10-8. When a car goes around a corner, the outside wheel must move a greater distance than the inside wheel. Thus, the drive wheels must move at different speeds and with different driving forces.

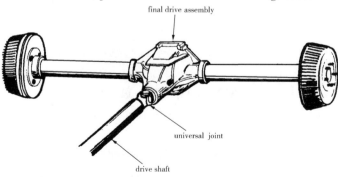

Figure 10-7 *The final drive transfers power from the drive shaft to the drive wheels*

If the two drive wheels moved at equal speeds, the wheels would skid as the car rounded the corner. This would cause the tires to wear rapidly. To avoid such wear, the final drive has a set of gears that can divide the power between the drive wheels. Thus, the wheels can turn at different speeds, if necessary. Because the gears allow a speed differential (or difference) between the two drive wheels, the gear mechanism is called the differential. Some people confuse the differential with the final drive. The differential is really only the power-dividing gears, while the final drive includes the differential plus other parts.

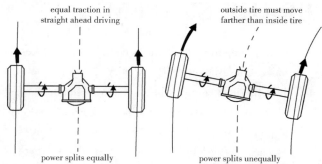

Figure 10-8 *The final drive splits the power equally when a car moves straight ahead. It splits the power unequally when a car goes around a corner.*

Dividing power unequally is difficult. It becomes even harder when one wheel loses traction, such as on ice or slippery pavement. The final drive assembly tends to transmit power to the wheel that spins and no power to the wheel that may have normal traction. Most differentials do not compensate for this situation and are called standard, open, or unlimited-slip differentials.

However, a more complex design avoids this problem. This type of final drive allows a certain amount of slip between the two drive wheels. When one drive wheel starts spinning at a much greater speed than the other wheel, the differential "senses" the change. The differential then transfers the power away from the wheel that spins and toward the one that does not spin. This type of differential is called a limited-slip differential.

NEW WORDS

1. pavement   ['peivmənt]   *n.* 人行道,公路
2. compensate   ['kɔmpenseit]   *v.* 抵消,弥补

PHRASES AND EXPRESSIONS

1. final drive   主减速器
2. drive wheel   驱动轮
3. limited-slip differential   防滑差速器

NOTES

1. The final drive assembly tends to transmit power to the wheel that spins and no power to the wheel that may have normal traction.

主减速器总成趋向于将动力传到旋转的驱动轮,而不传到能产生正常驱动力的驱动轮。

2. The differential then transfers the power away from the wheel that spins and toward the one that does not spin.

差速器就将动力不传到旋转的驱动轮,而传到不旋转的驱动轮。

UNIT 11　BRAKE SYSTEM

　　The brake system is the most important system in cars. If the brakes fail, the result can be disastrous. Brakes are actually energy conversion devices, which convert the kinetic energy (momentum) of the vehicle into thermal energy (heat). When stepping on the brakes, the driver commands a stopping force ten times as powerful as the force that puts the car in motion. The brake system can exert thousands of pounds of pressure on each of the four brakes.

　　The brake system is composed of the following basic components: the "master cylinder" which is located under the hood, and is directly connected to the brake pedal, converts driver foot's mechanical pressure into hydraulic pressure. Steel "brake lines" and flexible "brake hoses" connect the master cylinder to the "slave cylinders" located at each wheel. Brake fluid, specially designed to work in extreme conditions, fills the system. "Shoes" and "pads" are pushed by the slave cylinders to contact the "drums" and "rotors" thus causing drag, which (hopefully) slows the car.

　　The typical brake system consists of disk brakes in front and either disk or drum brakes in the rear connected by a system of tubes and hoses that link the brake at each wheel to the master cylinder (Figure 11-1).

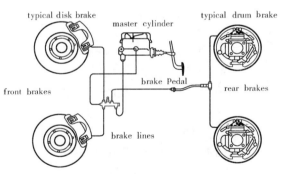

Figure 11-1　*Typical automobile braking system*

　　Stepping on the brake pedal, a plunger is actually been pushing against in the master cylinder which forces hydraulic oil (brake fluid) through a series of tubes and hoses to the braking unit at each wheel. Since hydraulic fluid (or any fluid for that matter) cannot be compressed, pushing fluid through a pipe is just like pushing a steel bar through a pipe. Unlike a steel bar, however, fluid can be directed through many twists and turns on its way to its destination, arriving with the exact same motion and pressure that it started with. It is very important that the fluid is pure liquid and that there are no air bubbles in it. Air can compress, which causes a sponginess to the pedal and severely reduced braking efficiency. If air is suspected, then the system must be bled to remove the air. There are "bleeder screws" at each wheel cylinder and caliper for this purpose.

On a disk brake, the fluid from the master cylinder is forced into a caliper where it presses against a piston. The piston, in-turn, squeezes two brake pads against the disk (rotor) which is attached to the wheel, forcing it to slow down or stop. This process is similar to a bicycle brake where two rubber pads rub against the wheel rim creating friction.

With drum brakes, fluid is forced into the wheel cylinder which pushes the brake shoes out so that the friction linings are pressed against the drum which is attached to the wheel, causing the wheel to stop.

In either case, the friction surfaces of the pads on a disk brake system, or the shoes on a drum brake convert the forward motion of the vehicle into heat. Heat is what causes the friction surfaces (linings) of the pads and shoes to eventually wear out and require replacement.

Brake fluid is a special oil that has specific properties. It is designed to withstand cold temperatures without thickening as well as very high temperatures without boiling. (If the brake fluid should boil, it will cause you to have a spongy pedal and the car will be hard to stop). Figure 11-2 shows a brake hydraulic system.

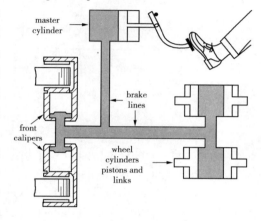

Figure 11-2 *The brake hydraulic system*

The brake fluid reservoir is on top of the master cylinder. Most cars today have a transparent reservoir so that you can see the level without opening the cover. The brake fluid level will drop slightly as the brake pads wear. This is a normal condition and no cause for concern. If the level drops noticeably over a short period of time or goes down to about two thirds full, have your brakes checked as soon as possible. Keep the reservoir covered except for the amount of time you need to fill it and never leave a can of brake fluid uncovered. Brake fluid must maintain a very high boiling point. Exposure to air will cause the fluid to absorb moisture which will lower that boiling point.

The brake fluid travels from the master cylinder to the wheels through a series of steel tubes and reinforced rubber hoses. Rubber hoses are only used in places that require flexibility, such as at the front wheels, which move up and down as well as steer. The rest of the system uses non-corrosive seamless steel tubing with special fittings at all attachment points. If a steel line requires a repair, the best procedure is to replace the complete line. If this is not practical, a line can be repaired using special splice fittings that are made for brake system repair. You must never use brass "compression" fittings or copper tubing to repair a brake system. They are dangerous and illegal.

Other Components in the Hydraulic System

Proportioning Valve or Equalizer Valve

These valves are mounted between the master cylinder and the rear wheels. They are designed to adjust the pressure between the front and rear brakes depending on how hard you are stopping. The shorter you stop, the more of the vehicle's weight is transferred to the front wheels, in some cases, causing the rear to lift and the front to dive. These valves are designed to direct more pressure to the front and less pressure to the rear the harder you stop. This minimizes the chance of premature lockup at the rear wheels.

Pressure Differential Valve

This valve is usually mounted just below the master cylinder and is responsible for turning the brake warning light on when it detects a malfunction. It measures the pressure from the two sections of the master cylinder and compares them. Since it is mounted ahead of the proportioning or equalizer valve, the two pressures it detects should be equal. If it detects a difference, it means that there is probably a brake fluid leak somewhere in the system.

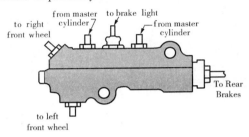

Combination Valve

The Combination valve (Figure 11-3) is simply a proportioning valve and a pressure differential valve that is combined into one unit.

The parking brake (a. k. a. emergency brake) system controls the rear brakes through a series of steel cables that are connected to either a hand lever or a foot pedal. The idea is that the system is fully

Figure 11-3 Combination valve

mechanical and completely bypasses the hydraulic system so that the vehicle can be brought to a stop even if there is a total brake failure.

On drum brakes, the cable pulls on a lever mounted in the rear brake and is directly connected to the brake shoes. This has the effect of bypassing the wheel cylinder and controlling the brakes directly.

Disk brakes on the rear wheels add additional complication for parking brake systems. There are two main designs for adding a mechanical parking brake to rear disk brakes. The first type uses the existing rear wheel caliper and adds a lever attached to a mechanical corkscrew device inside the caliper piston. When the parking brake cable pulls on the lever, this corkscrew device pushes the piston against the pads, thereby bypassing the hydraulic system, to stop the vehicle. This type of system is primarily used with single piston floating calipers, if the caliper is of the four piston fixed type, then that type of system can't be used. The other system uses a complete mechanical drum brake unit mounted inside the rear rotor. The brake shoes on this system are connected to a lever that is pulled by the parking brake cable to activate the brakes. The brake "drum" is actually the inside part of the rear brake rotor.

On cars with automatic transmissions, the parking brake is rarely used. This can cause a couple of problems. The biggest problem is that the brake cables tend to get corroded and eventually seize up causing the parking brake to become inoperative. By using the parking brake from time to time, the cables stay clean and functional. Another problem comes from the fact that the self adjusting mechanism on certain brake systems uses the parking brake actuation to adjust the brakes. If the parking brake is never used, then the brakes never get adjusted.

The power brake booster (Figure 11-4) is mounted on the firewall directly behind the master cylinder and, along with the master cylinder, is directly connected with the brake pedal. Its purpose is to amplify the available foot pressure applied to the brake pedal so that the amount of foot pressure required to stop even the largest vehicle is minimal. Power for the booster comes from engine vacuum. The automobile engine produces vacuum as a by-product of normal operation and is freely available for use in powering accessories such as the power brake booster. Vacuum enters the booster through a check valve on the booster. The check valve is connected to the engine with a rubber hose and acts as a one-way valve that allows vacuum to enter the booster but does not let it escape. The booster is an empty shell that is divided into two

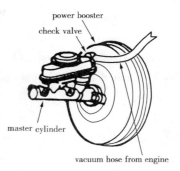

Figure 11-4 the power brake booster

chambers by a rubber diaphragm. There is a valve in the diaphragm that remains open while foot is off the brake pedal so that vacuum is allowed to fill both chambers. When stepping on the brake pedal, the valve in the diaphragm closes, separating the two chambers and another valve opens to allow air in the chamber on the brake pedal side. This is what provides the power assist. Power boosters are very reliable and cause few problems of their own. However, other things can contribute to a loss of power assist. In order to have power assist, the engine must be running. If the engine stalls or shuts off while you are driving, you will have a small reserve of power assist for two or three pedal applications but, after that, the brakes will be extremely hard to apply and you must put as much pressure as you can to bring the vehicle to a stop.

The last topic is the Anti-Lock Brakes (ABS). The most efficient braking pressure takes place just before each wheel lock up. When you slam on the brakes in a panic stop and the wheels lock up, causing a screeching sound and leaving strips of rubber on the pavement, you do not stop the vehicle nearly as short as it is capable of stopping. Also, while the wheels are locked up, you loose all steering control so that, if you have an opportunity to steer around the obstacle, you will not be able to do so. Another problem occurs during an extended skid is that you will burn a patch of rubber off the tire which causes a "flat spot" on the tread that will produce an annoying thumping sound as you drive.

Anti-lock brake systems solve this lockup problem by rapidly pumping the brakes whenever the system detects a wheel that is locked up. In most cases, only the wheel that is locked will be pumped, while full braking pressure stays available to the other wheels. This effect allows you to stop in the shortest amount of time while maintaining full steering control even if one or more wheels are on ice. The system uses a computer to monitor the speed of each wheel. When it detects that one or more wheels have stopped or are turning much slower than the remaining wheels, the computer sends a signal to momentarily remove and reapply or pulse the pressure to the affected wheels to allow them to continue turning. This "pumping" of the brakes occurs at ten or more times a second, far faster then a human can pump the brakes manually. If you step on the brakes hard enough to engage the anti-lock system, you may feel a strong vibration in the brake pedal. This is a normal condition and indicates that the system is working; however, it can be disconcerting to some people who don't expect it. If your vehicle has anti-lock brakes, read your owner's manual to find out more about it.

The system consists of an electronic control unit, a hydraulic actuator, and wheel speed sensors at each wheel. If the control unit detects a malfunction in the system, it will illuminate an ABS warning light on the dash to let you know that there is a problem. If there is a problem, the anti-lock system will not function but the brakes will otherwise function normally.

NEW WORDS

1. disastrous [diˈzɑːstrəs] *adj.* 灾难性的
2. plunger [ˈplʌndʒə] *n.* 活塞,柱塞,针阀
3. sponginess [ˌspʌdʒinis] *n.* 轻软有弹性,海绵性
4. malfunction [mælˈfʌŋkʃən] *n.* 故障
5. bypass [ˈbaipɑːs] *v.* 设旁路,迂回
6. corkscrew [ˈkɔːkskruː] *n.* 开塞钻,螺丝锥,活塞推杆
7. inoperative [inˈɔpərətiv] *adj.* 不起作用的
8. booster [ˈbuːstə] *n.* 调压器,(制动,转向)助力器,伺服装置
9. slam [slæm] *v.* 猛地踏下,猛力抨击,冲击
10. screech [skriːtʃ] *v.* 发出尖锐的声音
11. thumping [ˈθʌmpiŋ] *adj.* 极大的
12. momentarily [ˌməʊmənˈteərəliː] *adv.* 即刻,立即

PHRASES AND EXPRESSIONS

1. thermal energy 热能
2. master cylinder 制动主缸
3. brake pedal 制动踏板
4. brake hose 制动软管
5. slave cylinder 轮缸,分泵
6. drum brake 鼓式制动器
7. brake shoe 制动蹄(块),闸皮
8. bleeder screw (制动系统)放气螺钉
9. spongy pedal 踏板发软
10. panic stop 紧急停车,紧急制动
11. friction lining 摩擦衬片
12. proportioning valve 比例阀,定量阀,配合阀
13. equalizer valve 平衡阀
14. pressure differential valve 差压(调节)阀
15. combination valve 组合阀
16. a.k.a. = also known as 又名……,也叫作……
17. emergency brake 紧急制动器,紧急闸,应急制动
18. brake booster 制动助力器
19. flat spot (胎面)平点
20. hydraulic actuator 液压传动(操纵)机构,液压动力缸

UNIT 11 BRAKE SYSTEM

NOTES TO THE TEXT

1. Brakes are actually energy conversion devices, which convert the kinetic energy (momentum) of the vehicle into thermal energy (heat). When stepping on the brakes, the driver commands a stopping force ten times as powerful as the force that puts the car in motion.

制动器实际就是能量转换装置,它将汽车的动能(动量)转化成热能(热量)。当驾驶人踩下制动踏板,所产生的制动力是汽车运动时动力的十倍。

2. The typical brake system consists of disk brakes in front and either disk or drum brakes in the rear connected by a system of tubes and hoses that link the brake at each wheel to the master cylinder.

常见的制动系统布置有前后盘式,前盘后鼓式,各个车轮上的制动器通过一套管路系统连接到制动主缸上。

3. They are designed to adjust the pressure between the front and rear brakes depending on how hard you are stopping. The shorter you stop, the more of the vehicle's weight is transferred to the front wheels, in some cases, causing the rear to lift and the front to dive.

这些阀用于调节分配到前后轮制动管路的油压,而这些压力的大小取决于驾驶人制动的强度。制动越急促,则汽车的重心越靠近前轮,有些情况下,甚至能导致后轮抬起,出现点头现象。

4. The parking brake (a.k.a. emergency brake) system controls the rear brakes through a series of steel cables that are connected to either a hand lever or a foot pedal. The idea is that the system is fully mechanical and completely bypasses the hydraulic system so that the vehicle can be brought to a stop even if there is a total brake failure.

驻车制动(又称应急制动)系统通过一套与操纵手柄或踏板相连的钢缆来操纵后轮制动器。这套系统是机械式的,且与液压系统并联,从而保证在整个液压制动系统失灵的情况下汽车也能实现制动。

EXERCISES

I. Answer the following questions

1. Please explain the components of a brake system.
2. Please draw a Brake Hydraulic System.
3. Please explain the two main designs for adding a mechanical parking brake to rear disk brakes.
4. How does the power brake booster work?
5. Please indicate the importance of the Anti-Lock Brakes (ABS).

II. Translate the following into Chinese

1. The brake shoes and their waterproof linings must be strong enough to withstand high temperatures and thousands of brake applications. They must have just the right coefficient of friction to provide the proper braking force.

2. Two types of hydraulic brake systems are used. The manual brake system is the simplest.

Here, the force of the driver's foot on the pedal applies all the force to the hydraulic system. Another system, the power brake system, uses parts that assist a driver in applying force to the hydraulic system.

Reading Material: Disk Brake

Disc brakes, like many automotive innovations, were originally developed for auto racing, but are now standard equipment on virtually every car made. On most cars, the front brakes are of the disc type, and the rear brakes are of the "drum" type. Drum brakes use two semi-circular shoes to press outward against the inner surfaces of a steel drum. Older cars often had drum brakes on all four wheels, and many new cars now have 4-wheel disc brakes.

Though disc brakes rely on the same basic principles to slow a vehicle (friction and heat), their design is far superior to that of drum brakes. Because disc brakes can fling off water more easily than drum brakes, they work much better in wet conditions. This is not to say that water does not affect them, it definitely does. If you splash through a puddle and then try to apply the brakes, your brakes may not work at all for a few seconds! Disc brakes also allow better airflow cooling, which also increases their effectiveness. Some high performance disc brakes have drilled or slotted holes through the face of the rotor, which helps to prevent the pads from "glazing" (becoming hardened due to heat). Disc brakes were introduced as standard equipment on most cars in the early seventies.

The main components of a disk brake are the Brake Pads, Rotor (Disc), Caliper and Caliper Support (Figure 11-5).

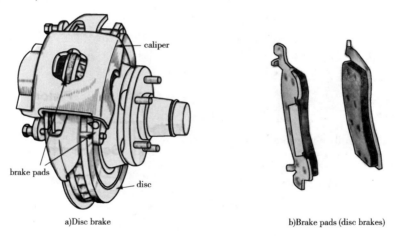

Figure 11-5   Disk brake parts

Brake Pads

There are two brake pads on each caliper. They are constructed of a metal "shoe" with the lining riveted or bonded to it. The pads are mounted in the caliper, one on each side of the rotor. Brake linings used to be made primarily of asbestos because of its heat absorbing properties and quiet operation; however, due to health risks, asbestos has been outlawed, so new materials are now being used. Brake pads wear out with use and must be replaced periodically. There are many types and qualities of pads available. The differences have to do with brake life (how long the new pads will last) and noise (how quiet they are when you step on the brake). Harder linings tend to last longer and stop better under heavy use but they may produce an irritating squeal when they are applied. Technicians that work on brakes usually have a favorite pad that gives a good compromise that their customers can live with.

Brake pads should be checked for wear periodically. If the lining wears down to the metal brake shoe, then a "Metal-to-Metal" condition will be had where the shoe rubs directly again "brake warning sensor" that will emit a squealing noise when the pads are worn to a point where they should be changed. This noise will usually be heard when your foot is off the brake and disappear when you step on the brake. If you hear this noise, have your brakes checked as soon as possible.

Rotor

The disk rotor is made of iron with highly machined surfaces where the brake pads contact it. Just as the brake pads wear out over time, the rotor also undergoes some wear, usually in the form of ridges and groves where the brake pad rubs against it. This wear pattern exactly matches the wear pattern of the pads as they seat themselves to the rotor. When the pads are replaced, the rotor must be machined smooth to allow the new pads to have an even contact surface to work with. Only a small amount of material can be machined off of a rotor before it becomes unusable and must be replaced. A minimum thickness measurement is stamped on every rotor and the technician doing the brake job will measure the rotor before and after machining it to make sure it doesn't go below the legal minimum. If a rotor is cut below the minimum, it will not be able to handle the high heat that brakes normally generate. This will cause the brakes to "fade", greatly reducing their effectiveness to a point where you may not be able to stop!

Caliper & Support

There are two main types of calipers: Floating calipers and fixed calipers. There are other configurations but these are the most popular. Calipers must be rebuilt or replaced if they show signs of leaking brake fluid.

Single Piston Floating Calipers (Figure 11-6) are the most popular and also least costly to manufacture and service. A floating caliper "floats" or moves in a track in its support so that it can center itself over the rotor. As driver applies brake pressure, the hydraulic fluid pushes in two directions. It forces the piston against the inner pad which in turn pushes against the rotor. It also pushes the caliper in the opposite direction against the outer pad, pressing it against the other side of the rotor. Floating calipers are also available on some vehicles with two pistons mounted on the same side. Two piston floating calipers are found on more expensive cars and can provide an improved braking "feel".

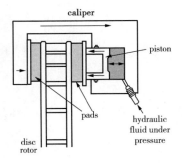

Figure 11-6 *Single piston floating caliper*

Four Piston Fixed Calipers are mounted rigidly to the support and are not allowed to move. Instead, there are two pistons on each side that press the pads against the rotor. Four piston calipers have a better feel and are more efficient, but are more expensive to produce and cost more to service. This type of caliper is usually found on more expensive luxury and high performance cars.

NEW WORDS

1. puddle   ['pʌdl]   n. 水坑,胶土,污水坑
2. glazing   ['gleiziŋ]   n. 上釉,上光
3. riveted   ['rivitid]   adj. 用铆钉钉牢的
4. outlaw   ['autlɔː]   v. 宣布……为不合法,法律规定禁用

PHRASES AND EXPRESSIONS

1. fling off   掷出,甩掉,扔掉
2. splash through   溅着水通过,涉水通过
3. slotted hole   长圆孔,长孔,缝槽,切口
4. Brake pads   制动块
5. do with   利用,忍受(满足)

NOTES

Brake linings used to be made primarily of asbestos because of its heat absorbing properties and quiet operation; however, due to health risks, asbestos has been outlawed, so new materials are now being used.

由于石棉的吸热特性和工作时噪声小,制动器摩擦片过去通常以石棉为主要材料;然而由于石棉对身体健康有害,已被法律禁止使用,所以新的材料被用在摩擦片中。

UNIT 12 STEERING SYSTEM

1. Steering System Principles

The steering system is the means by which the driver of a vehicle is able to control the position of the front wheels. The system must provide ease of handling, good directional control, and stability. This is achieved by the steering system in conjunction with the suspension.

For a car to turn smoothly, each wheel must follow a different circle. Since the inside wheel is following a circle with a smaller radius, it is actually making a tighter turn than the outside wheel. If you draw a line perpendicular to each wheel, the lines will intersect at the center point of the turn (Figure 12-1). The geometry of the steering linkage makes the inside wheel turn more than the outside wheel.

There are a couple different types of steering gears. The most common are rack-and-pinion and recirculating ball.

1.1 *Rack-and-pinion Steering*

Rack-and-pinion steering is quickly becoming the most common type of steering on cars, small trucks and SUVs. It is actually a pretty simple mechanism. A rack-and-pinion gear set is enclosed in a metal tube, with each end of the rack protruding from the tube. A rod, called a tie rod, connects to each end of the rack. The pinion gear is attached to the steering shaft. When you turn the steering wheel, the gear spins, moving the rack. The tie rod at each end of the rack connects to the steering arm on the spindle. Figure 12-2 shows the principle of rack-and-pinion.

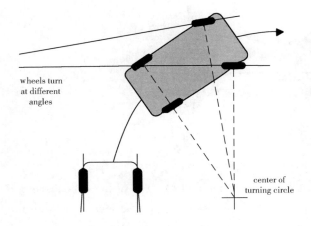

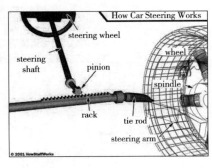

Figure 12-1 *The principle of a car steering*   Figure 12-2 *Shows the principle of rack-and-pinion*

The rack-and-pinion gearset does two things:

(a) It converts the rotational motion of the steering wheel into the linear motion needed to turn the wheels.

(b) It provides a gear reduction, making it easier to turn the wheels.

On most cars, it takes three to four complete revolutions of the steering wheel to make the wheels turn from lock to lock (from far left to far right).

The steering ratio is the ratio of how far you turn the steering wheel to how far the wheels turn. For instance, if one complete revolution (360 degrees) of the steering wheel results in the wheels of the car turning 20 degrees, then the steering ratio is 360 divided by 20, or 18:1. A higher ratio means that you have to turn the steering wheel more to get the wheels to turn a given distance. However, less effort is required because of the higher gear ratio.

Generally, lighter, sportier cars have lower steering ratios than larger cars and trucks. The lower ratio gives the steering a quicker response—you don't have to turn the steering wheel as much to get the wheels to turn a given distance—which is a desirable trait in sports cars. These smaller cars are light enough that even with the lower ratio, the effort required to turn the steering wheel is not excessive.

Some cars have variable-ratio steering, which uses a rack-and-pinion gearset that has a different tooth pitch (number of teeth per inch) in the center than it has on the outside. This makes the car respond quickly when starting a turn (the rack is near the center), and also reduces effort near the wheel's turning limits.

1.2 Power Rack-and-pinion

When the rack-and-pinion is in a power-steering system, the rack has a slightly different design. Figure 12-3 shows the principle of power rack-and-pinion.

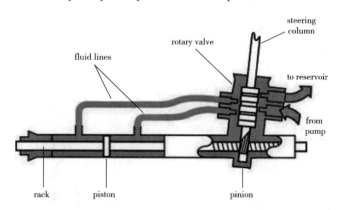

Figure 12-3 *The principle of power rack-and-pinion*

Part of the rack contains a cylinder with a piston in the middle. The piston is connected to the rack. There are two fluid ports, one on either side of the piston. Supplying higher-pressure fluid to one side of the piston forces the piston to move, which in turn moves the rack, providing the power assist.

1.3 Recirculating-ball Steering

Recirculating-ball steering is used on many trucks and SUVs today. The linkage that turns the wheels is slightly different than on a rack-and-pinion system.

The recirculating-ball steering gear contains a worm gear. You can image the gear in two parts. The first part is a block of metal with a threaded hole in it. This block has gear teeth cut into the outside of it, which engage a gear that moves the pitman arm (Figure 12-4).

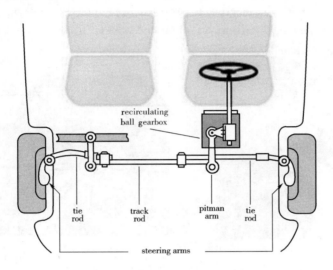

Figure 12-4 *Parts of recirculating-ball steering system*

The steering wheel connects to a threaded rod, similar to a bolt, which sticks into the hole in the block. When the steering wheel turns, it turns the bolt. Instead of twisting further into the block the way a regular bolt would, this bolt is held fixed so that when it spins, it moves the block, which moves the gear that turns the wheels.

Instead of the bolt directly engaging the threads in the block, all of the threads are filled with ball bearings (Figure 12-5) that recirculate through the gear as it turns. The balls actually serve two purposes: First, they reduce friction and wear in the gear; second, they reduce slope in the gear. Slope would be felt when you change the direction of the steering wheel—without the balls in the steering gear, the teeth would come out of contact with each other for a moment, making the steering wheel feel loose.

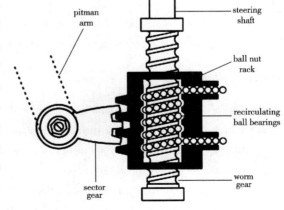

Figure 12-5 *Parts of recirculating-ball steering gear*

Power steering in a recirculating-ball system works similarly to a rack-and-pinion system. Assist is provided by supplying higher-pressure fluid to one side of the block.

2. Power Steering

There are a couple of key components in power steering in addition to the rack-and-pinion or recirculating-ball mechanism. Figure 12-6 shows the sketch of the power steering.

2.1 *Pump*

The hydraulic power for the steering is provided by a rotary-vane pump (see Figure 12-7). This pump is driven by the car's engine via a belt and pulley. It contains a set of retractable vanes that spin inside an oval chamber.

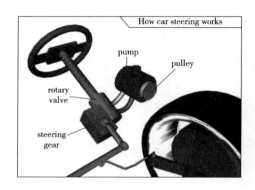
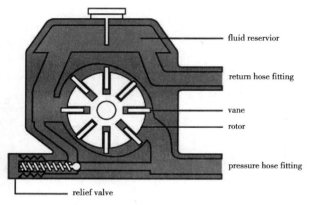

Figure 12-6 The sketch of the power steering   *Figure 12-7 The principle of the rotary-vane pump*

As the vanes spin, they pull hydraulic fluid from the return line at low pressure and force it into the outlet at high pressure. The amount of flow provided by the pump depends on the car's engine speed. The pump must be designed to provide adequate flow when the engine is idling. As a result, the pump moves much more fluid than necessary when the engine is running at faster speeds.

The pump contains a pressure-relief valve to make sure that the pressure does not get too high, especially at high engine speeds when so much fluid is being pumped.

2.2 *Rotary Valve*

A power-steering system should assist the driver only when he is exerting force on the steering wheel (such as when starting a turn). When the driver is not exerting force (such as when driving in a straight line), the system shouldn't provide any assist. The device that senses the force on the steering wheel is called the rotary valve (see Figure 12-8).

The key to the rotary valve is a torsion bar. The torsion bar is a thin rod of metal that twists when torque is applied to it. The top of the bar is connected to the steering wheel, and the bottom of the bar is connected to the pinion or worm gear (which turns the wheels), so the amount of torque in the torsion bar is equal to the amount of torque the driver is using to turn the wheels. The more torque the driver uses to turn the wheels, the more the bar twists.

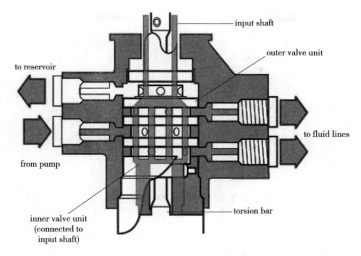

Figure 12-8   The principle of the rotary valve

The input from the steering shaft forms the inner part of a spool-valve assembly. It also connects to the top end of the torsion bar. The bottom of the torsion bar connects to the outer part of the spool valve. The torsion bar also turns the output of the steering gear, connecting to either the pinion gear or the worm gear depending on which type of steering the car has.

As the bar twists, it rotates the inside of the spool valve relative to the outside. Since the inner part of the spool valve is also connected to the steering shaft (and therefore to the steering wheel), the amount of rotation between the inner and outer parts of the spool valve depends on how much torque the driver applies to the steering wheel.

When the steering wheel is not being turned, both hydraulic lines provide the same amount of pressure to the steering gear. But if the spool valve is turned one way or the other, ports open up to provide high-pressure fluid to the appropriate line.

NEW WORDS

1. perpendicular   [ˌpɜːpənˈdikjələ]   *adj.* 垂直的, 正交的; *n.* 垂线
2. intersect   [ˌintəˈsekt]   *vi.* (直线)相交, 交叉
3. enclose   [inˈkləuz]   *vt.* 放入封套, 装入, 围绕
4. mechanism   [ˈmekənizəm]   *n.* 机械装置, 机构, 机制
5. rack   [ræk]   *n.* 齿条, 齿轨
6. spindle   [ˌspindl]   *n.* 轴, 杆, 心轴
7. revolution   [ˌrevəˈluːʃən]   *n.* 绕转, 旋转
8. slightly   [ˈslaitliː]   *adv.* 轻微地, 有一点, 略
9. fluid   [ˈfluːid]   *n.* 液体, 流质
10. linkage   [ˈliŋkidʒ]   *n.* 联结
11. threaded   [ˈθredid]   *adj.* 带螺纹的
12. engage   [inˈgeidʒ]   *vi.* 接合, 啮合
13. spin   [spin]   *vt. & vi.* 快速旋转, 回旋
14. recirculate   [riˈsəːkjuleit]   *vi.* 再[重复, 封闭, 回路]循环

15. slope	[sləup]	n. 斜坡，斜面，倾斜
16. oval	['əuvəl]	adj. 卵形的，椭圆的；n. 卵形，椭圆形
17. outlet	['autlet]	n. 出口，出路
18. exert	[ig'zə:t]	vt. 尽(力)，施加(压力等)；v. 发挥，竭尽全力
19. utilize	['ju:tilaiz]	vt. 利用
20. consumption	[kən'sʌmpʃən]	n. 消费，消费量，消耗
21. eliminate	[i'limineit]	vt. 除去，排[删，消]除，削减
22. spindle	['spindl]	n. 轴，杆，心轴

PHRASES AND EXPRESSIONS

1. steering system 转向系统
2. rack-and-pinion 齿条齿轮式
3. recirculating ball 循环球式
4. tie rod 转向横拉杆
5. steering ratio 转向减速比，转向变速比
6. variable-ratio steering 可变速比转向，可变传动比转向装置
7. tooth pitch 齿节，齿距
8. turning limit 转向限值
9. power-steering system 动力转向系统
10. worm gear 涡轮，螺杆
11. pitman arm 转向垂臂，转向摇臂，转向臂
12. threaded rod 螺杆
13. ball bearing 球轴承，滚球轴承
14. rotary-vane pump 回转式叶片泵，叶片泵
15. retractable vane 可伸缩叶片
16. pressure-relief valve 安全阀，卸压阀
17. rotary valve 回转阀，转阀
18. spool-valve 滑阀，柱式滑阀
19. electronic control system 电子控制系统

NOTES TO THE TEXT

1. On most cars, it takes three to four complete revolutions of the steering wheel to make the wheels turn from lock to lock (from far left to far right).

对于大多数汽车来说，使转向轮从一侧的极限位置偏转到另一侧的极限位置(从最左侧转到最右侧)，转向盘需要转动三到四圈。

2. Some cars have variable-ratio steering, which uses a rack-and-pinion gearset that has a different tooth pitch (number of teeth per inch) in the center than it has on the outside.

有些汽车采用可变传动比的转向器，在其齿轮齿条机构中，齿条中心与两端的齿距(每英寸的齿数)不同。

3. Instead of twisting further into the block the way a regular bolt would, this bolt is held fixed

so that when it spins, it moves the block, which moves the gear that turns the wheels.

由于转向螺杆的轴向是固定的,所以螺杆转动时,没有像通常那样螺杆向螺母深处前进,而是使螺母沿螺杆轴向移动,从而带动齿扇轴,最后偏转转向轮。

4. As the vanes spin, they pull hydraulic fluid from the return line at low pressure and force it into the outlet at high pressure.

随着叶片转动,从回油管吸入低压油然后把它压向出油口,以高压油输出。

5. Since the inner part of the spool valve is also connected to the steering shaft (and therefore to the steering wheel), the amount of rotation between the inner and outer parts of the spool valve depends on how much torque the driver applies to the steering wheel.

由于阀芯也与转向轴相连(也就是与转向盘相连),所以阀芯与阀体之间的转动量取决于驾驶人给转向盘所施加的转矩有多大。

EXERCISES

Ⅰ. Answer the following questions

1. Please list the types of the steering gears used in cars today.
2. Please list the parts of a recirculating ball steering system.
3. How does a rack-and-pinion steering system work?
4. How does a power steering pump operate?
5. Why are ball joints used in steering system?

Ⅱ. Translate the following into Chinese

1. Four-Wheel steering systems are offered today that keep the side slip angle small through deliberate counter-steering action of the rear wheels. For this purpose, the rear wheels must be turned in the same direction as the front wheels but at a much reduced steering angle.

2. The steering linkage is so designed as to prevent side-slip of all automobile wheels in cornering, thus ensuring ease of steering and minimizing wear of tire.

3. Some automobiles are equipped with a hydraulic power steering system intended to decrease the efforts spent by the driver to turn the wheels and to damp the road jolts transmitted to the steering wheel.

Reading Material: Wheel Alignment

The purpose of proper wheel alignment is to provide maximum safety, ease of handling, stability, and directional control of the vehicle. This requires each of the steering angles (steering geometry) be adjusted to the specifications recommended by the vehicles require different settings. Follow the specific shop manual for each vehicle. The wheels must also be in proper dynamic and static balance to achieve these purposes.

Steering geometry refers to the angels formed by the steering and suspension parts in relationship to the frame and body of the vehicle. These angles include camber, caster, steering axis inclination, toe in (toe out), and toe out on turn (turning radius). Ideally, the vehicle center line, geometric center line, and the thrust line would all be identical and the car would form a perfect 90° rectangle. Because of factory tolerances and the unitized construction common to today's cars, this is rarely, if ever, the case.

On all vehicles it is important to remember that the rear axle dictates the position of the front wheels. On frame-type vehicles, two-wheel alignments are taken from the frame and the rear axle is assumed to be in correct alignment. On unitized vehicles with four wheel independent suspension, there is no frame to work with, so we can no longer assume that rear wheels are in correct alignment; therefore, four-wheel alignment is necessary to give proper steering and handling.

Tracking and Wheelbase

For proper tracking, all four wheels must be parallel to the frame. This requires the wheelbase to be equal on both sides of the vehicle. The four wheels should be positioned to form a rectangle.

Camber

Camber is the inward or outward tilt of the wheel at the top. Inward tilt is negative camber and outward tilt is positive camber. The tilt of the wheel (camber) is measured in degrees and is adjustable on many vehicles.

Caster

Caster is the forward or backward tilt of the spindle or steering the knuckle at the top when viewed from the side. Forward tilt is negative caster and backward tilt is positive caster. Caster is measured in the number of degrees that it is forward or backward from true vertical and is adjustable on many vehicles.

Steering Axis Inclination

Steering axis inclination is the inward tilt of the steering knuckle at the top. Steering axis inclination is measure in degrees and is not adjustable. If incorrect, suspension parts are at fault and must be replaced.

Toe-In (Toe Out)

Toe-in occurs when the front wheels are slightly closer together at the front wheels are slightly closer together at the front than at the rear. Toe-in is measured in inches, millimeters, or degrees. A limited amount of toe-in or toe-out is needed to allow for the fact that the wheels spread apart or come together slightly at the front when driving down the road, depending on vehicle design. This provides a zero running toe and no tire scuffing.

Incorrect toe-in or toe-out is the most frequent cause of rapid tire-tread wearing. Toe setting is the last adjustment to be made when performing a wheel alignment. On most front-wheel-drive vehicles, toe-out setting is required to provide a zero running toe. This is because the driving front wheels are trying to go around the steering axis inclination pivot point with a negative scrub radius. Rear wheels are designed with zero to slight toe-in, depending on the vehicle. This provides straight running as driving forces tend to push back the rear spindles. Correct toe is important for increasing tire life.

Toe-Out on Turns

Toe-out on turns is the different turning radius of the two front wheels. When the car is in a turn, the inner wheel is turned more than the outer wheel, resulting in toe-out on turns. This is caused by the steering arms being bent inward where they connect to the steering linkage. It is needed to prevent tire scuffing (dragging sideways) during a turn. Since the inner wheel follows a

smaller circle than the outer wheel when in a turn, toe-out on turns is necessary. Toe-out on turns is not adjustable and is corrected by replacing steering arms.

Center Point Steering

Although not technically an alignment angle, this causes more customer complaints than any other condition. Customers generally know little about alignment and to them, when the steering wheel is not centered, the car is not aligned correctly.

Wheel Alignment Procedure

Customer and vehicle safety depend on the technician' ability to follow proper procedures and specifications. To achieve this, the following factors should be included.

(a) Perform all pre-alignment checks properly to determine extent of repairs required.

(b) The vehicle's steering and suspension system, including tires, should be in good condition before attempting alignment.

(c) Use all alignment equipment as recommended by manufacturer.

(d) Tighten all fasteners to specified torque.

(e) Install cotter pins wherever required.

(f) Observe all safety precautions when positioning the vehicle on the alignment machine.

NEW WORDS

1. specification [ˌspesifiˈkeiʃən] n. 详述, 规格, 说明书, 规范
2. camber [ˈkæmbə] n. (车轮)外倾, 外倾角
3. caster [ˈkɑːstə] n. 主销后倾(角)
4. wheelbase [ˈwiːlbeis] n. 前后轮的轮轴距离, 轴距
5. fastener [ˈfɑːsθnə] n. 扣件, 扣, 钩扣, 扣钉, 卡子, 夹子

PHRASES AND EXPRESSIONS

1. wheel alignment   车轮定位
2. steering geometry   转向梯形机构, 转向几何结构
3. steering angle   转向角
4. toe in   前轮前束
5. toe out   负前束, 后束
6. turning radius   转向半径
7. tire-tread   轮胎胎面
8. cotter pin   开口销

NOTES

1. The purpose of proper wheel alignment is to provide maximum safety, ease of handling, stability, and directional control of the vehicle.

车轮定位的作用是保证汽车有最好的安全性、操纵稳定性, 并且操纵轻便。

2. The wheels must also be in proper dynamic and static balance to achieve these purposes.

为实现上述功用, 车轮必须达到动平衡和静平衡的要求。

UNIT 13 SUSPENSION SYSTEM

1. Suspension System Principle

The suspension system supports the weight of the engine, transmission, car body, and whatever the car body is carrying. This system has parts that link the wheels and tires to the frame or unit body.

Springs are the key part of the suspension. They absorb the shocks of the road surface so that passengers have a comfortable ride.

The suspension system has two subsystems—the front suspension and the rear suspension. There are a number of different suspension system types. There also are different types of springs that absorb road shocks. This unit discusses the most common types of suspension system.

2. The Front Suspension

The front suspension is more complicated than the rear suspension. This is because the front wheels must move in several different directions. The wheels must move up and down with the suspension and turn left to right with the steering. Since the car goes in the direction in which the front wheels point, the alignment of the front wheels is important. The wheels must point in just the right direction for the car to move straight down the road and turn properly.

Modern cars use an independent front suspension. In this system, each wheel mounts separately to the frame and has its own individual spring and shock absorber. Thus, the wheels act independently of one another. When one wheel hits a bump or hole in the road, the other wheel does not deflect.

2.1 Types of Springs

The spring allows the suspension to deflect when it hits a bump. Consequently, the force of the bump does not pass directly to the passenger compartment. There are three basic types of springs in automotive suspensions—coil springs, leaf springs and torsion bars. Many cars use combinations of springs, with one type for the front suspension and another type for the rear suspension.

2.1.1 Coil Springs

The coil springs used in the suspension are the same as many other coil springs used on a car. The compressed spring when force is removed, returns to its original position. The distance that a spring compressed under force depends on the rate of the spring. This is a measurement or specification that describes how much force is needed to compress or deflect the spring a certain amount.

UNIT 13 SUSPENSION SYSTEM

The thicker the coils in a coil spring, the stiffer it is and the higher its rate. Higher rate springs are used on larger, heavier cars, while lower rate springs are used on lighter cars. You may have heard that a car "rides like a truck." It means that the springs are so stiff and have such a high rate that they compress very little. Thus, they pass the road shocks to the car body and the passengers. Trucks and station wagons have heavier springs because the spring size determines the total load that cars can carry. If a car carries too much of a load, the springs may compress so much that the car will sit several inches lower than normal.

2.1.2 *Leaf Springs*

Leaf springs are made of long, flat pieces of metal clamped together to form a spring. The spring has a friction action because the leaves slip against one another as the assembly bends in the middle. The front and rear ends of the spring are bent into circles to form spring eyes. Usually these springs are used in the rear suspension because of their length. Bolts hold the spring eyes to the frame. These bolts have rubber bushings that fit between the bolt heads and the spring eyes. The bushings allow for a small amount of twist in the spring. They also absorb some vibrations. The rear suspension mounts to the frame with a spring shackle. The spring shackle allows for changes in the length of the spring as it bends. The rear axle mounts near the middle of the spring so that force is applied at that point.

Like coil springs, leaf springs have a rate that describes the amount of deflection for each pound of force applied. The thickness of the leaves and the number of leaves set the rate of a leaf spring.

2.1.3 *Torsion Bar*

Torsion bar springs are the simplest type. Coil springs absorb force by compressing and leaf springs absorb force by bending. A torsion bar is simply a long straight bar that absorbs force by twisting.

Torsion bars normally connect to the car so that one end is fixed in place and the other attaches to lever arm. When a force acts on the end of this lever arm, it bends up, causing the torsion bar to twist and absorb the force. When the force is released, the bar untwists to force the lever back to its original position. Thus, the twisting and untwisting of the torsion bar provides the same type of springing action as the coil spring and leaf spring.

Torsion bars also have a spring rate. The rate depends on the diameter and length of the bar. Torsion bar front suspension is used on many Chrysler and some GM products. Torsion bar suspensions are compact and give good handling and ride control. Also, torsion bars are easy to adjust for the car height.

2.2 *Types of Front Suspension*

Four types of front suspension are used with the different types of springs. These types are A-arm front suspension, alternate coil spring suspension, torsion bar front suspension, and MacPherson strut suspension.

2.2.1 *A-arm Front Suspension*

Many American cars use the A-arm suspension system. As mentioned, the steering knuckle supports the wheel and pivots about the steering axis so that the wheels can turn. The steering knuckle also is important. The knuckle mounts between the upper control arm and the lower control arm. The arms usually are triangular-shaped (like the letter A). The wide end is mounted to the car frame and the pointed end is mounted to the steering knuckle.

Ball joints hold the pointed end of the control arms to the steering knuckle and provide for multi-axis motion. Because of their shape, the arms are called A-arms. To reduce tire scuff, the upper arm is shorter than the lower arm. Thus, the shorter upper arm pulls in the top of the tire as the spring deflects. Therefore, the bottom of the tire stays at the same line on the road, resulting in less scuff.

In this suspension, a coil spring mounts near the knuckle. The bottom of the spring presses down on the lower control arm. The top of the spring pushes up on the frame of the car. A shock absorber usually mounts in the center of each coil spring. Most cars use a stabilizer bar (also called an anti-sway bar) that runs across the car, connecting one lower control arm to the other.

When a tire hits a bump, it is deflected, or moved up, making the control arms pivot. The lower control arm squeezes the spring up against the frame. After the wheel is deflected, the coil spring rebounds, moving down. The wheel and the control arms then return to their original position. There is a similar action if a wheel hits a hole. Then, the coil spring moves down before returning to its original position. When a car stands still, each coil spring is partially compressed because the spring supports the weight of the car on that wheel.

The stabilizer bar acts as a torsion bar between the front wheels. It helps balance the load between the wheels. For example, if a car corner sharply to the left, the cornering force shifts toward the outside front wheel. Thus, the right front wheel is heavily loaded and the left front wheel is lightly loaded. The high deflection of the right-side lower control arm pushes on the stabilizer bar, causing it to twist as a torsion bar. The bar now applies some of the force to the inside lower control arm, distributing the load more evenly. This prevents the car from leaning badly on turns.

2.2.2 *Alternate Coil Spring Suspension*

Another type of coil spring front suspension places the spring between the top surface of the upper control arm and a part of the car body. The part of the sheet metal body is the upper wheel housing. Often, the shock absorber mounts inside the coil spring between the upper arm and the housing. The top part of the wheel housing that supports the spring is called the spring tower.

This system works in the same way as the A-arm system. However, the upper control arm, rather than the lower arm, compressed the spring against the car body. In some cars, the coil spring mounts between the lower arm and frame. The shock absorber sits above the upper arm. Instead of an A-arm, some cars have a lower control rod that mounts to the frame with one bolt. A long rod called a strut mounts to the control arm near its outer end. The strut connects the arm to the frame at a point ahead of the main control arm mounting bolt. This is called a brake-reaction strut because it keeps the lower control arm from moving rearward when a driver applies the brakes. Together, the strut and lower control arm form the "A" shape.

2.2.3 *Torsion Bar Front Suspension*

Some cars use fully-independent torsion bar suspension systems. Here the torsion bars replace the standard coil springs. Torsion bars may be installed lengthwise or across (transverse to) the car. A

UNIT 13 SUSPENSION SYSTEM

lock ring anchors the rear end of the torsion bar to the frame. The front end of the bar attaches to the lower control arm at its inner pivot point. Up and down motion of the lower control arm twists the bar. This design also uses an upper and lower control arm. Ball joints mount the steering knuckle to the arms. The shock absorber mounts between the lower control arm and the frame. Upper motion of the lower control arm compresses the shock absorber against the car frame, as in the coil spring system.

In the torsion bar system, a mechanic can easily adjust the amount of preload on the torsion bar. This is done by tightening or loosening an anchor adjust bolt on the lower control arm. This adjusts the ride height.

2.2.4 *MacPherson Strut Suspension*

Many cars use the MacPherson strut suspension system. This system, which is used most often on the front, combines the shock absorber and spindle into a single unit. Sometimes the coil spring is also part of unit. The unit replaces the upper control arm because it mounts to the frame or body above the wheel housing. A ball joint connects the lower control arm to the steering arm and the strut.

The MacPherson system is simpler than other systems. However, it needs a longer, stronger shock tube. Furthermore, since the shock and spindle is a unit, replacement of either part is more expensive than is a standard coil spring or torsion bar suspension system. The MacPherson system is often used on cars with transverse engines. It allows additional underhood space.

The MacPherson system uses coil springs. However, some cars combine the MacPherson strut with torsion bars. The strut and spindle mount to the strut tower. The torsion bar mounts to the lower control arm at pivot point. The upward motion of the control arm causes the torsion bars to twist and then untwist to return the parts to their original positions.

3. The Rear Suspension

Rear suspensions may be of the solid axle or independent design. Many cars have solid axle rear suspension. Either design may have different kinds of springs, including torsion bars. However, the coil spring and leaf spring types are most popular.

3.1 *Solid Axle Rear Suspension with Coil Springs*

A common type of rear suspension uses the solid axle design and coil springs. This is called the link-type or four-link rear suspension (Figure 13-1). In most instances, two links mount to the top side of the axle tubes. The other two mount to the bottom side of the axle tubes. These are trailing links because they normally mount ahead of the rear axle and then extend either straight rearward or rearward at an angle.

Rubber bushings are placed between the bolts and the links. These bushings dampen vibrations. The links hold the axle in place and keep it from moving from side to side or forward and backward. The links also control the reaction of the axle tubes during acceleration and braking. The rubber bushings permit a small amount of twist. However, too much twist changes the pinion angle and could cause U-joint wear.

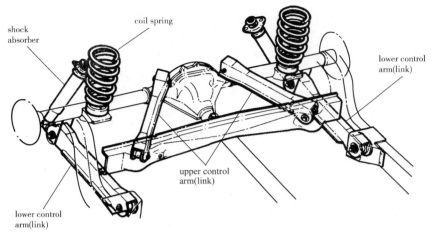

Figure 13-1 *This link-type solid axle uses coil springs between the axle tubes and the frame*

The coil springs are between brackets on the axle tube and the frame, some times in the center of the spring. The weight of the car and the shock absorbers hold the springs in place. The shock absorbers limit axle movement during rebound. Thus, the axle can freely move in the up-and-down direction caused by road surface irregularities. Such motion makes the links pivot at their mounting points because the springs and shocks compress and expand. The wheels are not independent of one another. Thus, a bump at one rear wheel causes a reaction in both rear wheels.

3.2 *Solid Axle with Leaf Springs*

Solid axle rear suspensions with leaf springs are also popular. This design needs fewer parts but gives a slightly harsher ride. The springs are asymmetrical, semielliptical leaf springs. This means that the springs are not symmetrical and the axle housing is not at the midpoint of the spring. Furthermore, the springs are slightly curved. The springs attach firmly to the axle tubes by means of large U-bolts (Figure 13-2).

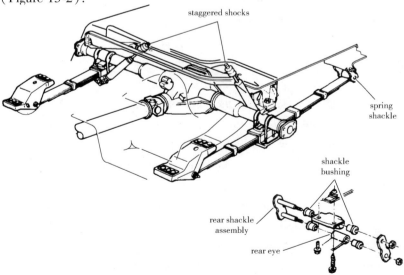

Figure 13-2 *Most leaf springs do two jobs. They position the axle and support the car*

The lower end of each shock absorber mounts to a plate that attaches to the springs at the same point. The leaf springs mount to the frame at the front eye and at the rear by means of a spring-shackle. The leaf springs provide the axle location in both the side-to-side and fore-and-aft directions. The springs permit up-and-down motion of the axle twist. In most cars, the mounting of the shock absorbers lessens axle twist. Some axles use staggered shocks, where one shock mounts to the suspension ahead of the rear axle. The other shock mounts behind the axle housing.

NEW WORDS

1. alignment   [ə'lainmənt]   n. 校直，调正，调准，定线
2. bump   [bʌmp]   n. 碰撞，猛击
3. deflect   [di'flekt]   vt. & vi （使）偏斜，（使）转向，（使）弯曲
4. clamp   [klæmp]   n. 夹子，夹具，夹钳；vt. 夹住，夹紧
5. pivot   ['pivət]   n. 枢，枢轴，支点
6. rebound   ['riː'baʊnd, ri-]   n. 回弹；v. 回弹
7. strut   [strʌt]   n. 支柱，压杆
8. lengthwise   ['leŋθwaiz]   adj. 纵长的，纵向长的
9. vibration   [vai'breiʃən]   n. 振动，颤动，摇动，摆动
10. asymmetrical   [ˌeisi'metrikl]   adj. 不均匀的，不对称的
11. semielliptical   [semii'liptikəl]   adj. 半椭圆的
12. bracket   ['brækit]   n. 托架
13. staggered   ['stægəd]   adj. 错列的，叉排的

PHRASES AND EXPRESSIONS

1. unit body   组合车身
2. coil spring   螺旋弹簧
3. leaf spring   钢板弹簧，片弹簧
4. torsion bar   扭力杆，扭杆弹簧
5. station wagons   客货两用轿车，旅行车
6. spring eye   钢板弹簧卷耳
7. rubber bushing   橡胶衬套
8. bolt head   螺栓头
9. spring shackle   板簧吊环
10. A-arm front suspension   叉形控制臂前悬架
11. torsion bar front suspension   扭杆弹簧前悬架
12. MacPherson strut suspension   麦弗逊滑柱悬架
13. upper control arm   上控制臂
14. ball joint   球形接头，球节，球窝关节
15. stabilizer bar   稳定杆，防止车厢侧倾稳定杆
16. cornering force   回转力，侧向反力
17. shock absorber   减振器，阻尼器

18. trailing links (悬架)纵(拖)臂,纵向连杆
19. pinion angle 小齿轮角
20. U-joint 万向节,万向接头
21. U-bolt U形螺栓
22. fore-and-aft 纵向的,前后的

NOTES TO THE TEXT

1. The compressed spring when force is removed, returns to its original position. The distance that a spring compressed under force depends on the rate of the spring.

当压紧力撤除时,被压紧的弹簧恢复到初始的(长度)状态。在压力作用时,弹簧的压缩变形量取决于该弹簧的刚度。

2. Rubber bushings are placed between the bolts and the links. These bushings dampen vibrations. The links hold the axle in place and keep it from moving from side to side or forward and backward.

在螺栓和控制臂之间装有橡胶衬套,这些衬套可缓解振动。这些控制臂确保后桥工作在正确的位置,防止它左右或前后移动。

EXERCISES

Ⅰ. Answer the following questions

1. List the three basic types of springs used in automobile suspension.
2. Please list the parts of an A-arm front suspension.
3. How does a MacPherson strut suspension operate?
4. What does a stabilizer bar do?
5. List the parts of Solid Axle Rear Suspension with Coil Springs.

Ⅱ. Translate the following into Chinese

1. When the road surface is not smooth, so jerky motion due to ups and downs of the road creates shocks to the vehicle parts, the suspension system prevents these shocks from being transmitted to the vehicle components.

2. The chassis is connected to the road wheels through the medium of springs and axles, and it is this medium which, with the wheels and tyres, constitutes the suspension system of any car or commercial vehicle.

3. An extremely flexible spring, or too soft, would allow too much movement, while a stiff or hard spring would give too rough a ride.

Reading Material: An Introduction to Active Suspension Systems

Background

Traditionally automotive suspension designs have been a compromise between the three conflicting criteria of road holding, load carrying and passenger comfort.

The suspension system must support the vehicle, provide directional control during handling

UNIT 13 SUSPENSION SYSTEM

manoeuvres and provide effective isolation of passengers/payload from road disturbances. Good ride comfort requires a soft suspension, whereas insensitivity to applied loads requires stiff suspension. Good handling requires a suspension setting somewhere between the two.

Due to these conflicting demands, suspension design has to be something of a compromise, largely determined by the type of use for which the vehicle was designed. Active suspensions are considered to be a way of increasing the freedom which has to specify independently the characteristics of load carrying, handling and ride quality.

A passive suspension system has the ability to store energy via a spring and to dissipate it via a damper. Its parameters are generally fixed, being chosen to achieve a certain level of compromise among road holding, load carrying and comfort.

An active suspension system has the ability to store, dissipate and to introduce energy to the system. It may vary its parameters depending upon operating conditions and can have knowledge other than the strut deflection the passive system is limited to.

High bandwidth systems

In a high bandwidth (or "fully active") suspension system we generally consider an actuator connected between the sprung and unsprung masses of the vehicle. A fully active system aims to control the suspension over the full bandwidth of the system. In particular this means that we aim to improve the suspension response around both the "rattle-space" frequency (10 to 12 Hz) and "tyre-hop" frequency (3 to 4Hz). The terms rattle-space and tyre-hop may be regarded as resonant frequencies of the system. A fully active system will consume a significant amount of power and will require actuators with a relatively wide bandwidth. These have been successfully implemented in Formula One cars and by, for example, Lotus.

Low bandwidth systems

They are also known as slow-active or band-limited systems. In this class the actuator will be placed in series with a road spring and/or a damper. A low bandwidth system aims to control the suspension over the lower frequency range, and specifically around the rattle space frequency. At higher frequencies the actuator effectively locks-up and hence the wheel-hop motion is controlled passively. With these systems we can achieve a significant reduction in body roll and pitch during manoeuvres such as cornering and braking, with lower energy consumption than a high bandwidth system.

Preview Systems

These aim to increase the bandwidth of a band-limited system by using feed-forward or knowledge of future road inputs. Some systems aim to measure road disturbances ahead of the car (using perhaps a laser system), and then use both standard feedback control and feed-forward from the sensor to achieve a superior response. Others e.g. aim to use the information available from the front strut deflection to improve the performance of the rear suspension.

Current Technology and Applications

Active suspension systems that have been successfully implemented include the high-profile examples found on Formula One racing cars. Most major motor manufacturers are researching their own systems and some are near to fruition. These include Jaguar, Mercedes Benz, and Toyota, etc.

Formula One cars represent the extreme of active suspension implementation, being fully active systems using high bandwidth aerospace specification components. For wide spread commercial use much cheaper actuators and control valves must be used, and so semi-active or low bandwidth systems are the norm here. The oleo-pneumatic actuator is a popular choice, giving both a low frequency active element and a high frequency passive element in one unit.

NEW WORDS

1. conflicting　　　　[kən'fliktiŋ]　　　　*adj.* 相冲突的，不一致的，相矛盾的
2. payload　　　　　['pei,ləud]　　　　　*n.* 有效载荷
3. handling　　　　　['hændliŋ]　　　　　*n.* 操纵稳定性
4. compromise　　　['kɔmprəmaiz]　　　 *n.* 妥协，折中
5. via　　　　　　　 ['vaiə]　　　　　　　*prep.* 经，通过，经由
6. resonant　　　　　['rezənənt]　　　　　*adj.* 引起共鸣的
7. roll　　　　　　　[rəul]　　　　　　　 *n.* 侧倾
8. pitch　　　　　　 [pitʃ]　　　　　　　 *n.* 俯仰

PHRASES AND EXPRESSIONS

1. active suspension system　　　　主动悬架系统
2. road holding　　　　　　　　　（车辆动力学）行车方向稳定性
3. load carrying　　　　　　　　　承载能力
4. passenger comfort　　　　　　　（汽车）乘客舒适性
5. ride comfort　　　　　　　　　 乘坐舒适性
6. sprung mass　　　　　　　　　 簧载质量
7. unsprung mass　　　　　　　　 非簧载质量
8. oleo-pneumatic actuator　　　　　油气（液压—空气）执行机构

NOTES

1. Traditionally automotive suspension designs have been a compromise between the three conflicting criteria of road holding, load carrying and passenger comfort.

传统上，在设计汽车悬架时，要综合考虑行车方向稳定性、承载能力和乘坐舒适性这三个互相矛盾的评价指标，采用折中的方案。

2. The oleo-pneumatic actuator is a popular choice, giving both a low frequency active element and a high frequency passive element in one unit.

通常选用油气（液压—空气）执行机构，它在一个部件上同时提供低频有源元件和高频无源元件。

UNIT 14　ABS AND TCS

1. Braking System Fundamentals, Foundation Brakes

There are two usual force inputs to a motor vehicle: engine torque to provide acceleration (+ X acceleration) and brake friction to provide deceleration (− X acceleration).

When an operator actuates the brake pedal, he or she is actually pushing on a lever that pushes a piston in a master cylinder to generate hydraulic pressure that is transmitted through the brake lines to the wheel actuators (either wheel cylinders or caliper pistons). The wheel actuators force a friction material (brake shoes or disk pads) against a rotating surface (brake drums or disk rotors) to generate a force that stops the vehicle. The energy to stop the vehicle is normally dissipated as heat in the drums or rotors. Thus, applying the brakes is really the act of dissipating the rolling energy of the vehicle as heat, hence slowing the vehicle down. A simplified schematic of a foundation brake system is shown in Figure 14-1.

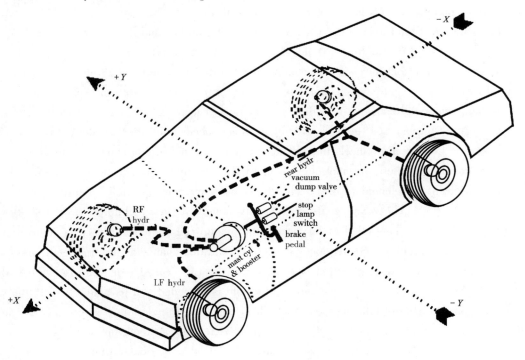

Figure 14-1　Foundation brake system

The operation of the braking system depends on the integrity of the hydraulic system. Modern boosted master cylinders can generate 2,000 psi or more, and the hydraulic system must distribute that pressure without leaking. Almost all modern braking systems use a booster (or operator force amplifier) that uses engine vacuum to increase the force the brake lever applies to the master cylinder. Generally, disk brakes require higher application pressure than drums because they are not self-actuating. When drum brakes are combined with disk brakes in a vehicle (usually with drums in the rear), there is always "a proportioning valve" to proportionally reduce the effective hydraulic pressure at the drum brake wheel cylinders and to always keep the rear wheels turning to preserve directional stability.

2. Antilock Braking Systems

A vehicle braking system, including the tires, is most effective, i.e., produces the optimum retarding force, when the wheel speeds are approximately 85% to 90% of the vehicle speed. The difference (100% − 85% = 15%) is called the percent slip of a particular wheel. The 10% to 15% slip retarding force is greater than the locked wheel retarding force, so optimum braking is achieved when the slip is 10% to 15% and no more. Over-applying foundation brakes can cause wheels to lock (100% slip), so a system that prevents this can improve braking effectiveness. Antilock braking systems (ABS) have been developed to do this.

However, prevention of lock to improve braking effectiveness is not the most important reason for ABS. Once a wheel is locked, it does not provide any lateral control of the vehicle (+/-Y axis), and, if multiple wheels lock, the vehicle will start to yaw. This means that if the rear wheels lock, the vehicle will tend to spin out (rear end moving forward), and if the front wheels lock, the vehicle cannot be steered. Control of vehicle track is the most important reason for the use of ABS.

It has been shown that for poor road conditions (sand, ice, snow, water, etc.), a system that prevented wheel lockup and gave significantly increased directional control, in exchange for a small loss of absolute stopping distance, provided a major benefit to overall vehicle performance. This is accomplished by using an ECU to sense individual wheel speeds, and then isolate and reduce brake fluid pressure to the wheel or wheels that are locking up. A schematic of such a feedback system is shown in Figure 14-2, where the controller is an ECU, the controlled parameter is wheel cylinder pressure (via electrical solenoid valves), and the feedback elements are individual electronic wheel speed sensors (WSS). The WSS signals are typically generated via a pickup coil mounted adjacent to a toothed ring at each controlled wheel, where the pickup coil generates a varying voltage output proportional to the amplitude and frequency of the magnetic flux change as the ring teeth pass by it.

By monitoring the frequency output of each WSS, the ECU can decide if an individual wheel slip exceeds a desired threshold. When such a threshold is exceeded at a particular wheel, the ECU directs the hydraulic control unit to isolate that wheel and reduce hydraulic pressure at that wheel, so that the wheel can resume rotation. Once the wheel is rotating at about optimum slip (assuming the brakes are still applied) again, pressure is reapplied to that particular wheel. Typically, each wheel control circuit is called a channel and the hydraulic control unit is typically called a hydraulic modulator. Hydraulic modulators typically include three functions for each controlled wheel circuit: isolation, pressure-dump, and pressure-reapply. This control sequence causes a pulsed apply/

release/apply as ABS is controlling a wheel in an emergency stop, often up to ten times per second.

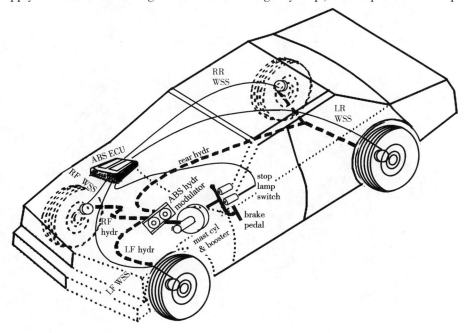

Figure 14-2 Basic ABS schematic

Because of practical slip-threshold tradeoffs, ABS equipped vehicles may show a slightly increased stopping distance, but a marked increase in track control over the ensemble of many emergency braking situations. That trade off is deemed to be beneficial for the average driver on modern vehicles. Thus, the primary purpose of ABS is to preserve directional stability and allow the driver to continue steering during emergency braking, with an acceptable tradeoff of slightly longer stopping distance. Also, because wheel slip is limited with ABS vehicles, hard braking stops will not produce typical tire scrub artifacts on road surfaces, thus, complicating traditional accident reconstruction methods. When ABS is not activated, the foundation brakes operate normally; thus, normal stops are unaffected by ABS.

3. Traction Control Systems

In the past few years, selected manufacturers have introduced systems that add traction and tracking control functions during acceleration as well as braking. ABS releases the brakes momentarily whenever wheel speed sensors indicate a locked wheel during braking, whereas traction control applies the brakes momentarily to one of the drive wheels whenever the wheel speed sensors indicates a wheel is going faster than the others during acceleration. Figure 14-3 shows a schematic of a basic TCS (traction control system) architecture. Note that the TCS is designed to operate only in the engine-acceleration mode, and its function is suspended if the operator applies the brake.

Some TCS systems also have the capability to reduce engine power via electronic control of fuel injectors and/or spark timing. This is accomplished via bidirectional communications between the

TCS ECU and the PCM.

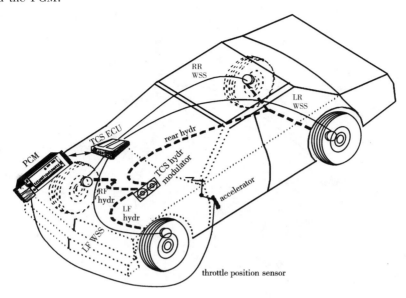

Figure 14-3 Basic TCS schematic

4. Combined ABS and TCS

Since the primary function of both TCS and ABS is the control of a wheel whose speed significantly varies from the averaged speed of the other wheels (+ for TCS, − for ABS), where both features are incorporated in a vehicle, these functions are usually combined into one hydraulic control unit, sharing a common ECU. Figure 14-4 shows such a combined system architecture, with its combined ABS/TCS ECU. The objective of both ABS and TCS is to operate transparently to the consumer operator so as to provide enhanced vehicle tracking stability under both braking and acceleration under adverse road surface conditions. This feature provides the ordinary driver with advanced tracking stability that was previously accomplished only by skilled racing and police drivers.

Thus, for combined ABS/TCS ECUs with the brake applied in ABS modes, if the speed of one wheel drops significantly compared with the other wheels, the brake pressure on that wheel is momentarily reduced (using isolation and dump valves) to stop the wheel from locking, and it is reapplied (using a motor/pump) when the wheel speed is near the average of the other wheel speeds. With no brake applied and under acceleration in TCS modes, if the speed of one wheel increases significantly compared to the other wheels, that wheel brake is momentarily applied to reduce that wheel speed (and with differential systems to redistribute traction power to the opposite wheel). Braking is removed when that wheel speed returns to near the average of the other wheel speeds.

Given that ABS, TCS, and ABS/TCS systems variously monitor parameters such as wheel speeds, brake application, accelerator application, etc. for normal operation, there is an obvious capability to save them in event triggered snapshot/freeze frames. These parameters can indicate critical aspects of operator-vehicle interaction and, thus, become an important element of the analysis of post-crash vehicle data.

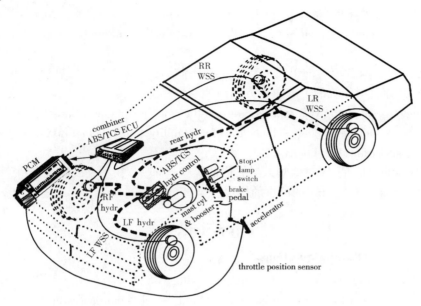

Figure 14-4 Basic combined ABS/TCS schematic

NEW WORDS

1. dissipate   ['disipeit]   v. 消耗,耗尽,散失
2. schematic   [ski:'mætik]   n. 简图,示意图,原理图,图解
3. integrity   [in'tegriti]   n. 完整性,完善,综合性,统一性
4. amplitude   ['æmplitu:d]   n. 振幅
5. threshold   ['θreʃhəuld]   n. 临界(值),阈(值),极限值
6. modulator   ['mɔdjuleitə]   n. 调节器
7. ensemble   [an'sɑ:mbl]   n. 整体,总效果
8. momentarily   [,məumən'teərəli:]   adv. 即刻

PHRASES AND EXPRESSIONS

1. ABS (Antilock Braking System)   防抱死制动系统
2. TCS (Traction Control System)   牵引力控制系统
3. combine with   与……结合
4. retarding force   制动力,减速力
5. in exchange for   交换,以此易彼
6. magnetic flux   磁通量
7. tracking stability   直线行驶(方向)稳定性
8. dump valve   减(降、卸)压阀
9. PCM (power control module)   动力系统控制模块
   (powertrain control module)   传动系统控制模块

NOTES TO THE TEXT

1. Also, because wheel slip is limited with ABS vehicles, hard braking stops will not produce typical tire scrub artifacts on road surfaces, thus, complicating traditional accident reconstruction methods.

同时,由于带有 ABS 车辆的车轮滑转率受到限制,猛烈制动时不会在路面上留下常见的轮胎摩擦痕迹,因而,给传统的事故重建方法造成麻烦。

2. The objective of both ABS and TCS is for them to operate transparently to the consumer operator so as to provide enhanced vehicle tracking stability under both braking and acceleration under adverse road surface conditions.

ABS 和 TCS 的目的是,通过驾驶人对它们的操作,(即使)在不利的路面条件下,无论是制动还是加速,都能保证车辆有更加可靠的操纵稳定性。

EXERCISES

Ⅰ. Answer the following questions

1. What are the benefits for a vehicle equipped with ABS?
2. Which characteristics will be influenced due to a vehicle equipped with ABS?
3. How does a traction control system work?
4. What are the benefits for a vehicle equipped with combined ABS and TCS?

Ⅱ. Translate the following into Chinese

1. When the ABS system is in operation you will feel a pulsing in the brake pedal; this comes from the rapid opening and closing of the valves. Some ABS systems can cycle up to 15 times per second.

2. Anti-lock braking systems use different schemes depending on the type of brakes in use.

3. Four-channel, four-sensor ABS—This is the best scheme. There is a speed sensor on all four wheels and a separate valve for all four wheels. With this setup, the controller monitors each wheel individually to make sure it is achieving maximum braking force.

4. The slip angle of the tire is defined as the angle between the wheel plane and the direction of the wheel hub velocity.

Reading Material: Components of ABS/TCS Units

Common Components

All ABS-equipped vehicles have certain common components. These consist of an electronic control unit (ECU), one or more hydraulic modulator assemblies, one or more wheel speed sensors, and a wiring harness. The ABS system is transparent to the operator in normal operation, except for the (ABS) malfunction indicator lamp (MIL) in the instrument cluster. The ABS MIL is normally activated during key on diagnostic checks and remains off unless a system problem is detected. In general, each channel operates with a dedicated wheel sensor circuit, hydraulic modulator subassembly, and sense/control portion of the ECU.

Wheel Sensors

Wheel sensors are the key components of both ABS and TCS systems. In order to determine vehicle wheel speeds, a wheel speed sensor (WSS) is placed on each wheel. Figure 14-5 shows a wheel speed sensor using an electrical coil to detect a change in the magnetic field of its magnetic core as a toothed wheel attached to the brake disk/drum rotates past it. As the teeth pass by the pickup core, a sinusoidal pulse train is generated with a frequency proportional to the speed of the wheel. This generated frequency is directly proportional to wheel revolutions/time and is said to be an analog of the wheel ground speed (at the circumference of the tire). Scaling arithmetic in the ECU microprocessor software is used to convert the input frequency analog to commonly understood units of ground speed. That wheel pulse train is monitored by the ABS/TCS ECU, which compares it to the speeds (frequencies) of the other wheels in order to determine individual wheel slip.

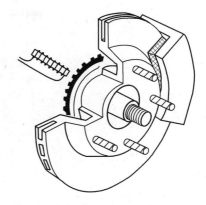

Figure 14-5 Wheel speed sensor on a disk brake

Pumps, Valves, Accumulators, and Motors

ABS and TCS hydraulic control units (HCUs) contain pumps, valves, accumulators, and motors that perform the ECU commanded functions for system operation. Most HCUs are relatively insulated from crash damage, but a few are located in the frontal crush zone, like the front wheel speed sensors.

ABS and TCS ECUs

Similarly, most ABS and TCS ECUs are relatively insulated from crash damage. Thus, it is often the case that crash damage to a wheel sensor, causing a DTC and a snapshot/freeze frame, is available after a crash.

NEW WORDS

1. subassembly ['sʌbə'sembli] n. 部件，组件
2. sinusoidal [ˌsainə'sɔidl] adj. 正弦曲线
3. accumulator [ə'kjuːmjuleitə] n. 〈英〉蓄电池，积聚者，蓄压器
4. investigation [inˌvesti'geiʃən] n. 调查，研究

PHRASES AND EXPRESSIONS

1. wiring harness 线束
2. malfunction indicator lamp (MIL) 故障指示灯
3. instrument cluster 仪表板，仪表组，组合仪表
4. freeze frame 停帧，停格，冻结帧，凝固画面
5. DTC (diagnostic test code) 诊断故障码

NOTES

That wheel pulse train is monitored by the ABS/TCS ECU, which compares it to the speeds (frequencies) of the other wheels in order to determine individual wheel slip.

ABS/TCS ECU 监测该车轮的脉冲信号顺序,并且把该车轮的速度(频率)与其他车轮的加以比较,以确定车轮的滑转率。

UNIT 15 ADAPTIVE CRUISE CONTROL SYSTEM

1. Introduction

Adaptive Cruise Control (ACC) is an automotive feature that allows a vehicle's cruise control system to adapt the vehicle's speed to the traffic environment. A radar system attached to the front of the vehicle is used to detect whether slower moving vehicles are in the ACC vehicle's path. If a slower moving vehicle is detected, the ACC system will slow the vehicle down and control the clearance, or time gap, between the ACC vehicle and the forward vehicle. If the system detects that the forward vehicle is no longer in the ACC vehicle's path, the ACC system will accelerate the vehicle back to its set cruise control speed. This operation allows the ACC vehicle to autonomously slow down and speed up with traffic without intervention from the driver. The method by which the ACC vehicle's speed is controlled is via engine throttle control and limited brake operation.

2. Definitions and Physical Overview (Figure 15-1)

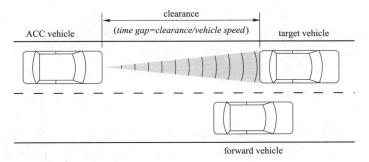

Figure 15-1 ACC vehicle relationships

2.1 Definitions

(1) **Adaptive Cruise Control (ACC).** An enhancement to a conventional cruise control system which allows the ACC vehicle to follow a forward vehicle at an appropriate distance.

(2) **ACC vehicle.** The subject vehicle equipped with the ACC system.

(3) **Active brake control.** A function which causes application of the brakes without driver application of the brake pedal.

(4) **Clearance.** Distance from the forward vehicle's trailing surface to the ACC vehicle's leading

surface.

(5) **Forward vehicle.** Any one of the vehicles in front of and moving in the same direction and traveling on the same roadway as the ACC vehicle.

(6) **Set speed.** The desired cruise control travel speed set by the driver and is the maximum desired speed of the vehicle while under ACC control.

(7) **System states (Figure 15-2).**

(a) ACC off state. Direct access to the "ACC active" state is disabled.

(b) ACC standby state. System is ready for activation by the driver.

(c) ACC active state. The ACC system is in active control of the vehicle's speed.

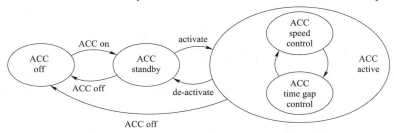

Figure 15-2 *ACC states and transitions*

(d) ACC speed control state. A substate of "ACC active" state in which no forward vehicles are present such that the ACC system is controlling vehicle speed to the "set speed" as is typical with conventional cruise control systems.

(e) ACC time gap control state. A substate of "ACC active" state in which time gap, or clearance, between the ACC vehicle and the target vehicle is being controlled.

(8) **Target vehicle.** One of the forward vehicles in the path of the ACC vehicle that is closest to the ACC vehicle.

(9) **Time gap.** The time interval between the ACC vehicle and the target vehicle. The "time gap" is related to the "clearance" and vehicle speed by:

$$time\ gap = clearance/ACC\ vehicle\ speed$$

2.2 Physical Layout

As shown in Figure 15-3, the ACC system consists of a series of interconnecting components and systems. The method of communication between the different modules is via a serial communication network known as the Controller Area Network (CAN).

(1) **ACC Module.** The primary function of the ACC module is to process the radar information and determine if a forward vehicle is present. When the ACC system is in "time gap control", it sends information to the Engine Control and Brake Control modules to control the clearance between the ACC Vehicle and the Target Vehicle.

(2) **Engine Control Module.** The primary function of the Engine Control Module is to receive information from the ACC module and Instrument Cluster and control the vehicle's speed based on this information. The Engine Control Module controls vehicle speed by controlling the engine's throttle.

UNIT 15 ADAPTIVE CRUISE CONTROL SYSTEM

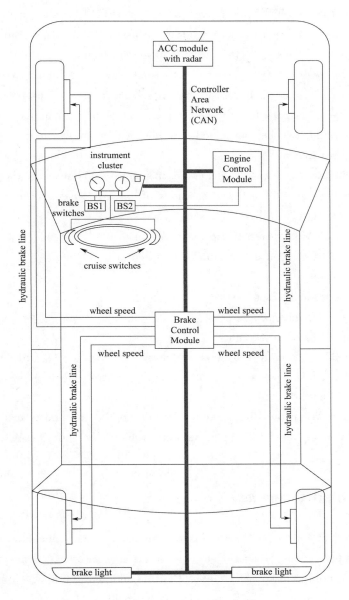

Figure 15-3 *Physical layout*

(3) **Brake Control Module.** The primary function of the Brake Control Module is to determine the vehicle's speed via each wheel and to decelerate the vehicle by applying the brakes when requested by the ACC Module. The braking system is hydraulic with electronic enhancement, such as an ABS brake system, and is not full authority brake by wire.

(4) **Instrument Cluster.** The primary function of the Instrument Cluster is to process the Cruise Switches and send their information to the ACC and Engine Control Modules. The Instrument Cluster also displays text messages and telltales for the driver so that the driver has information regarding the state of the ACC system.

(5) **CAN.** The Controller Area Network (CAN) is an automotive standard network that utilizes a

2-wire bus to transmit and receive data. Each node on the network has the capability to transmit 0 to 8 bytes of data in a message frame. A message frame consists of a message header, followed by 0 to 8 data bytes, and then a checksum. The message header is a unique identifier that determines the message priority. Any node on the network can transmit data if the bus is free. If multiple nodes attempt to transmit at the same time, an arbitration scheme is used to determine which node will control the bus. The message with the highest priority, as defined in its header, will win the arbitration and its message will be transmitted. The losing message will retry to send its message as soon as it detects a bus free state.

(6) **Cruise Switches.** The Cruise Switches are mounted on the steering wheel and have several buttons which allow the driver to command operation of the ACC system. The switches include:

(a) "On": place system in the "ACC standby" state;
(b) "Off": cancel ACC operation and place system in the "ACC off" state;
(c) "Set +": activate ACC and establish set speed or accelerate;
(d) "Coast": decelerate;
(e) "Resume": resume to set speed;
(f) "Time Gap +": increase gap;
(g) "Time Gap −": decrease gap.

(7) **Brake Switches.** There are two brake switches, Brake Switch 1 (BS1) and Brake Switch 2 (BS2). When either brake switch is activated, cruise control operation is deactivated and the system enters "ACC standby" state.

(8) **Brake Lights.** When the Brake Control Module applies the brakes in response to an ACC request, it will illuminate the brake lights to warn vehicles behind the ACC vehicle that it is decelerating.

3. Operational Overview

The driver interface for the ACC system is very similar to a conventional cruise control system. The driver operates the system via a set of switches on the steering wheel. The switches are the same as for a conventional cruise control system except for the addition of two switches to control the time gap between the ACC vehicle and the target vehicle. In addition, there are a series of text messages that can be displayed on the instrument cluster to inform the driver of the state of the ACC system and to provide any necessary warnings. The driver engages the ACC system by first pressing the ON switch which places the system into the "ACC standby" state. The driver then presses the Set switch to enter the "ACC active" state at which point the ACC system attempts to control the vehicle to the driver's set speed dependent upon the traffic environment.

3.1 *Control System Interfaces*

Figure 15-4 shows the information and signal flows between the different systems for ACC operation.

UNIT 15　ADAPTIVE CRUISE CONTROL SYSTEM

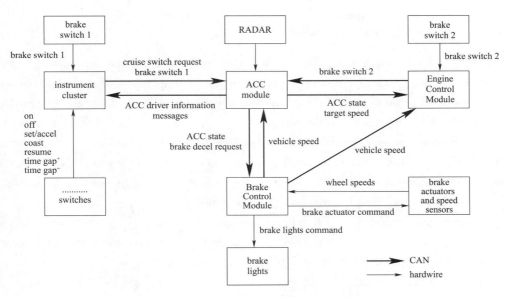

Figure 15-4　ACC signals and information flow

3.2　Initialization

When the ignition key is in the off position, no power is applied to any of the systems. When the key is cycled to the on position, the ACC system initializes to the "ACC off" state.

3.3　Engaging Cruise Control

(1)**Entering "ACC standby"**. Before active cruise control can be engaged the driver must first enter "ACC standby". This is performed by the driver pressing the ACC "On" button. If no system faults are present, the ACC system will transition to the "ACC standby" state.

(2)**Entering "ACC active"**. The driver enters the "ACC active" state by pressing the "Set" or "Resume" button. If a prior set speed is present in memory, the system uses this prior value as the target speed when Resume is pressed, else, the current speed of when the Set button was pressed will become the target speed. The following conditions must be true for the system to enter "ACC active" in response to the cruise switches:

$$\text{Brake Switch 1} = \text{brake not applied}$$
$$\text{Brake Switch 2} = \text{brake not applied}$$
$$\text{Vehicle Speed} > = 25 \text{ mile/h}$$

When entering active ACC control, the vehicle speed is controlled either to maintain a set speed or to maintain a time gap to a forward vehicle, whichever speed is lower.

3.4　Operation During Speed Control Mode (ACC Speed Control)

Operation during this mode is equivalent to that of conventional speed control. If no forward vehicle is present within the Time Gap or clearance of the system, the vehicle's speed is maintained at the target speed. The engine control system controls the engine output via throttle control to maintain the vehicle speed at the target speed.

3.5 Operation During Follow Mode (ACC Time Gap Control)

The ACC system enters follow mode or "ACC time gap control" if the radar detects a forward vehicle at or within the clearance distance. During this mode of operation, the ACC system sends a target speed to the Engine Control Module and deceleration commands to the Brake Control Module to maintain the set time gap between the vehicles.

(1) **Deceleration control.** The ACC system decelerates the vehicle by lowering the target speed sent to the Engine Control Module and sending a brake deceleration command to the Brake Control Module. The maximum allowed braking effort of the system is 0.2 g. During brake deceleration events, the Brake Control Module activates the brake lights.

(2) **Acceleration control.** The ACC system accelerates the vehicle by increasing the target speed sent to the Engine Control Module. The Engine Control Module tries to maintain the target speed and can accelerate the vehicle at a rate of up to 0.2 g of acceleration.

(3) **Adjusting the time gap.** The driver can adjust the time gap via the "Time Gap +" and "Time Gap -" switches. Pressing the "Time Gap +" switch causes the time gap value to increase and therefore the clearance between the two vehicles to increase. Pressing the "Time Gap -" switch causes the time gap value to decrease and therefore the clearance between the two vehicles to decrease.

(4) **Reaction to a slow moving or stopped vehicle.** Situations may occur such that the ACC system is not able to maintain the time gap within the deceleration authority of the system, 0.2 g. The clearance between the ACC vehicle and the forward vehicle may be rapidly decreasing or the minimum vehicle speed of 25 mile/h may be reached. Under these situations the ACC system enters "ACC standby" and alerts the driver by displaying a "Driver Intervention Required" text message on the instrument cluster and by turning on an audible chime. If the brakes were being applied by the ACC system, they will be slowly released. At this point the driver must take control of the vehicle.

3.6 Transitioning Between Speed Control and Follow Modes

The ACC system automatically transitions between Speed Control and Time Gap (Follow) Modes. The mode of operation is determined by the lower of the set speed for Speed Control Mode and the target speed to maintain the gap between the ACC vehicle and a forward vehicle. Basically, if no vehicle is present within the clearance distance, the system will operate in Speed Control Mode, else, it will operate in Time Gap Mode.

3.7 Canceling Cruise Control Operation

Cruise Control operation may be canceled by the operator or automatically via the ACC system. Either of the following conditions will deactivate ACC:

Brake pedal is pressed
"Off" button is pressed
Vehicle Speed < 25 mile/h
An ACC system fault is detected

UNIT 15 ADAPTIVE CRUISE CONTROL SYSTEM

NEW WORDS

1. intervention   [ˌɪntəˈvenʃn]   n. 干涉,干预
2. checksum   [ˈtʃeksʌm]   n. 检验和(用以校验数据项的和)
3. clearance   [ˈklɪərəns]   n. 间距
4. priority   [praɪˈɒrəti]   n. 优先级,优先权
5. arbitration   [ˌɑːbɪˈtreɪʃn]   n. 仲裁
6. standby   [ˈstændbaɪ]   n. 备用品; adj. 备用的
7. resume   [rɪˈzjuːm]   vt. 恢复,再继续,重新开始,再用

PHRASES AND EXPRESSIONS

1. Adaptive Cruise Control (ACC)   自适应巡航控制
2. time gap   时间间隔
3. serial communication network   串行通信网络
4. Controller Area Network (CAN)   控制器局域网
5. Instrument Cluster   仪表盘,仪表组
6. arbitration scheme   仲裁程序,仲裁方案

NOTES TO THE TEXT

The message with the highest priority, as defined in its header, will win the arbitration and its message will be transmitted. The losing message will retry to send its message as soon as it detects a bus free state.

消息头中定义的具有最高优先级的消息将赢得仲裁,其消息将被传输。一旦检测到总线处于空闲状态,那些丢失的消息将被重新发送。

EXERCISES

I. Answer the following questions

1. What are the purposes of adaptive cruise control systems?
2. How to engage adaptive cruise control system?
3. How to transit between speed control and follow modes?
4. How does adaptive cruise control system work?

II. Translate the following into Chinese

1. The ACC system uses a radar sensor, which projects a beam directly forward of the vehicle to detect objects ahead. The radar sensor is mounted centrally behind the bumper cover above the cooling aperture, to provide a clear view forward for the radar beam.

2. The set speed and gap can be overridden by pressing the accelerator pedal when cruising at constant speed or in follow mode. If the vehicle is in follow mode, the instrument warning indicator will go out when the ACC is overridden by the driver using the accelerator and "CRUISE OVERRIDE" will be displayed on the message center. When the accelerator is released the ACC

function will operate again and vehicle speed will decrease to the set speed, or a lower speed if follow mode is active.

Reading Material: Air Bags

For years, the trusty seat belt provided the sole form of passive restraint in our cars. There were debates about their safety, especially relating to children, but over time, much of the country adopted mandatory seat-belt laws. Statistics have shown that the use of seat belts has saved thousands of lives that might have been lost in collisions.

Air bags have been under development for many years. The attraction of a soft pillow to land against in a crash must be very strong. In the 1980s, the first commercial air bags appeared in automobiles.

Since model year 1998, all new cars have been required to have air bags on both driver and passenger sides. (Light trucks came under the rule in 1999.) To date, statistics show that air bags reduce the risk of dying in a direct frontal crash by about 30 percent. Some experts say that within the next few years, our cars will go from having dual air bags to having six or even eight air bags!

What an air bag wants to do is to slow the passenger's speed to zero with little or no damage. The constraints that it has to work within are huge. The air bag has the space between the passenger and the steering wheel or dash board and a fraction of a second to work with. Even that tiny amount of space and time is valuable, however, if the system can slow the passenger evenly rather than forcing an abrupt halt to his or her motion.

There are three parts to an air bag that help to accomplish this feat:

(1) The bag itself is made of a thin, nylon fabric, which is folded into the steering wheel or dashboard or, more recently, the seat or door.

(2) The sensor is the device that tells the bag to inflate. Inflation happens when there is a collision force equal to running into a brick wall at 10 to 15 miles per hour (16 to 24 km per hour). A mechanical switch is flipped when there is a mass shift that closes an electrical contact, telling the sensors that a crash has occurred. The sensors receive information from an accelerometer built into a microchip.

(3) The air bag's inflation system reacts sodium azide (NaN_3) with potassium nitrate (KNO_3) to produce nitrogen gas. Hot blasts of the nitrogen inflate the air bag.

The inflation system (Figure 15-5, Figure 15-6) is not unlike a solid rocket booster. The air bag system ignites a solid propellant, which burns extremely rapidly to create a large volume of gas to inflate the bag. The bag then literally bursts from its storage site at up to 200 mile/h (322 km/h)—faster than the blink of an eye! A second later, the gas quickly dissipates through tiny holes in the bag, thus deflating the bag so you can move.

Even though the whole process happens in only one-twenty-fifth of a second, the additional time is enough to help prevent serious injury. The powdery substance released from the air bag, by the way, is regular cornstarch or talcum powder, which is used by the air bag manufacturers to keep the bags pliable and lubricated while they're in storage.

UNIT 15   ADAPTIVE CRUISE CONTROL SYSTEM

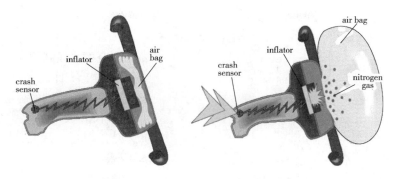

Figure 15-5   *The air bag and inflation system*

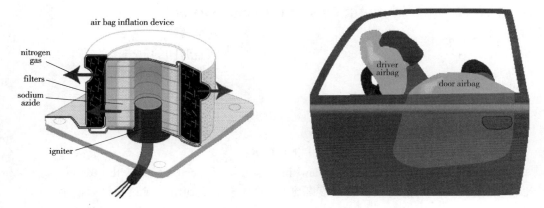

Figure 15-6   *The inflation system uses a solid propellant and an igniter*

The Future of Air Bags

Activities aimed at maintaining and improving the lifesaving benefits of air bags are in full swing. New NHTSA-sponsored tests use improved "dummy" injury criteria based on new knowledge and research.

Until recently, most of the strides made in auto safety were in front and rear impacts, even though 40 percent of all serious injuries from accidents are the result of side impacts, and 30 percent of all accidents are side-impact collisions. Many carmakers have responded to these statistics (and the resulting new standards) by beefing up doors, door frames and floor and roof sections. But cars that currently offer side air bags represent the new wave of occupant protection. Engineers say that designing effective side air bags is much more difficult than designing front air bags. This is because much of the energy from a front-impact collision is absorbed by the bumper, hood and engine, and it takes almost 30 to 40 milliseconds before it reaches the car's occupant. In a side impact, only a relatively thin door and a few inches separate the occupant from another vehicle. This means that door-mounted side air bags must begin deploying in mere five or six milliseconds!

The head air bag, or Inflatable Tubular Structure (ITS), was featured in all of BMW's 1999 models (except convertibles). The head bags look a little like big sausages and, unlike other air bags, are designed to stay inflated for about five seconds to offer protection against second or third impacts. Working with the side air bag, the ITS is supposed to offer better protection in some side collisions.

NEW WORDS

1. mandatory ['mændə,tɔːriː] *adj.* 命令的，强制的
2. statistics [stə'tistiks] *n.* 统计学，统计表
3. abrupt [ə'brʌpt] *adj.* 突然的，陡峭的，生硬的
4. dashboard ['dæʃbɔːd] *n.* 汽车仪表板
5. feat [fiːt] *n.* 技艺，功绩，武艺，壮举
6. dummy ['dʌmiː] *n.* 假人
7. cornstarch ['kɔːnstaːtʃ] *n.* 玉米淀粉

PHRASES AND EXPRESSIONS

1. air bag 安全气囊
2. over time 随着时间的过去
3. to date 到此为止
4. beef up 加强，补充
5. talcum powder 滑石粉

NOTES

1. What an air bag wants to do is to slow the passenger's speed to zero with little or no damage.

安全气囊所要做的是将乘客的速度降到零，并且不会受到伤害或只受轻微伤害。

2. The bag then literally bursts from its storage site at up to 200 mile/h (322 km/h)—faster than the blink of an eye!

安全气囊就以高达200英里/小时(322 km/h)的速度从储藏处爆炸充气而出——比一眨眼的时间还短。

UNIT 16 ELECTRIC CARS

An electric car is a car powered by an electric motor rather than a gasoline engine.

Under the hood, there are a lot of differences between gasoline and electric cars:

(1) The gasoline engine is replaced by an electric motor.

(2) The electric motor gets its power from a controller.

(3) The controller gets its power from an array of rechargeable batteries.

A gasoline engine, with its fuel lines, exhaust pipes, coolant hoses and intake manifold, tends to look like a plumbing project. An electric car is definitely a wiring project.

This electric vehicle began its life as a normal, gasoline-powered 1994 Geo Prism. Here are the modifications that turned it into an electric car:

(1) The gasoline engine, along with the muffler, catalytic converter, tailpipe and gas tank, was all removed.

(2) The clutch assembly was removed. The existing manual transmission was left in place, and it was pinned in second gear.

(3) A new AC electric motor was bolted to the transmission with an adapter plate.

(4) An electric controller was added to control the AC motor.

(5) A battery tray was installed in the floor of the car.

(6) Fifty 12-volt lead-acid batteries were placed in the battery tray (two sets of 25 to create 300 volts DC).

(7) Electric motors were added to power things that used to get their power from the engine: the water pump, power steering pump, air conditioner.

(8) A vacuum pump was added for the power brakes (which used engine vacuum when the car had an engine).

(9) The shifter for the manual transmission was replaced with a switch, disguised as an automatic transmission shifter, to control forward and reverse.

(10) A small electric water heater was added to provide heat.

(11) A charger was added so that the batteries could be recharged. This particular car actually has two charging systems—one from a normal 120-volt or 240-volt wall outlet, and the other from a magna-charge inductive charging paddle.

(12) The gas gauge was replaced with a volt meter.

Everything else about the car is stock. When you get in to drive the car, you put the key in the ignition and turn it to the "On" position to turn the car on. You shift into "Drive" with the shifter, push on the accelerator pedal and go. It performs like a normal gasoline car. Here are some interesting statistics:

(1) The range of this car is about 50 miles (80 km).

(2) The 0 to 60 mile/h time is about 15 seconds.

(3) It takes about 12 kilowatt-hours of electricity to charge the car after a 50-mile trip.

(4) The batteries weigh about 1,100 pounds (500 kg).

(5) The batteries last three to four years.

The Controller is the the heart of an electric car is the combination of (Figure 16-1):

(1) The electric motor.

(2) The motor's controller.

(3) The batteries.

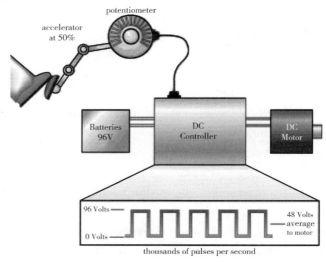

Figure 16-1 A simple DC controller

The controller takes power from the batteries and delivers it to the motor. The accelerator pedal hooks to a pair of potentiometers (variable resistors), and these potentiometers provide the signal that tells the controller how much power it is supposed to deliver. The controller can deliver zero power (when the car is stopped), full power (when the driver floors the accelerator pedal), or any power level in between.

Figure 16-2 The 300-volt, 50-kilowatt controller

In this car, the controller takes in 300 volts DC from the battery pack. It converts it into a maximum of 240 volts AC, three-phase, to send to the motor. It does this using very large transistors that rapidly turn the batteries' voltage on and off to create a sine wave.

The controller normally dominates the scene when you open the hood, as you can see in Figure 16-2.

When you push on the gas pedal, a cable from the pedal connects these two potentiometers:

The signal from the potentiometers tells the controller how much power to deliver to the electric car's motor. There are two potentiometers for safety's sake. The controller reads both potentiometers and makes sure that their signals are equal. If they are not, then the controller does not operate. This arrangement guards against a situation where a potentiometer fails in the full-on position.

The controller's job in a DC electric car is easy to understand. Let's assume that the battery pack contains 12 12-volt batteries, wired in series to create 144 volts. The controller takes in 144 volts DC, and delivers it to the motor in a controlled way.

The very simplest DC controller would be a big on/off switch wired to the accelerator pedal. When you push the pedal, it would turn the switch on, and when you take your foot off the pedal, it would turn it off. As the driver, you would have to push and release the accelerator to pulse the motor on and off to maintain a given speed.

Obviously, that sort of on/off approach would work but it would be a pain to drive, so the controller does the pulsing for you. The controller reads the setting of the accelerator pedal from the potentiometers and regulates the power accordingly. If that you have the accelerator pushed halfway down. The controller reads that setting from the potentiometer and rapidly switches the power to the motor on and off so that it is on half the time and off half the time. If you have the accelerator pedal 25 percent of the way down, the controller pulses the power so it is on 25 percent of the time and off 75 percent of the time.

Most controllers pulse the power more than 15,000 times per second, in order to keep the pulsation outside the range of human hearing. The pulsed current causes the motor housing to vibrate at that frequency, so by pulsing at more than 15,000 cycles per second, the controller and motor are silent to human ears.

In an AC controller (Figure 16-3), the job is a little more complicated, but it is the same idea. The controller creates three pseudo-sine waves. It does this by taking the DC voltage from the batteries and pulsing it on and off. In an AC controller, there is the additional need to reverse the polarity of the voltage 60 times a second. Therefore, you actually need six sets of transistors in an AC controller, while you need only one set in a DC controller. In the AC controller, for each phase you need one set of transistors to pulse the voltage and another set to reverse the polarity. You replicate that three times for the three phases—six total sets of transistors.

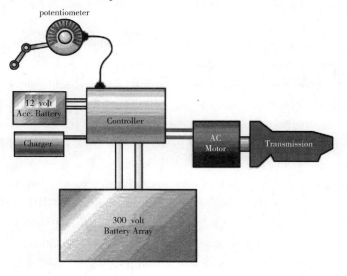

Figure 16-3 *An AC controller*

1. The Motor

Electric cars can use AC or DC motors:

(1) If the motor is a DC motor, then it may run on anything from 96 to 192 volts. Many of the DC motors used in electric cars come from the electric forklift industry.

(2) If it is an AC motor, then it probably is a three-phase AC motor running at 240 volts AC with a 300 volt battery pack.

DC installations tend to be simpler and less expensive. A typical motor will be in the 20,000-watt to 30,000-watt range. A typical controller will be in the 40,000-watt to 60,000-watt range (for example, a 96-volt controller will deliver a maximum of 400 or 600 amps). DC motors have the nice feature that you can overdrive them (up to a factor of 10-to-1) for short periods of time. That is, a 20,000 watt motor will accept 100,000 watts for a short period of time and deliver 5 times its rated horsepower. This is great for short bursts of acceleration. The only limitation is heat build-up in the motor. Too much overdriving and the motor heats up to the point where it self-destructs.

AC installations allow the use of almost any industrial three-phase AC motor, and that can make finding a motor with a specific size, shape or power rating easier. AC motors and controllers often have a regenerator feature. During braking, the motor turns into a generator and delivers power back to the batteries.

2. The Batteries

Right now, the weak link in any electric car is the batteries. There are at least six significant problems with current lead-acid battery technology:

(1) They are heavy (a typical lead-acid battery pack weighs 1,000 pounds or more).

(2) They are bulky (the car we are examining here has 50 lead-acid batteries, each measuring roughly 6" x 8" by" 6").

(3) They have a limited capacity (a typical lead-acid battery pack might hold 12 to 15 kilowatt-hours of electricity, giving a car a range of only 50 miles or so).

(4) They are slow to charge (typical recharge times for a lead-acid pack range between four to 10 hours for full charge, depending on the battery technology and the charger).

(5) They have a short life (three to four years, perhaps 200 full charge/discharge cycles).

(6) They are expensive (perhaps $2,000 for the battery pack shown in the sample car).

You can replace lead-acid batteries with NiMH batteries. The range of the car will double and the batteries will last 10 years (thousands of charge/discharge cycles), but the cost of the batteries today is 10 to 15 times greater than lead-acid. In other words, an NiMH battery pack will cost $20,000 to $30,000 (today) instead of $2,000. Prices for advanced batteries fall as they become mainstream, so over the next several years it is likely that NiMH and lithium-ion battery packs will become competitive with lead-acid battery prices. Electric cars will have significantly better range at that point.

3. Accessory Battery

Just about any electric car has one other battery on board. This is the normal 12-volt lead-acid battery that every car has. The 12-volt battery provides power for accessories—things like headlights, radios, fans, computers, air bags, wipers, power windows and instruments inside the car. Since all of these devices are readily available and standardized at 12 volts, it makes sense from an economic standpoint for an electric car to use them.

Therefore, an electric car has a normal 12-volt lead-acid battery to power all of the accessories. To keep the battery charged, an electric car needs a DC-to-DC converter. This converter takes in the DC power from the main battery array (at, for example, 300 volts DC) and converts it down to 12 volts to recharge the accessory battery. When the car is on, the accessories get their power from the DC-to-DC converter. When the car is off, they get their power from the 12-volt battery as in any gasoline-powered vehicle.

The DC-to-DC converter is normally a separate box under the hood, but sometimes this box is built into the controller.

4. The Charging System

Any electric car that uses batteries needs a charging system to recharge the batteries. The charging system has two goals:

(1) To pump electricity into the batteries as quickly as the batteries will allow.

(2) To monitor the batteries and avoid damaging them during the charging process.

The most sophisticated charging systems monitor battery voltage, current flow and battery temperature to minimize charging time. The charger sends as much current as it can without raising battery temperature too much. Less sophisticated chargers might monitor voltage or amperage only and make certain assumptions about average battery characteristics. A charger like this might apply maximum current to the batteries up through 80 percent of their capacity, and then cut the current back to some preset level for the final 20 percent to avoid overheating the batteries.

NEW WORDS

1. wiring ['waiəriŋ] n. 线路,配线,接线,布线,架线
2. muffler ['mʌflə] n. 消声器
3. tailpipe ['teilpaip] n. 排气管
4. inductive [in'dʌktiv] adj. 感应式的,感应的
5. disguise [dis'gaiz] v. 假装,伪装,掩饰;n. 伪装
6. potentiometer [pə,tenʃi'ɔmitə] n. 电位计,分压计
7. dominate ['dɔmineit] v. 支配,占优势
8. transistor [træn'sistə] n. 晶体管
9. sake [seik] n. 为了……之好处,缘故,理由

10. pseudo	[ˈsuːdəu]	*adj.* 假的，冒充的
11. replicate	[ˈrepliˌkeit]	*v.* 复制
12. forklift	[ˈfɔːklift]	*n.* 铲车，叉式升降机
13. bulky	[ˈbʌlkiː]	*adj.* 大的，容量大的，体积大的
14. mainstream	[ˈmeinˌstriːm]	*n.* 主流
15. standpoint	[ˈstændpɔint]	*n.* 立场，观点

PHRASES AND EXPRESSIONS

1. catalytic converter	（汽车等的）催化式排气净化器
2. gas gauge	汽油表，燃油表
3. adapter plate	安装板，转接（器）板
4. battery tray	蓄电池组合箱，蓄电池（安装）托架
5. battery pack	蓄电池组

NOTES TO THE TEXT

1. The very simplest DC controller would be a big on/off switch wired to the accelerator pedal.
最简单的直流控制器是一个通过电线连接到加速踏板的 on/off 开关。

2. Most controllers pulse the power more than 15,000 times per second, in order to keep the pulsation outside the range of human hearing.
大多数控制器提供的动力脉冲频率高于15,000Hz，以确保其脉冲频率在人的听觉范围之外。

3. During braking, the motor turns into a generator and delivers power back to the batteries.
在制动过程中，电动机转变为发电机，给蓄电池充电。

EXERCISES

Ⅰ. Answer the following questions

1. What's the difference between gasoline and electric cars?
2. Please list the key parts of electric car.
3. Why the battery is the weak link in any electric car?
4. What are the differences between the most sophisticated charge systems and the less sophisticated chargers?
5. Why electric cars are green cars?

Ⅱ. Translate the following into Chinese

1. A few electric vehicles are on the road already, but these are limited in capability by the state of battery technology. Currently available batteries are expensive, heavy, and store little power.

2. Electric vehicles are sometimes referred to as "zero-emission vehicles" because they produce essentially no pollution from the tailpipe or through fuel evaporation. This is important, for it means that the use of electric vehicles could greatly reduce emissions of carbon monoxide and smog-forming

pollutants in cities with dirty air.

3. Electric drive systems are virtually non-polluting and extremely energy efficient. Whereas only about 20% of the chemical energy in gasoline gets converted into useful work at the wheels of an internal combustion vehicle, 75% or more of the energy from a battery reaches its wheels.

Reading Material: The Tesla Roadster

Unlike a traditional gasoline-powered car, the Tesla Roadster doesn't contain hundreds of moving parts. It's powered by just four main systems:

(a) The Energy Storage System (ESS);
(b) The Power Electronics Module (PEM);
(c) An electric motor;
(d) A sequential manual transmission.

In place of an internal combustion engine, the Tesla Roadster sports a bank of batteries — the Energy Storage System (ESS). In developing a power source befitting such a high-performance car, Tesla went with technology proven in the laptop computer field — rechargeable lithium-ion batteries. The Roadster contains 6,831 of them. They weigh about 1,000 pounds in total, and Tesla claims that they provide "four to five times the energy-density stores of other batteries". The batteries fit into 11 sectors with 621 batteries each. A separate computer processor controls each sector to make sure all of the charging and discharging is handled smoothly.

The Power Electronics Module (PEM) is a power inverter and charging system that converts DC power to AC power using 72 insulated gate bipolar transistors (IGBTs). This results in a marked increase in power output compared to first-generation electric cars. Under peak acceleration, the batteries can crank out 200 kW of energy —— enough to light 2,000 incandescent light bulbs.

In addition to controlling charge and discharge rates, the Power Electronics Module controls voltage levels, the motor's RPM (revolutions per minute), torque and the regenerative braking system. This braking system captures the kinetic energy usually lost through braking and transfers it back into the ESS. The efficiency and integration of the battery, PEM and motor systems is between 85 and 95 percent, allowing the motor to put out up to 185 kW of power. Aluminum heat dissipation fins and a rear-mounted ventilation port keep the power transistors from overheating.

You can recharge the Roadster in two different ways. An electrician can install a recharging station in your garage. This 220 volts, 70 amps outlet allows for a full recharge in 3.5 hours from a completely dead battery. Tesla likens charging your car to charging your cell phone; you can plug it in at night and have a fully-charged car in the morning. There's also a mobile kit that allows recharging at any electrical outlet, no matter where you are. The length of time it takes to charge using the mobile kit depends on the outlet configuration that you're using (110 volts or 220 volts).

Although auto owners have been driving around for decades with tankfulls of volatile, flammable gasoline in their cars, having 1,000 pounds of batteries behind their head gives some people pause. The recent recalls of lithium-ion batteries used in laptop computers have increased those fears. Tesla has gone to great lengths to ensure the safety of the Roadster's energy system. The battery system was extensively "catastrophe tested", which involved heating individual cells until they burst into flames. Each cell is isolated enough from adjacent cells to prevent any damage to them. If one cell overheats, it will not start a chain reaction explosion.

A host of sensors detects acceleration, deceleration, tilt, temperature and smoke. If one senses an abnormal event, like a crash, it immediately shuts down and disconnects the power system. Similar anti-fault protections and sensors are part of the charging system.

Tesla Roadster Motor and Other Features

The heart of the Tesla Roadster is its 3 phases, 4 poles electric induction motor, which weighs just 70 pounds. Tesla's claims and independent testing show that the Roadster can reach 60 mile/h in about four seconds and its speed will top out somewhere around 130 mile/h. But the Roadster's performance isn't just about speed and acceleration. The unique properties of an electric motor give it a huge advantage over a combustion engine in terms of torque, force that tends to rotate or turn things, and power band, the range of operating speeds under which the engine operates efficiently. The Roadster can generate large amounts of torque even at very low RPM, and the motor can always turn out major horsepower. It can reach over 13,000 RPM, something very few large combustion engines can do.

That kind of motor response eliminates the need for a complicated transmission, so the Roadster has just three gears — two forward gears and one reverse gear. Shifting is manual, but there's no clutch. That also means there's no stalling or "jerk" when you shift between gears.

The Tesla Roadster can go a lot faster than previous electric cars, but perhaps more importantly, it can go a lot farther. The Roadster's estimated range is 250 miles on a single charge, at least 100 miles more than General Motors' EV1, which could go almost 150 miles under optimal conditions.

Most of the hype surrounding the Roadster is about its status as an electric vehicle. But while earlier electric cars tended to be cramped and lacking in features, the Tesla Roadster looks and feels like a sports car. In addition to basics like heated seats, a stereo with CD player, ABS brakes and dual airbags, the Roadster has a few unique features:

(a) A unique PIN to start the car and prevent hot-wiring;

(b) A Homelink transceiver you can program to control radio-frequency controlled devices such as your community gate and garage door;

(c) A dock connector for your iPod;

(d) Electrically-controlled door handles (there's no mechanical lock, which makes it more difficult to break into the car).

Since it's a convertible, the Roadster comes standard with a soft top. Options include a hard top as well as features like a full leather interior and a satellite navigation system.

Tech Specs:

(a) Acceleration: zero to 60 in about 4 seconds;

(b) Dimensions: 155.4 inches long, 73.7 inches wide, 44.4 inches tall with a 92.6 inches wheelbase;

(c) Weight: 2,500 pounds (subject to change due to safety regulations);

(d) Top Speed: Over 130 mile/h;

(e) Range: 250 miles EPA highway;
(f) Battery Life: Useful battery life in excess of 100,000 miles.

NEW WORDS

1. catastrophe　　　[kəˈtæstrəfi]　　　*n.* 灾难,横祸
2. transceiver　　　[trænˈsiːvə(r)]　　　*n.* 无线电收发机,收发器,收发报机
3. convertible　　　[kənˈvɜːtəbl]　　　*n.* 敞篷车,活动顶篷式汽车

PHRASES AND EXPRESSIONS

1. insulated gate bipolar transistors (IGBTs)　　　绝缘栅双极晶体管
2. Tech Specs　　　技术规格

NOTES

1. A host of sensors detects acceleration, deceleration, tilt, temperature and smoke. If one senses an abnormal event, like a crash, it immediately shuts down and disconnects the power system.

许多传感器检测加速度、减速度、倾斜度、温度和烟雾。如果一个传感器监测到一个异常事件(比如撞车)它会立即关闭并断开电力系统。

2. The unique properties of an electric motor give it a huge advantage over a combustion engine in terms of torque, force that tends to rotate or turn things, and power band, the range of operating speeds under which the engine operates efficiently.

电动机的独特性能使其在转矩、旋转或转动物体的力、功率带(发动机高效运行的工作转速范围)方面与内燃机相比具有巨大优势。

UNIT 17　HYBRID ELECTRIC VEHICLES

A vehicle that has two or more energy sources and energy converters is called a hybrid vehicle. A hybrid vehicle with an electrical power train (energy source energy converters) is called an HEV.

A hybrid vehicle drive train usually consists of no more than two power trains. More than two power train configurations will complicate the system. For the purpose of recapturing part of the braking energy that is dissipated in the form of heat in conventional ICE vehicles, a hybrid drive train usually has a bidirectional energy source and converter. The other one is either bidirectional or unidirectional. Figure 17-1 shows the concept of a hybrid drive train and the possible different power flow routes.

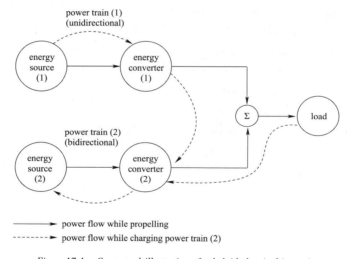

Figure 17-1　Conceptual illustration of a hybrid electric drive train

Hybrid drive trains supply the required power by an adapted power train. There are many available patterns of combining the power flows to meet load requirements as described below:

(a) Power train 1 alone delivers power to the load;
(b) Power train 2 alone delivers power to the load;
(c) Both power train 1 and 2 deliver power to load at the same time;
(d) Power train 2 obtains power from load (regenerative braking);
(e) Power train 2 obtains power from power train 1;
(f) Power train 2 obtains power from power train 1 and load at the same time;
(g) Power train 1 delivers power to load and to power train 2 at the same time;
(h) Power train 1 delivers power to power train 2, and power train 2 delivers power to load;
(i) Power train 1 delivers power to load, and load delivers power to power train 2.

In the case of hybridization with a liquid fuel IC engine (power train 1) and a battery-electric

UNIT 17 HYBRID ELECTRIC VEHICLES

machine (power train 2), pattern (a) is the engine-alone propelling mode. This may be used when the batteries are almost completely depleted and the engine has no remaining power to charge the batteries, or when the batteries have been fully charged and the engine is able to supply sufficient power to meet the power demands of the vehicle. Pattern (b) is the pure electric propelling mode, in which the engine is shut off. This pattern may be used in situations where the engine cannot operate effectively, such as very low speed, or in areas where emissions are strictly prohibited. Pattern (c) is the hybrid traction mode and may be used when a large amount of power is needed, such as during sharp acceleration or steep hill climbing. Pattern (d) is the regenerative braking mode, by which the kinetic or potential energy of the vehicle is recovered through the electric motor functioning as a generator. The recovered energy is stored in the batteries and reused later on. Pattern (e) is the mode in which the engine charges the batteries while the vehicle is at a standstill, coasting, or descending a slight grade, in which no power goes into or comes from the load. Pattern (f) is the mode in which both regenerative braking and the IC engine charge the batteries simultaneously. Pattern (g) is the mode in which the engine propels the vehicle and charges the batteries simultaneously. Pattern (h) is the mode in which the engine charges the batteries, and the batteries supply power to the load. Pattern (i) is the mode in which the power flows into the batteries from the heat engine through the vehicle mass. The typical configuration of this mode is two power trains separately mounted on the front and the rear axle of the vehicle. The varied operation modes in a hybrid vehicle create more flexibility over a single power train vehicle. With proper configuration and control, applying the specific mode for each special operating condition can optimize overall performance, efficiency, and emissions. However, in a practical design, deciding which mode should be implemented depends on many factors, such as the physical configuration of the drive train, the power train efficiency characteristics, load characteristics, etc.

Operating each power train in its optimal efficiency region is essential for the overall efficiency of the vehicle. An IC engine generally has the best efficiency operating region with a wide throttle opening. Operating away from this region will cause the efficiency to suffer a lot. On the other hand, efficiency suffering in an electric motor is not as detrimental when compared to an IC engine that operates away from its optimal region.

The load power of a vehicle varies randomly in real operation due to frequent acceleration, deceleration, and climbing up and down grades. Actually, the load power is composed of two components: one is steady (average) power, which has a constant value, and the other is dynamic power, which has a zero average. In hybrid vehicle strategy, one power train that favors steady-state operation, such as an IC engine, can be used to supply the average power. On the other hand, other power trains such as an electric motor can be used to supply the dynamic power. The total energy output from the dynamic power train will be zero in a whole driving cycle. This implies that the energy source of the dynamic power train does not lose energy capacity at the end of the driving cycle. It functions only as a power damper.

1. Architectures of Hybrid Electric Drive Trains

The architecture of a hybrid vehicle is loosely defined as the connection between the components that define the energy flow routes and control ports. Traditionally, HEVs were classified into two basic types: series and parallel. It is interesting to note that, in 2000, some newly introduced HEVs could not be classified into these kinds. Therefore, HEVs are now classified into four kinds: series hybrid, parallel hybrid, series-parallel hybrid, and complex hybrid, which are functionally shown in Figure 17-2. In Figure 17-2, a fuel tank IC engine and a battery-electric motor are taken, respectively, as examples of the primary power source (steady power source) and secondary power source (dynamic power source). Of course, the IC engine can be replaced by other types of power sources, such as fuel cells. Similarly, the batteries can be replaced by ultracapacitors or by flywheels and their combinations.

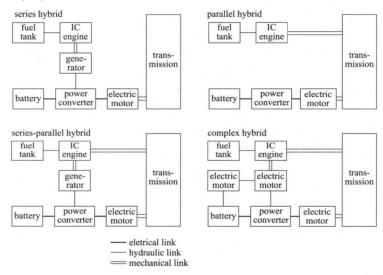

Figure 17-2 Classification of hybrid electric vehicles

2. Series Hybrid Electric Drive Trains

A series hybrid drive train is a drive train where two power sources feed a single powerplant (electric motor) that propels the vehicle. The most commonly found series hybrid drive train is the series hybrid electric drive train shown in Figure 17-3. The unidirectional energy source is a fuel tank and the unidirectional energy converter is an engine coupled to an electric generator. The output of the electric generator is connected to an electric power bus through an electronic converter (rectifier). The bidirectional energy source is an electrochemical battery pack, connected to the bus by means of a power electronics converter (DC/DC converter). The electric power bus is also connected to the controller of the electric traction motor. The traction motor can be controlled either as a motor or a generator, and in forward or reverse motion. This drive train may need a battery charger to charge the batteries by a wall plug-in from the power network.

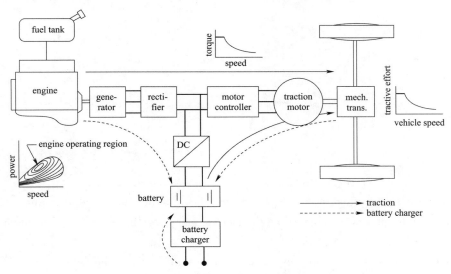

Figure 17-3 Configuration of a series hybrid electric drive train

Series hybrid electric drive trains potentially have the following operation modes:

(a) Pure electric mode: The engine is turned off and the vehicle is propelled only by the batteries;

(b) Pure engine mode: The vehicle traction power only comes from the engine-generator, while the batteries neither supply nor draw any power from the drive train. The electric machines serve as an electric transmission from the engine to the driven wheels;

(c) Hybrid mode: The traction power is drawn from both the engine-generator and the batteries;

(d) Engine traction and battery charging mode: The engine-generator supplies power to charge the batteries and to propel the vehicle;

(e) Regenerative braking mode: The engine-generator is turned off and the traction motor is operated as a generator. The power generated is used to charge the batteries;

(f) Battery charging mode: The traction motor receives no power and the engine-generator charges the batteries;

(g) Hybrid battery charging mode: Both the engine-generator and the traction motor operate as generators to charge the batteries.

3. Parallel Hybrid Electric Drive Trains

A parallel hybrid drive train is a drive train in which the engine supplies its power mechanically to the wheels like in a conventional ICE-powered vehicle. It is assisted by an electric motor that is mechanically coupled to the transmission. The powers of the engine and electric motor are coupled together by mechanical coupling, as shown in Figure 17-4. The mechanical combination of the engine and electric motor power leaves room for several different configurations, detailed hereafter.

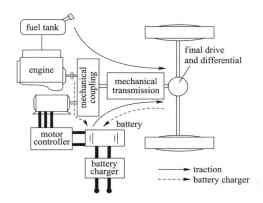

Figure 17-4　Configuration of a parallel hybrid electric drive train

The mechanical coupling in Figure 17-4 may be a torque or speed coupling. The torque coupling adds the torques of the engine and the electric motor together or splits the engine torque into two parts: propelling and battery charging.

Another torque coupling parallel hybrid drive train is the separated axle architecture, in which one axle is powered by the engine and another is powered by the electric motor (Figure 17-5). The tractive efforts from the two power trains are added through the vehicle chassis and the road.

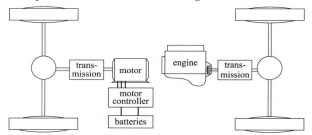

Figure 17-5　Separated axle torque combination parallel hybrid electric drive train

The separated axle architecture offers some of the advantages of a conventional vehicle. It keeps the original engine and transmission unaltered and adds an electrical traction system on the other axle. It also has four-wheel drive, which optimizes traction on slippery roads and reduces the tractive effort on a single tire.

However, the electric machines and the eventual differential gear system occupy considerable space and may reduce the available passenger and luggage space. This problem may be solved if the motor transmission is single gear and the electric motor is replaced by two small-sized electric motors that can be placed within two driven wheels. It should be noted that the batteries cannot be charged from the engine when the vehicle is at a standstill.

NEW WORDS

1. recapture　　　[ˌriːˈkæptʃə(r)]　　　vt. 重新捕获,夺回,回收
2. pattern　　　　[ˈpætn]　　　　　　　n. 模式,范例
3. detrimental　　[ˌdetrɪˈmentl]　　　　adj. 有害的,不利的
4. dynamic　　　 [daɪˈnæmɪk]　　　　　adj. 动力的,动态的

| 5. architecture | [ˈɑːkitektʃə(r)] | n. 结构,架构 |
| 6. standstill | [ˈstændstil] | n. 停顿,停止 |

PHRASES AND EXPRESSIONS

1. hybrid vehicle　　　　　　　混合动力汽车
2. hybrid electric vehicle　　　　油电混合动力汽车
3. dynamic power　　　　　　　动态功率
4. torque coupling　　　　　　　转矩耦合器

NOTES TO THE TEXT

On the other hand, other power trains such as an electric motor can be used to supply the dynamic power.

另一方面,可以由其他动力传动系统(如电动机)来提供动态功率。

EXERCISES

Ⅰ. Answer the following questions

1. How does the hybrid electric vehicle work?
2. How many patterns of combining the power flows to meet HEV load requirements?
3. How many kinds are now HEVs classified into? What are they?
4. Can the batteries in the separated axle architecture HEV be charged from the engine when the vehicle is at a standstill?
5. Why hybrid electric vehicles are higher efficiency?

Ⅱ. Translate the following into Chinese

1. A gas-powered car has a fuel tank, which supplies gasoline to the engine. The engine then turns a transmission, which turns the wheels. An electric car, on the other hand, has a set of batteries that provides electricity to an electric motor. The motor turns a transmission, and the transmission turns the wheels. The hybrid is a compromise. It attempts to significantly increase the mileage and reduce the emissions of a gas-powered car while overcoming the shortcomings of an electric car. Lifecycle GHG emissions for an FCV are the sum of emissions from the production and distribution of hydrogen, the production of the vehicle, and vehicle operation.

2. The gas engine on a conventional car is sized for the peak power requirement (those few times when you floor the accelerator pedal). In fact, most drivers use the peak power of their engines less than one percent of the time. The hybrid car uses a much smaller engine, one that is sized closer to the average power requirement than to the peak power.

Reading Material: Automatic Emergency Braking (AEB) Systems

There's a lot of complexities involved in Automatic Emergency Braking (AEB) systems on today's vehicles. Depending on the OEM, AEBs can take on various names, including Collision Mitigation Braking System, Autonomous Emergency Braking, Forward Collision Plus, Forward

Collision Warning Plus, and Pre-Sense Front.

Although the names are very different, the way that these systems work is quite similar. Sure, the software and specific hardware may be unique to each OEM and even to a specific model, but the sequence of events that transpire during the application of the AEB system is quite common among vehicle makers regardless of the OEM.

The AEB system will typically work in stages to detect a potential collision, provide warnings and avoid a collision or reduce the severity of an impact in the event a collision cannot be avoided entirely. These stages are not independent and will often chronologically overlap as to when they are initiated. These can typically be broken down into four stages.

Pre-Stage and Vehicle Conditioning

This category is first in the sequence and is implemented at the first recognition of a potential collision by the AEB system. By gathering information from sensors and cameras, the system can detect within milliseconds if an emergency braking situation exists. It includes the following actions by the system:

(a) Adjustment of electronically controlled steering and suspension components;

(b) Selecting a braking diagram based on the initial sensor/camera information;

(c) Pre-charging of the braking system.

This means that the AEB system automatically adjusts the steering and/or suspension to tighten it up to limit body roll and weight transfer. This limiting of weight transfer helps to maximize the braking by reducing the amount of weight that moves off of the rear wheels and onto the front wheels. Keeping the weight balanced means that more brake pressure can be applied to the rear without locking up the brakes and causing the ABS to activate.

Limiting body roll will have a similar effect as reducing front to back weight transfer, except here the benefit is seen not so much with braking but with the steering. Sometimes in an emergency braking situation the driver will attempt to avoid the potential collision with a sharp steering maneuver that will involve steering in one direction and then immediately in the opposite direction. This causes a tremendous amount of force to be applied left and right. Limiting the amount the body can roll during this maneuver reduces the side-to-side weight transfer, which can help avoid skidding and loss of vehicle control.

The braking diagram chooses the best braking scenario based on the initial inputs and can change scenarios in milliseconds as the data from the input's changes. Pre-charging of the brakes puts pressure in the braking system ahead of any braking. This can allow for full pressure to be applied to the brakes even when only light pressure is applied to the pedal by the driver. This will allow shorter stopping times when the driver or the system brakes the vehicle.

Driver Warning

There can be a number of different means to bring attention to the driver that a collision may be eminent. These may be independent, or they may be simultaneous. Warnings include visual, acoustic, haptic, and steering wheel jolt.

Typically, the visual is a warning light or icon that will display on the instrument cluster or a head-up display. This is often the first warning the system will give, with an acoustic or audible

UNIT 17 HYBRID ELECTRIC VEHICLES

warning next. This beep or alarm is often activated along with the visual warning as a way to intensify the importance of the warning to the driver. A haptic (vibration) warning may also be used with visual and acoustic. Next is a jolt to the steering wheel. This is typically the last warning before braking intervention by the AEB system. Warnings typically continue until automatic braking is applied or until the eminent collision is avoided.

Active Brake Intervention

The system will apply partial braking to the vehicle if there is zero or insufficient drive braking. Partial braking is typically done in two stages: standard and extended.

The difference in these two stages is that extended braking is roughly double the braking force than that of standard braking. Sufficient driver braking will override the AEB partial braking and often will cause the stop lamps to blink as a warning to other drivers that emergency braking is taking place with the vehicle ahead.

Automatic Emergency Braking

This is typically the last resort for AEB, although in some cases it may be the first and only depending upon the situation. For example, if a vehicle suddenly pulled in front from a different lane or pulled out from a side street, it may trigger full braking by the AEB system. Full braking will typically be three times as much braking force as the standard braking with active brake intervention and may apply up to 100% of the braking force of the vehicle.

Again, it is important to remember that these stages do not occur separately but simultaneously to a certain degree and that this overlap in stages will constantly vary depending upon the specific emergency braking situation.

With a better understanding of how AEB works and the speed and complexity of the decision making of the system, consider now the importance of the inputs and how even the slightest misalignment of these inputs could have negative results on the AEB system.

For example, if a front radar sensor or camera is not calibrated correctly and is only off by say one degree, the system may continue to operate and no warning light or DTCs may be set, but that does not mean that the system will be operating as it should or as it was intended. Even one degree off will mean that the radar or camera is not "looking" where it was intended to. This may cause false alerts and unexpected braking or even worse, delayed or non-existent detection of an eminent collision.

Drivers come to expect the AEB to function in a specific and consistent manner. Having a small amount of misalignment of a sensor or camera will inevitably change the manner in which the system works. This will increase the risk for a collision if the AEB does not react as expected or as it did before.

When dealing with angles and degrees, a change in a degree of measurement does not seem like much. However, the further you move out from the apex of an angle (the point where the two lines meet) the distance between those lines increases.

To visualize this, take a flashlight and shine it on the wall at a close distance (a foot or less). Now move it slightly to the right or left; see how the beam moves only slightly. Now back up 10 to 15 feet and move the light the same amount to the right or left. Observe how much greater the distance is that the beam of light moves. Now imagine that beam of light is the field of view for a camera or the sensing area for a radar — it now should be clear how even a slight misalignment can make a huge impact.

This means that for a long-range radar, that "sees" out many feet in front of the vehicle, one degree of misalignment at a one-foot distance is only potentially inches off, but at 20 feet out that same degree of error is now off in many inches and potentially even feet and can drastically change the field of view. There is a reason OEMs provide measurement specifications for certain inputs and very specific instructions on how to calibrate those inputs back to the OEM specification.

NEW WORDS

1. chronologically   [ˌkrɒnəˈlɒdʒikli]   *adv.* 按时间的前后顺序排列地
2. implement   [ˈimpliment, ˈimplimənt]   *vt.* 实施,执行,使生效
3. acoustic   [əˈkuːstik]   *adj.* 听觉的,声学的,声音的
4. haptic   [ˈhæptik]   *adj.* 触觉的
5. jolt   [dʒəʊlt]   *vt. & n.* 颠簸,震动
6. drastically   [ˈdrɑːstikli]   *adv.* 彻底地,激烈地

PHRASES AND EXPRESSIONS

1. Automatic Emergency Braking (AEB)   自动紧急制动
2. Collision Mitigation Braking System   碰撞缓解制动系统
3. extended braking   增强制动
4. full braking   全力制动
5. Diagnostic Trouble Code (DTC)   诊断故障代码

NOTES

1. This limiting of weight transfer helps to maximize the braking by reducing the amount of weight that moves off of the rear wheels and onto the front wheels.

限制质量转移有助于通过减少从后轮移动到前轮上的质量来最大化制动。

2. Sufficient driver braking will override the AEB partial braking and often will cause the stop lamps to blink as a warning to other drivers that emergency braking is taking place with the vehicle ahead.

充分的驾驶人制动将超越 AEB 部分制动,通常会导致停车灯闪烁,以警告其他驾驶人前方车辆正在进行紧急制动。

UNIT 18 FUEL CELL

1. Fuel Cell Principles

In principle, a fuel cell operates like a battery. Unlike a battery, a fuel cell does not run down or require recharging. It will produce energy in the form of electricity and heat as long as fuel is supplied.

A fuel cell consists of two electrodes sandwiched around an electrolyte. Oxygen passes over one electrode and hydrogen over the other, generating electricity, water and heat. Figure 18-1 shows the Fuel cell principle.

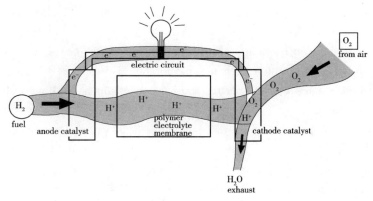

Figure 18-1 *Fuel cell principle*

Hydrogen fuel is fed into the "anode" of the fuel cell. Oxygen (or air) enters the fuel cell through the cathode. Encouraged by a catalyst, the hydrogen atom splits into a proton and an electron, which take different paths to the cathode. The proton passes through the electrolyte. The electrons create a separate current that can be utilized before they return to the cathode, to be reunited with the hydrogen and oxygen in a molecule of water.

The fuel cell will compete with many other types of energy conversion devices, including the gas turbine in city's power plant, the gasoline engine in car and the battery in laptop. Combustion engines like the turbine and the gasoline engine burn fuels and use the pressure created by the expansion of the gases to do mechanical work. Batteries store electrical energy by converting it into chemical energy, which can be converted back into electrical energy when needed.

A fuel cell provides a DC (direct current) voltage that can be used to power motors, lights or any number of electrical appliances. There are several different types of fuel cells, each using a different chemistry. Fuel cells are usually classified by the type of electrolyte they use. Some types of fuel cells show promise for use in power generation plants. Others may be useful for small portable applications or for powering cars.

The proton exchange membrane fuel cell (PEMFC) is one of the most promising technologies. This is the type of fuel cell that will end up powering cars, buses and maybe even your house.

2. Proton Exchange Membrane (PEM)

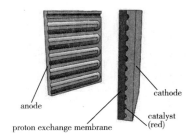

Figure 18-2 *The parts of a PEM fuel cell*

The proton exchange membrane fuel cell (PEMFC) uses one of the simplest reactions of any fuel cell. First, let's take a look at what's in a PEM fuel cell; Figure 18-2 shows four basic elements of a PEMFC:

(1) The anode, the negative post of the fuel cell, has several jobs. It conducts the electrons that are freed from the hydrogen molecules so that they can be used in an external circuit. It has channels etched into it that disperse the hydrogen gas equally over the surface of the catalyst.

(2) The cathode, the positive post of the fuel cell, has channels etched into it that distribute the oxygen to the surface of the catalyst. It also conducts the electrons back from the external circuit to the catalyst, where they can recombine with the hydrogen ions and oxygen to form water.

(3) The electrolyte is the proton exchange membrane. This specially treated material, which looks something like ordinary kitchen plastic wrap, only conducts positively charged ions. The membrane blocks electrons.

(4) The catalyst is a special material that facilitates the reaction of oxygen and hydrogen. It is usually made of platinum powder very thinly coated onto carbon paper or cloth. The catalyst is rough and porous so that the maximum surface area of the platinum can be exposed to the hydrogen or oxygen. The platinum-coated side of the catalyst faces the PEM.

Chemistry of a Fuel Cell

Anode side:
$$2H_2 \Rightarrow 4H^+ + 4e^-$$

Cathode side:
$$O_2 + 4H^+ + 4e^- \Rightarrow 2H_2O$$

Net reaction:
$$2H_2 + O_2 \Rightarrow 2H_2O$$

The pressurized hydrogen gas (H_2) enters the fuel cell on the anode side. This gas is forced through the catalyst by the pressure. When an H_2 molecule comes in contact with the platinum on the catalyst, it splits into two H^+ ions and two electrons (e^-). The electrons are conducted through the anode, where they make their way through the external circuit (doing useful work such as turning a motor) and return to the cathode side of the fuel cell.

Meanwhile, on the cathode side of the fuel cell, oxygen gas (O_2) is being forced through the catalyst, where it forms two oxygen atoms. Each of these atoms has a strong negative charge. This negative charge attracts the two H^+ ions through the membrane, where they combine with an oxygen atom and two of the electrons from the external circuit to form a water molecule (H_2O).

This reaction in a single fuel cell produces only about 0.7 volts. To get this voltage up to a reasonable level, many separate fuel cells must be combined to form a fuel-cell stack.

PEMFCs operate at a fairly low temperature (about 176 degrees Fahrenheit, 80 degrees Celsius), which means they warm up quickly and don't require expensive containment structures. Constant improvements in the engineering and materials used in these cells have increased the power density to a level where a device about the size of a small piece of luggage can power a car.

3. Problems with Fuel Cells

Since a fuel cell uses oxygen and hydrogen to produce electricity. The oxygen required for a fuel cell comes from the air. In fact, in the PEM fuel cell, ordinary air is pumped into the cathode. The hydrogen is not so readily available, however. Hydrogen has some limitations that make it impractical for use in most applications. For instance, you don't have a hydrogen pipeline coming to your house, and you can't pull up to a hydrogen pump at your local gas station.

Hydrogen is difficult to store and distribute, so it would be much more convenient if fuel cells could use fuels that are more readily available. This problem is addressed by a device called a reformer. A reformer turns hydrocarbon or alcohol fuels into hydrogen, which is then fed to the fuel cell. Unfortunately, reformers are not perfect. They generate heat and produce other gases besides hydrogen. They use various devices to try to clean up the hydrogen, but even so, the hydrogen that comes out of them is not pure, and this lowers the efficiency of the fuel cell.

Some of the more promising fuels are natural gas, propane and methanol. Many people have natural-gas lines or propane tanks at their house already, so these fuels are the most likely to be used for home fuel cells. Methanol is a liquid fuel that has similar properties to gasoline. It is just as easy to transport and distribute, so methanol may be a likely candidate to power fuel-cell cars.

4. Efficiency of Fuel Cells

4.1 Fuel-Cell-Powered Electric Car

If the fuel cell is powered with pure hydrogen, it has the potential to be up to 80-percent efficient. That is, it converts 80 percent of the energy content of the hydrogen into electrical energy. But, as we learned in the previous section, hydrogen is difficult to store in a car. When we add a reformer to convert methanol to hydrogen, the overall efficiency drops to about 30 to 40 percent.

We still need to convert the electrical energy into mechanical work. This is accomplished by the electric motor and inverter. A reasonable number for the efficiency of the motor/inverter is about 80 percent. So we have 30 to 40 percent efficiency at converting methanol to electricity, and 80-percent efficiency converting electricity to mechanical power. That gives an overall efficiency of about 24 to 32 percent.

4.2 Gasoline-Powered Car

The efficiency of a gasoline-powered car is surprisingly low. All of the heat that comes out as exhaust or goes into the radiator is wasted energy. The engine also uses a lot of energy turning the various pumps, fans and generators that keep it going. So the overall efficiency of an automotive gas engine is about 20 percent. That is, only about 20 percent of the thermal-energy content of the gasoline is converted into mechanical work.

4.3 Battery-Powered Electric Car

This type of car has a fairly high efficiency. The battery is about 90-percent efficient (most batteries generate some heat, or require heating), and the electric motor/inverter is about 80-percent efficient. This gives an overall efficiency of about 72 percent.

But that is not the whole story. The electricity used to power the car had to be generated somewhere. If it was generated at a power plant that used a combustion process (rather than nuclear, hydroelectric, solar or wind), then only about 40 percent of the fuel required by the power plant was converted into electricity. The process of charging the car requires the conversion of alternating current (AC) power to direct current (DC) power. This process has an efficiency of about 90 percent.

So, if we look at the whole cycle, the efficiency of an electric car is 72 percent for the car, 40 percent for the power plant and 90 percent for charging the car. That gives an overall efficiency of 26 percent. The overall efficiency varies considerably depending on what sort of power plant is used. If the electricity for the car is generated by a hydroelectric plant for instance, then it is basically free (we didn't burn any fuel to generate it), and the efficiency of the electric car is about 65 percent.

5. Other Types of Fuel Cells

There are several other types of fuel-cell technologies being developed for possible commercial uses:

(1) Alkaline fuel cell (AFC): This is one of the oldest designs. It has been used in the U.S. space program since the 1960s. The AFC is very susceptible to contamination, so it requires pure hydrogen and oxygen. It is also very expensive, so this type of fuel cell is unlikely to be commercialized.

(2) Phosphoric-acid fuel cell (PAFC): The phosphoric-acid fuel cell has potential for use in small stationary power-generation systems. It operates at a higher temperature than PEM fuel cells, so it has a longer warm-up time. This makes it unsuitable for use in cars.

(3) Solid oxide fuel cell (SOFC): These fuel cells are best suited for large-scale stationary power generators that could provide electricity for factories or towns. This type of fuel cell operates at very high temperatures (around 1,832 ℉, 1,000 ℃). This high temperature makes reliability a problem, but it also has an advantage: The steam produced by the fuel cell can be channeled into turbines to generate more electricity. This improves the overall efficiency of the system.

(4) Molten carbonate fuel cell (MCFC): These fuel cells are also best suited for large stationary power generators. They operate at 1,112 °F (600℃), so they also generate steam that can be used to generate more power. They have a lower operating temperature than the SOFC, which means they don't need such exotic materials. This makes the design a little less expensive.

NEW WORDS

1. electrode	[i'lek,trəʊd]	n.	电极
2. anode	['æn,əʊd]	n.	阳极
3. cathode	['kæθ,əʊd]	n.	阴极,负极
4. electrolyte	[i'lektrə,lait]	n.	[化]电解液,电解质
5. membrane	['mem,brein]	n.	膜,隔膜
6. catalyst	['kætlist]	n.	催化剂,接触剂
7. porous	['pɔːrəs, 'pəʊr-]	adj.	多孔的,有气孔的
8. reformer	[ri'fɔːmə]	n.	转化器
9. propane	['prəʊpein]	n.	[化]丙烷
10. methanol	['meθənɔl]	n.	甲醇,木醇
11. inverter	[in'vəːtə]	n.	逆变器
12. susceptible	[sə'septəbl]	adj.	易受影响的,易受感染的
13. contamination	[kən,tæmə'neiʃən]	n.	玷污,污染,污染物
14. exotic	[ig'zɔtik]	adj.	外国产的,进口的

PHRASES AND EXPRESSIONS

1. fuel cell	燃料电池
2. end up	最终成为,最后处于
3. PEMFC	质子交换膜燃料电池
4. even so	虽然如此,即使如此
5. alkaline fuel cell	碱性燃料电池
6. phosphoric-acid fuel cell	磷酸燃料电池
7. solid oxide fuel cell	固态[体]氧燃料电池
8. molten carbonate fuel cell	熔碳酸盐燃料电池

NOTES TO THE TEXT

1. Unlike a battery, a fuel cell does not run down or require recharging.
与普通电池不同,燃料电池电能不会耗尽,也不用充电。

2. Constant improvements in the engineering and materials used in these cells have increased the power density to a level where a device about the size of a small piece of luggage can power a car.
由于这些电池中采用的材料和工艺技术的不断改进,已经使功率密度提高到相当的水平,也就是说,一个小行李舱大小的燃料电池就可以驱动一辆汽车。

3. They use various devices to try to clean up the hydrogen, but even so, the hydrogen that comes out of them is not pure, and this lowers the efficiency of the fuel cell.

转化器使用各种装置试图使氢纯净化，但即便如此，转化器产出的氢并不纯净，并且这使得燃料电池效率下降。

EXERCISES

I. Answer the following questions

1. How does the fuel cell works?
2. What are the functions of the proton exchange membrane?
3. What are the problems with fuel cells?
4. How much is the overall efficiency of fuel cells according to this text?
5. Why fuel cell cars are green cars?

II. Translate the following into Chinese

1. Polymer Electrolyte Membrane (PEM) fuel cells used in automobiles—also called Proton Exchange Membrane fuel cells—use hydrogen fuel and oxygen from the air to produce electricity.

2. Hydrogen fuel cell vehicles (FCVs) have a significant potential to reduce emissions from the transportation sector, because they do not emit any greenhouse gases (GHGs) during vehicle operation. Their lifecycle GHG emissions depend on how the hydrogen fuel is made.

3. Lifecycle GHG emissions for an FCV are the sum of emissions from the production and distribution of hydrogen, the production of the vehicle, and vehicle operation.

Reading Material: Hydrogen Cars

Although hydrogen-powered cars have a science fiction quality to them, the idea isn't really new. Actually, the technology for using hydrogen to generate power has been around since the first part of the 19th century —— that's longer than cars have been around. What's new is a hydrogen powered car on the road, with steam coming out of its exhaust pipe instead of foul-smelling gases. Several hydrogen cars are now in existence, but most of them are concept cars. These eco-friendly driving machines include the Chevrolet Equinox, the BMW 745h and the one that's currently available for lease in California, the Honda FCX.

What makes a hydrogen car possible is a device called a fuel cell, which converts hydrogen to electricity, giving off only heat and water as byproducts. Because it's non-polluting, hydrogen seems like the ideal fuel for the 21st century. A lot of people in the government and the auto industry are excited about its potential. Hydrogen cars have the potential to be fuel-efficient and offer the hope of eco-friendly, green driving. But there are still a lot of problems that need to be overcome and questions that need to be answered before hydrogen becomes the fuel of choice for enough people to make much difference in our current use of fossil fuels. For instance, where will we get the hydrogen? How expensive will these fuel-efficient cars be to purchase? Will you be able to find a hydrogen fueling station to refill your tank? And, perhaps most importantly, as a fuel, is hydrogen really as non-polluting as it seems?

Hydrogen Car Production

Hydrogen car production is not vastly different from producing typical cars. Of course, the drive train and the electrical systems will be somewhat unique because a fuel cell creates electricity. Therefore, a hydrogen-powered car and electric car have a lot in common in that respect. Perhaps a more important question is how the hydrogen itself will be produced.

What hydrogen remains on this planet is bound with other elements in molecular form, most commonly in water (H_2O) molecules. And there is a lot of H_2O on the surface of the Earth. But how to separate the hydrogen molecules in the water from the oxygen molecules? And if not use water as a hydrogen source, where else can we get hydrogen?

The simplest way of getting hydrogen from water is electrolysis. Pass an electric current through water, the H_2O molecules break down. Similar to fuel cell operation, this process uses an anode and a cathode, usually made from inert metals. When an electric current is applied to the water, hydrogen forms at the cathode, and oxygen forms at the anode. Although this process is slow, it can be done on a large scale.

An alternative source for hydrogen is natural gas, which consists of naturally occurring hydrocarbons. A process called steam reformation can be used to separate the hydrogen in the gas from the carbon. At present, this is the most common method of industrial-scale production of hydrogen and would likely be the first method used to produce the hydrogen for fuel-cell vehicles. Unfortunately, this process uses fossil fuels-the natural gas. So if the point of building cars that run on hydrogen is to avoid depleting fossil fuel reserves, natural gas would be the worst possible source of this fuel.

Some experts have suggested that it might be possible to build miniature hydrogen plants that will fit in the average person's garage, so it won't even be necessary to drive to the local fueling station to fill up the car's hydrogen tank. The most extreme form of this idea has been the suggestion that electrolysis could be performed inside the car itself, which would make possible the astounding idea of a car that runs on water. However, the power for the electrolysis has to come from some sort of battery, so a water-powered car would need to be periodically recharged.

So, are green driving machines like fuel-cell equipped vehicles really the cars of the future? Many people hope so, but there are several potential roadblocks on the way to a world where people get around in cars that run on hydrogen.

Hydrogen Car Setbacks

A lot of people believe that hydrogen fuel cells are the most important alternative fuel technology currently under development. It is not, however, without problems, and it may be decades before fuel cell technology is in wide use. We can roughly group the problems with hydrogen into three categories: the costs of developing the technology, difficulties and dangers with hydrogen storage and the possibility that this "non-polluting technology" isn't so non-polluting after all. Here are some of the hydrogen car setbacks need to deal with in the near future.

The costs of developing hydrogen technology are high. Not only have to design and develop the fuel cells and the cars, but have to develop an infrastructure to support these fuel-efficient vehicles. Some of the more pessimistic estimates have placed the cost of building an infrastructure that will allow a significant number of hydrogen cars to be as high as $500 billion, and the time to produce the infrastructure as long as four decades.

The cost of the cars is high, too. With platinum as the most widely used catalyst in the fuel cells, the price of a single fuel cell vehicle is currently more than $100,000 and even perhaps considerably more, which is why the only hydrogen cars available for you to drive at the moment are for lease, not for sale. Few people are in a position to afford such an expensive car. Other catalysts are being developed which will probably be less expensive than platinum, but nobody knows how soon they'll be available for large-scale use.

The storage problem is also a thorny one. Hydrogen is a gas and it likes to spread out. Putting it in a car means squeezing it down to a reasonable size, and that isn't easy. Furthermore, hydrogen gets warm while it's sitting in the tank of a parked car, which causes the gas to expand. This means that the tanks have to vent the hydrogen periodically from the car. Leave a hydrogen car sitting around for more than a few days and all the fuel will be gone. Hydrogen is also highly flammable, the spectacular explosion of the dirigible Hindenburg in the 1930s is believed by some to have been the result of a hydrogen fire. So, if the hydrogen gets out of the tank, it has the potential to be dangerous. Fortunately, hydrogen fires aren't as hot as gasoline fires and are less likely to start secondary fires. And because hydrogen rises, most escaped hydrogen will float away before it can actually do any harm.

And is hydrogen really non-polluting? A fuel cell produces only heat and water as exhaust, but the processes used to create the hydrogen are not necessarily as clean. Electrolysis uses electricity and that electricity will often come from plants that burn coal, a highly polluting source. And when hydrogen is extracted from natural gas, it produces carbon emissions, which is exactly what we're trying to avoid by using hydrogen in the first place.

Many people think that we'll overcome these obstacles eventually, but it's going to be difficult. Others believe that our best bet for fuel efficiency and eco-friendly driving in the near future lies not in hydrogen but in hybrid electric vehicles, like the Toyota Prius, the Ford Fusion hybrid and other similar hybrid cars. Still, it's possible that within the next couple of decades, you just might own a hydrogen fuel cell car.

NEW WORDS

1. electrolysis [iˌlek'trɒləsɪs] n. 电解
2. inert [ɪ'nɜːt] adj. 不活泼的，[化]惰性的
3. astounding [ə'staʊndɪŋ] adj. 使人震惊的
4. thorny ['θɔːni] adj. 痛苦的，棘手的
5. dirigible ['dɪrɪdʒəbl] n. 飞船

PHRASES AND EXPRESSIONS

1. Hydrogen Cars 氢动力汽车
2. steam reformation 蒸汽重整

NOTES

Others believe that our best bet for fuel efficiency and eco-friendly driving in the near future lies not in hydrogen but in hybrid electric vehicles, like the Toyota Prius, the Ford Fusion hybrid and other similar hybrid cars.

其他人认为,在不久的将来,我们在燃油效率和环保驾驶方面的最佳选择不是氢气,而是混合动力电动汽车,如丰田 Prius、福特 Fusion hybrid 和其他类似的混合动力汽车。

UNIT 19　ADVANCED DRIVER-ASSISTANCE SYSTEMS

Advanced driver-assistance systems (ADASs) have become a salient feature for safety in modern vehicles. They are also a key underlying technology in emerging autonomous vehicles. State-of-the-art ADASs are primarily vision based, but light detection and ranging (lidar), radio detection and ranging (radar), and other advanced-sensing technologies are also becoming popular. A survey of different hardware and software ADAS technologies and their capabilities and limitations will be presented here.

Overview of Automotive System Safety

Safety in automotive systems has been a major concern since the early days of on-road vehicles. Several original equipment manufacturers (OEMs) have attempted to address this issue by developing various safety systems to protect occupants within a vehicle as well as prevent injuries to people outside the vehicle. These systems are mainly classified into two types: passive (or reactive) and active (or proactive). Passive safety systems protect vehicle occupants from injuries after a crash, e. g. , seat belts, air bags, and padded dashboards. Due to a consistent consumer demand for safer vehicles, passive safety systems that have been under continuous development for many decades have been augmented by active safety systems, which seek to prevent a crash from happening altogether. Active systems are one of the main areas of interest and have seen major growth in today's vehicles. Examples of such systems include lane keeping, automatic braking, and adaptive cruise control. These systems are commonly known as ADASs and are becoming increasingly popular as a way for automotive manufacturers to differentiate their offerings while promoting consumer safety.

With the increasing number of electronic control units and integration of various types of sensors, there are now sufficient computing capabilities in vehicles to support ADAS deployments. The different types of sensors, such as cameras, lidar, radar, and ultrasonic sensors, enable a variety of different ADAS solutions. Among them, the vision-based ADAS, which primarily uses cameras as vision sensors, is popular in most modern-day vehicles. Figure 19-1 shows some of the state-of-the-art ADAS features and the sensors used to implement them.

Modern-day ADASs are also key technologies to realize autonomous vehicles. But several challenges with the design, implementation, and operation of ADASs remain to be overcome. Some of these challenges include minimizing energy consumption, reducing response latency, adapting to changing weather conditions, and security.

UNIT 19　ADVANCED DRIVER-ASSISTANCE SYSTEMS

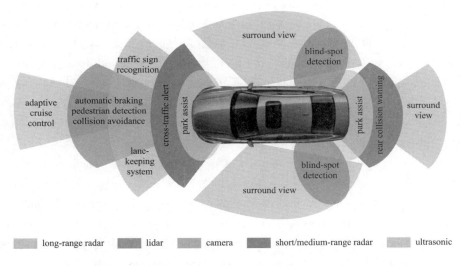

Figure 19-1　The state-of-the-art ADAS sensors used

ADAS Taxonomy

We propose a taxonomy of ADASs based on the type of sensors they use (Figure 19-2), as discussed next.

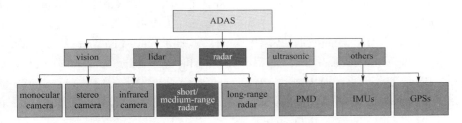

Figure 19-2　The taxonomy of an ADAS

PMD: photonic mixer device; IMUs: inertial measurement units; GPSs: global positioning systems

Vision Sensors

Cameras are the most commonly used vision sensors in vehicles. Vision-based ADAS uses one or more cameras to capture images and an embedded system to detect, analyze, and track different objects in them. In high-end ADAS, cameras are used to monitor both the inside and outside of the vehicle. Camera integration in modern vehicles is becoming more common because of its low cost and easy installation. At the 2018 Consumer Electronics Show, Mobileye stated that it is introducing smart cameras in millions of cars hitting the streets in 2018. In addition, laws such as (that mandate all vehicles manufactured from 1 May 2018 onward use vision-based ADAS) will further aid in camera integration. Cameras capture information such as color, contrast, and texture, which gives them a unique advantage over other sensors. Two types of cameras are often used in vision-based ADAS: monocular and stereo.

(1) Monocular Cameras. These camera systems have only one lens. As these systems have only one image output at any point of time, they have low image-processing requirements compared to those of other camera types. These cameras can be used for multiple applications, such as the detection of obstacles, pedestrians, lanes, and traffic signs. They can also be used for monitoring the driver inside a vehicle, e.g., for face and eye detection and head-pose analysis. But monocular camera images lack depth information and are, therefore, not reliable sensors for distance estimation. Some techniques allow approximating distance by identifying key features in the captured image frame and tracking their position when the camera is in motion.

(2) Stereo Cameras. These systems consist of two or more lenses, each with image sensors, separated by a certain distance (known as stereo base). Stereo cameras are useful in extracting three-dimensional (3-D) information from two or more two-dimensional images by matching stereo pairs (images from left and right sensors) and using a disparity map to estimate the relative depth of a scene. These cameras can be used for a variety of applications, such as traffic sign recognition, lane, pedestrian, and obstacle detection as well as distance estimation, with much greater accuracy compared to monocular cameras.

Stereo systems can be relied upon for accurate distance (depth) estimation over short distances, up to 30 m. In most production vehicles with stereo cameras, the cameras are located inside the vehicle, behind the rear-view mirror, angled slightly downward, and facing the road.

(3) IR Cameras. There are two main types of IR cameras. Active IR cameras use a near-IR light source (with wavelengths from 750 to 1,400 nm) built in the vehicle to illuminate the scene (which cannot be seen by the human eye) and a standard digital camera sensor to capture the reflected light. Passive IR cameras use an IR sensor, where every pixel on the IR sensor can be considered as a temperature sensor that can capture the thermal radiation emitted by any material. Unlike active IR cameras, passive IR cameras do not require any special illumination of the scene. Still, popular night-vision solutions mainly use active IR cameras to assist the driver by displaying video data on a screen during low light conditions.

Lidar

Lidar works by firing a laser beam at an object and then measuring the time taken for the light to bounce back to the sensor, to calculate the distance of an object. These systems can achieve high-resolution 3-D images and operate at longer ranges than camera systems. Some of the lidar scanners support surround-view sensors (that fire laser beams continuously in all directions), which can generate a 360° 3-D image of the surroundings with extremely accurate depth information. Lidar is becoming very popular in autonomous vehicles. Several prototype vehicles, have demonstrated the advantages of using lidar in autonomous driving. Lidar is useful for systems implementing automatic braking, object detection, collision avoidance, and more. Depending on the type of sensor, lidars for cars can have a range of up to 60m. Despite the aforementioned advantages, lidars are heavy, bulky in size, and expensive. Moreover, atmospheric conditions such as rain or fog can impact the coverage and accuracy of these systems. Emerging solid-state lidars have opened the possibility of powerful lidars that are significantly smaller and relatively inexpensive.

UNIT 19　ADVANCED DRIVER-ASSISTANCE SYSTEMS

Radar

Radar systems emit microwaves and estimate the speed and distance of an object by measuring the change in the frequency of the reflected wave as per the Doppler effect. Due to the longer wavelength of microwaves, they can travel much farther than optical light (e. g. , with lidar) and can detect objects at a longer distance. Unlike lidar, radar is not affected by foggy or rainy weather conditions and is relatively inexpensive. Depending on their operating distance range, radar systems can be classified as short range (0.2 to 30m), medium range (30 to 80m), or long range (80 to 200m). Cross-traffic alerts and blind-spot detection are some of the applications of short-/medium-range radars. These systems are often located at the corners of a vehicle. Adaptive cruise control is a long-range radar application, with the system located behind the front grill or under the bumper. Researchers have been developing algorithms to improve the performance of radar and reliability all while attempting to reduce the cost and power of the system.

Ultrasonic Sensors

Ultrasonic sensors use sound waves to measure the distance to an object. These sensors are mainly used for detecting objects very close to the vehicle. Some example applications include automatic parking and parallel parking assist. These sensors are mainly located under the front and rear bumper of the vehicle.

Others

A few other sensors are used to complement and improve the functionalities of those discussed earlier. For instance, photonic mixer device (PMD) cameras consist of an array of smart sensors that enable fast optical sensing and demodulation of incoherent light signals simultaneously. PMDs can support parallel target pixelwise distance measurement without scanning, thus resulting in faster imaging, high lateral resolution, and depth information. IMUs and GPSs are examples of systems that help improve the distance measurements with lidar and radar.

Vision-based ADASs

Vision-based ADASs rely on images from cameras and use computer vision principles to extract useful information.

Computer Vision Data Flow for ADASs

Figure 19-3 shows the steps involved in a vision-based system, each of which is discussed.

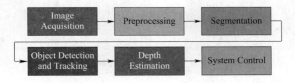

Figure 19-3　*The vision data flow for the ADAS used*

Image Acquisition

This refers to the process of capturing a frame from a video. The frame is often represented as a matrix of pixel data where each frame contains three channels of information, e. g., red, green, and blue (RGB) sets of pixels. Typical frame rates in ADASs range from 5 frames per second (fps) to 60 fps depending on the application. Applications that involve detection of vehicle proximity need a higher frame rate due to the rapid change in distance for cars on the road. In contrast, traffic sign detection does not demand a higher frame rate because only one frame of the sign needs to be captured for the sign to be detected.

Preprocessing

There are several common preprocessing steps needed to prepare an image for various computer vision algorithms, e. g., denoising, color enhancement, color space conversion, and image stabilization. A typical example of color space conversion is to convert the RGB color space to hue, saturation, and value to separate color from the intensity. Moreover, the hue channel is often used to separate out adverse effects (e. g., shadows, uneven lighting, and over-and underexposure) in the image to make tracking and detection easier.

Segmentation

This is the process of separating features from a frame. In analyzing an image, it is helpful to partition it into recognizable objects, e. g., identifying the road and sky in a frame as two different features. Various thresholding techniques are used to filter one class of pixels (e. g., the road) from another (e. g., the sky). One of the methods, e. g., exploits color information to detect a stop sign, where an algorithm may look for red in the image (typical for stop signs in the United States). Any pixels in that red range will be turned white, and anything that is not will be turned black, as shown in Figure 19-4a). This results in a binary image that is often used as a mask for finding the area of interest on the original image.

a) Binary stop signs　　b) Stop sign classification using optical character recognition

Figure 19-4　The stop sign detection

UNIT 19　ADVANCED DRIVER-ASSISTANCE SYSTEMS

Object Detection and Tracking

This is the process of classifying an object in an image (e.g., determining if an object ahead is a vehicle, sign, or pedestrian) and predicting its movement. It is often accomplished with various machine-learning (ML) algorithms. ML algorithms are provided large training data sets (thousands of images) to learn and differentiate between vehicles and common objects found around them. An example of an object detection method is called the cascade classifier, which was first presented in for face detection, on low-performance hardware systems.

Another common technique to train and classify images is using a convolutional neural network (CNN), which typically consists of an input layer, multiple hidden layers, and an output layer. The hidden layers consist of convolution and pooling layers that are used for feature extraction and a fully connected layer for classification. Examples of CNN frameworks used for vision applications include Caffe, Darknet, and MATLAB.

Depth Estimation

This step involves estimating the distance of an object in the image frame relative to the camera. There are two common methods for depth estimation: the use of a stereo camera to create a stereo pair and develop them to make a depth map and 3-D point cloud that allow a real-world reconstruction of the scene; and the use of a monocular camera and several state-of-the art techniques that use a subset of optical flow, calibration, and least squares techniques.

System Control

This is the last step in the vision data flow, which involves interpretation of the outputs from previous layers, as shown in the vision data flow diagram in Figure 19-3. This step requires a weighing of each layer in the vision pipeline to come up with a confidence value that can be used to make decisions. A major challenge at this step is a false detection with high confidence that would take priority over other information obtained from the previous layers. Thus, training with data that is correct and contains many orientations of the object to be classified is crucial to achieve high accuracy.

NEW WORDS

1. lidar	['laidɑː]	n.	激光雷达
2. taxonomy	[tæk'sɒnəmi]	n.	分类学,分类法
3. contrast	['kɒntrɑːst, kən'trɑːst]	n.	图像明暗对比度,反差
4. texture	['tekstʃə(r)]	n.	纹理,质地
5. bumper	['bʌmpə(r)]	n.	(汽车前后的)保险杠
6. algorithm	['ælgəriðəm]	n.	算法,计算程序
7. hue	[hjuː]	n.	色彩,色调
8. saturation	[ˌsætʃə'reiʃn]	n.	饱和状态,饱和度

PHRASES AND EXPRESSIONS

1. Advanced driver-assistance system（ADAS） 先进的驾驶人辅助系统
2. autonomous vehicle 自动驾驶车辆,无人驾驶汽车
3. State-of-the-art 最先进的,艺术级的
4. lane keeping 车道保持
5. ultrasonic sensor 超声波传感器
6. inertial measurement unit（IMU） 惯性测量单元
7. vision sensor 视觉传感器
8. monocular camera 单目摄像头（机）
9. stereo camera 立体摄像头（机）
10. convolutional neural network（CNN） 卷积神经网络

NOTES TO THE TEXT

1. There are several common preprocessing steps needed to prepare an image for various computer vision algorithms, e. g., denoising, color enhancement, color space conversion, and image stabilization.

对不同的计算机视觉算法,准备图像需要几个常见的预处理步骤,例如去噪、颜色增强、颜色空间转换和图像稳定。

2. Moreover, the hue channel is often used to separate out adverse effects (e. g., shadows, uneven lighting, and over-and underexposure) in the image to make tracking and detection easier.

此外,色调通道通常用于分离图像中的不利因素(例如阴影、不均匀照明、过度曝光和曝光不足),以使跟踪和检测更容易。

EXERCISES

Ⅰ. Answer the following questions

1. List the types of sensors for an ADAS.
2. Which types of cameras are often used in vision-based ADAS?
3. What are the advantages of lidar?
4. What are the steps of computer vision data flow involved in a vision-based system?

Ⅱ. Translate the following into Chinese

1. The most difficult function for intelligent vehicles is road scene understanding. This includes locating key landmarks: the road, other vehicles, pedestrians, traffic signals, road signs, and other unstructured obstacles. A more difficult challenge is speed control following the detection of event in the road scene.

2. Radar is generally used for obstacle detection at a distance, while infrared and ultrasound are used for close proximity obstacle detection. Laser ranging and image processing are used to more robustly recognize the road scene under various weather conditions. Certain road scene conditions such as road signs and traffic lights can only be understood using vision sensing.

UNIT 19　ADVANCED DRIVER-ASSISTANCE SYSTEMS

Reading Material: Blind Spot Detection (BSD) System

Blind spots consist of areas that cannot be seen by the driver from the back mirrors. Blind spot areas usually refer to the rear quarter blind spots, which are found in the rear of the vehicle in both sides. The biggest blind spot areas appear at the rear and right-hand side of the vehicle in case the drivers sit on the left-hand side and vice versa. In the meantime, other areas at the lower parts in the front and back of the vehicle can also be considered as blind spots (Figure 19-5). These areas are not visible from the driver's position due to the shape of the vehicle. For instance, such blind spots become larger when calculated for a truck driver. Moreover, vehicles in the adjacent lanes can be a part of the blind spots, thus making it very difficult or even impossible for the driver to see them only using the car's available mirrors. Finally, blind spots might arise in the right or the left side of the vehicle because of incidents or conditions that hinder the driver's vision for the respective sides.

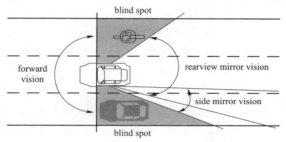

Figure 19-5　*Main Blind Spot areas* (*Mahapatra, Kumar, Khurana, & Mahajan*, 2008)

Considering the difficulty of drivers to detect vehicles in the vehicles' blind spots, there is a certain need to enhance safety around all types of vehicles. The Blind Spot Detection system aims in gathering information about objects and obstacles in blind spots of the vehicle's driver. Specifically, the system identifies whether a vehicle is present in the so-called "blind spot" area when the vehicle performs a lane change or overtaking manoeuvres. A variety of methods has been developed throughout the last decades in order to help drivers avoiding blind spot cause collisions.

Depending on the system's mechanism, the way the data is obtained may differ from infrared light techniques to cameras.

To obtain the required information the distance between the vehicle and the object, the speed of the object and the identity of the identified object have to be measured.

To begin with, the placement of extra mirrors and wide-angle lenses is the simplest applied method. The installation of such devices aims in broadening the driver's range of view. However, despite the method's simplicity, continuous alertness is still one of the driver's main responsibilities, while the blind spot areas are not totally reduced. In addition, in cases where additional mirrors are placed into trucks, areas of the truck are magnified in different ways. As a consequence, although some objects are found to be next to the truck, they only occupy a small part of the mirror's area and cannot be clearly observable.

A second approach for estimating the distance of an approaching vehicle is the use of radar sensors, which collect information from the surrounding road environment, translate it into quantitative data which is being processed, resulting to a warning to the driver in case a hazard or a collision is approaching. To be more specific, the radar uses either an ultrasonic distance detection system or an infrared distance detection radar to estimate the distance. In the first stage, when an object is detected, radio waves are spread and received at receiver-end of the sensors, while in the second stage of the system, the radio waves activate the circuit, the output of which is displayed by glowing LED's and audible signals. In certain cases, the detection of the vehicle's and object's shape is also possible. However, several system's drawbacks have been reported. Specifically, the low angular resolution of the range sensors is considered as the system's core disadvantage, while they provide a smaller view of the surrounding area. The range and the covered area of the blind spots is highly dependent on the number of the vehicular radars installed. Finally, such radars have restricted detection distance, increasing the difficulty of detecting a moving vehicle in a large area.

Another type of sensor offering higher angular resolution is the laser scanner. Nevertheless, due to the fact that laser range sensors are able to detect objects only in a thin two-dimensional plane, their use in this application is quite limited.

As far as ultrasonic sensors are concerned, on the one hand, this category of sensors has been advantageous in terms of cost-efficiency. On the other hand, a lot of factors have contributed to its limited use. The system's sensitivity to external instabilities such as specific environmental conditions (e.g. rain, wind) has been hindering the use of the sensor to high-speed applications. Another issue raised in the use of ultrasonic sensors is the small amount of information that is included in the signal given to the drivers. Compared to more expensive sensor systems, like radar or lidar, which offer a sufficient angular resolution, ultrasonic sensors usually have a huge aperture. As a result, the difficulty is distinguishing the location of a sound.

Given the deficiencies of the aforementioned methods, developments with other directions have taken place in order to detect moving obstacles. Matuszyk et al. (2004) suggested a different approach for monitoring vehicle blind spots, called computer vision. In their study, stereo panoramic vision has proved to be able to create disparity maps from which objects can be separated. According to the study's results, a stereo panoramic sensor can be used to reliably estimate the location of a vehicle with perfect angular accuracy in the direction of the azimuth. Finally, this kind of sensor owns the benefit of providing higher angular resolution and sensitivity than the other driver assistance systems.

Image or vision-based methods consist another widely applied vehicle detection system. In contrast to the previously described sensors, cameras are cheap passive devices operating with no beams or waves. Given that, they are more suitable for mass production in the automotive industry and substantial application on roads and highways.

In vision-based systems, cameras are installed on both sides of the vehicle attempting to gather images of blind spots. A display device allows the driver to watch the images of the blind spots. A variety of detection and tracking technologies for image-based detection system development have been found in literature. The latter refer to motion information, knowledge based as well as optical flow methods.

To elaborate on the differences between the latter techniques, knowledge-based ways implement color and edge information so as to identify approaching moving vehicles from a single image. On the

UNIT 19　ADVANCED DRIVER-ASSISTANCE SYSTEMS

other hand, motion information methods use a series of images in order to achieve vehicle detections, while employing homogeneous optical flow has been used to detect overtaking vehicle, providing more robust results than camera shocks and vibrations. Sotelo et al. (2007), elaborate on the way a vehicle is detected with optical flow analysis. Any object whose front part looks like the frontal part of a vehicle is considered to be one. In this way, a big enough object in the image that produces optical flow in the direction of the system equipped vehicle and has a frontal part similar to the previously described one, is validated as car entering the blind spot. As for the vehicle's position, the image is analyzed and the position in it is computed and tracked with the help of a Kalman filter. Vehicle tracking carries on until the vehicle disappears, leading to an alarm signal that informs the driver that a vehicle has entered the blind spot.

Given the fact that these three technologies require the consumption of a huge number of resources to process the needed images, Chen and Chen (2009) have proposed a new method. The method includes the transfer of two-dimensional road data into one-dimension lane information through the use of the estimation of the image entropy, followed by a differentiation process which determines the vehicle's position. Afterwards, the position of a moving object is determined by the data of two lanes which is taken from images of time series. Based on their experiment, the authors claim that the accuracy of the system reaches more than 90%, while the mean distance for the warning area is approximately 8 meters. Thus, the results present a system which is satisfactory enough as well as a perfect algorithm for the detection of an approaching vehicle from an imaging system. Hence, the technology is becoming broadly applied both for its low cost and the wide area of vision.

Having collected the necessary data, control of the vehicle is influenced by an audio or visual warning device or a steering wheel control device. In other cases, a controller is coupled to the indicator. The former creates a size signal and position signal for a rear-approaching vehicle. The controller activates an indicator when a rear-approaching vehicle enters a blind spot in accordance to the size signal and position signal.

In contrast with ACC, BSD is applied for the lateral control of the vehicle and may also result in undesirable events in case of the system's malfunctions or due to inappropriate driver response. The probabilities for that increase when the system has to be used by novice drivers. Besides speed and distance adaptation, they lack the experience and the cognitive skills to perceive the surrounding hazards. Thus, their reaction and behavior regarding the use of a blind spot detection system will be tested and studied.

NEW WORDS

1. Obstacle　　　　['ɒbstəkl]　　　　　n. 障碍物(绊脚石,障碍栅栏)
2. hinder　　　　　['hɪndə(r)]　　　　vt. & vi. 阻碍,妨碍
3. approach　　　　[ə'prəʊtʃ]　　　　　v. 接近,临近
4. aperture　　　　['æpətʃə(r)]　　　　n. (照相机、望远镜等的)光圈,孔径
5. azimuth　　　　['æzɪməθ]　　　　　n. 方位角,航向

PHRASES AND EXPRESSIONS

1. blind spot detection　　　　　　　　盲点侦测系统,盲区检测
2. vice versa　　　　　　　　　　　　反之亦然,反过来也一样
3. angular resolution　　　　　　　　　角坐标分辨率,角度分辨率
4. stereo panoramic vision　　　　　　立体全景视觉
5. disparity map　　　　　　　　　　　视差图
6. image entropy　　　　　　　　　　　图像熵

NOTES

A second approach for estimating the distance of an approaching vehicle is the use of radar sensors, which collect information from the surrounding road environment, translate it into quantitative data which is being processed, resulting to a warning to the driver in case a hazard or a collision is approaching.

第二种估算接近车辆距离的方法是使用雷达传感器,该传感器从周围道路环境收集信息,将其转换为正在处理的定量数据,在危险或碰撞临近时向驾驶人发出警告。

UNIT 20　CONNECTED VEHICLES

Next generation of vehicle safety applications will hinge on connectivity. It is also widely accepted notion that connectivity will be key enabling technology for autonomous driving. That connectivity may include Vehicle to Vehicle (V2V), Vehicle to Infrastructure (V2I), and Vehicle to Pedestrian (V2P) communications. One of the questions is "what technology will prevail?" Lower layers of Dedicated Short-Range Communication (DSRC) are defined in IEEE 802.11. The automotive industry, academia, and government have been evaluating DSRC since late 1990s. On the other side, recently the cellular industry has taken an interest in developing standards for vehicular usage. DSRC is based on relatively old physical layer protocol. But, it has been tested and proven to meet requirements for the vast majority of the cooperative safety applications in term of range and latency. The newer 5G cellular approach is not thoroughly tested for cooperative vehicle safety. It does offer potentially better communication performance and a path for system upgradeability. Whichever technology prevails, safety communication requirements will remain unchanged: high availability and low latency. Vehicle to everything (V2X) communications needs to accommodate fast-moving vehicles. Vehicles in various traffic situations need to communicate with low latency. End to end latency should be in the order of 100 ms. It is necessary for V2X communications to be highly available. In other words, V2X is not to compete with other crowded communications networks such as Wi-Fi and cellular networks.

DSRC historically evolved from Wi-Fi. In late 1990s, when the DSRC research was in its infancy, the best wireless technology was Wi-Fi. The researchers used Wi-Fi chipsets for the V2X communication development. More recently dedicated chipsets for DSRC started to take a foothold. IEEE task force introduced DSRC physical layer modifications in 802.11 as an 802.11p amendment. The amendment was fully integrated into 2012 version of the 802.11 standard. Aims of modifications are to reduce overhead, to limit out of band interference, and make provisions for outdoor multi-path and higher vehicle speeds. In the US, IEEE standards define lower layers of DSRC. SAE documents define the application layer. IEEE 802.11 details physical and lower Media Access Control (MAC) layers. IEEE 1609.4 describes upper MAC layer. IEEE 802.4 covers logical link control (LLC) layer. IEEE 1609.3 defines Network and Transportation layers. IEEE 1609.2 covers security. Finally, SAE J2735 and J2945 specify application layer. Federal Communications Commission (FCC) allocated 75 MHz for V2X communication in 1999. At that time FCC crafted the usage for manually driven vehicles. The main usage of V2X indents to improve travelers' safety. Other approved usages include decreasing traffic congestion, air pollution, and fuel consumption. In the future, V2X communication may extend to include the needs of the autonomous vehicles.

V2X communication is a set of communication protocols, experiments, and pilot deployments.

As such, V2X communications are addressing the needs of current and future travelers. It is important that V2X is a direct communication. For example, V2V communication is the exchange of the information directly between vehicles without intermediaries such as cell-phone infrastructure or Wi-Fi hotspot. DSRC-V2V does not require infrastructure to facilitate the communication between vehicles. Another mode of communication is Vehicle to Infrastructure (V2I). V2I communication is the exchange of information between vehicles and roadside infrastructure. For example, a RoadSide Unit (RSU) can be connected to a signal controller at an intersection. RSU sends out intersection map (MAP) message and traffic signal status message know as Signal Phase and Timing (SPaT) message. Next in line is Vehicle to Pedestrian (V2P) communication. V2P involves exchanging information between vehicles and pedestrians. For example, DSRC enabled smartphone can serve as a pedestrian communication device. Implementation of the V2X in a vehicle consists of the several standard components. The components include localization device, computation platform, HMI interface and DSRC transceiver. Collection of these components is commonly called On-Board Equipment (OBE). Fully implemented OEM V2X system may include connections to the internal vehicle bus. Aftermarket devices may not have access to the internal vehicle bus.

The most important message in V2V communication is Basic Safety Message (BSM). A DSRC equipped vehicle broadcasts BSMs to all other vehicles in its vicinity. BSM consists of crucial information about the vehicle such as position and vehicle dynamics. Some elements of the BSM are latitude, longitude, elevation, speed, heading, brake status, accelerations, dimensions, and path history and path prediction. Once a vehicle receives BSM from a remote vehicle it is able to compute collision probability and if needed warns the driver.

V2V cooperative safety applications are addressing immediate situations. These situations include collision avoidance and traffic scene awareness. For example, a very typical V2V application is Electronic Emergency Brake Light (EEBL). EEBL informs the driver when a vehicle in front brakes hard. EEBL helps the driver by giving an early notification that the leading vehicle is braking hard. EEBL warns even in the case of limited driver's visibility (e.g. a large truck is blocking the driver's view, heavy fog or rain). Another V2V example is cooperative Forward Collision Warning (FCW). FCW issues a warning to the driver of the host vehicle in case of an impending front-end collision. For example, a slow-moving vehicle ahead in the same lane and direction of travel is a candidate for FCW warning. FCW helps drivers avoid a collision in the forward path of travel. Blind Spot Warning (BSW) provides a notification to the driver when a remote vehicle is in its blind spot. Left Turn Assist (LTA) warns the driver in case it is unsafe to make a left turn at an intersection. For example, a remote vehicle approaches from the opposite direction in the adjacent lane. Intersection Movement Assist (IMA) issues a warning to the driver in case of an impending side collision. A remote vehicle driving in a perpendicular direction to the ego vehicle is a candidate for IMA warning. This often happens at an intersection. Control Loss Warning (CLW) issues a warning in case of a possible collision with a remote vehicle of which the driver has lost control. CLW helps avoid or mitigate collisions in a variety of traffic scenarios.

Like BSM, a Pedestrian Safety Message (PSM) is being transmitted from a smartphone. PSM consists of vital pedestrian data. The data include latitude, longitude, elevation, speed, heading,

UNIT 20   CONNECTED VEHICLES

and dimensions. PSM has similar but less information than BSM. V2P collision avoidance application works in a similar fashion to V2V. An aim of V2P cooperative safety applications is an increase in driver awareness. Candidates for V2P applications are vulnerable road users (generally pedestrians and cyclists). Pedestrian collision avoidance application warns the driver of impending pedestrians. For example, a vehicle would warn the driver in case a pedestrian, crossing the street, jumps in front of the moving vehicle.

V2I applications are usually local in character. An example is Cooperative Intersection Collision Avoidance Systems (CICAS). CICAS can issue traffic signal violation warning to the driver if he is about to run the red light. Pothole Detection is an example collaborative V2I application. Pothole Detection leverage collaboration from many vehicles and the infrastructure. Vehicles share information with infrastructure about their location and sudden events. One type of events includes maneuvers the driver is taking to avoid the pothole. Another type of events includes a sudden change in vertical acceleration of the vehicle going over a pothole. The infrastructure analyzes many such reports from vehicles. The infrastructure then sends aggregated data informing the vehicles about the existence of a pothole.

A unique feature of the V2X technology is the ability to detect threats in nonline of sight situations. Many safety applications such as FCW, BSW and pedestrian collision warning are implemented using a traditional line of sight sensors such as camera or radars. However, cameras and radars cannot detect vehicles and pedestrians in nonline of sight scenarios such as a blind intersection or obstructed traffic. V2X is envisioned to fill "the gap" and enhance the sensing ability of the vehicle. A traditional line-of-sight sensor (e.g. camera or radar) is estimating information such as relative position, speed, direction and infer the braking status of the targets whereas V2X is actually getting this information from the best possible sensors, from the remote vehicle internal bus itself.

Positioning

Benefits of connectivity in Intelligent Transportation Systems (ITS), including safety and convenience, arise from information shared between connected vehicles, other connected traffic participants, and road infrastructure. An essential shared set of information includes position (location) and velocity because they allow the connected device to know the presence and predict behavior of other relevant traffic, even by relying solely on the exchanged data in absence of other sensors. This further enables an in-vehicle system to warn the human driver, or even automatically initiate corrective actions. Satellite-based positioning systems, including the American Global Positioning System (GPS) and also other such Global Navigation Satellite Systems (GNSS), provide globally referenced location and velocity that are often sufficiently accurate for many ITS applications, but their performance suffers in obstructed skies. Integration of other positioning-relevant data through sensor fusion, such as that from inertial, ranging, and vision sensors, but also from maps, improves positioning robustness across diverse environments. Application of advanced satellite-based positioning algorithms, such as Differential GPS (DGPS), Real-Time Kinematic (RTK), and precise point positioning (PPP), to data received from ground reference stations, allows decimeter-level global positioning accuracy and improved integrity measures that further extend the scope of supported ITS applications. The DSRC standards, intended for ITS applications, conveniently provide for sharing of basic position data, local high-definition map data, as well as data for enabling high accuracy positioning. Planned improvements and expansions of GNSS systems, and trends of increasing performance-to-cost ratio of positioning-aiding sensors, suggest future gains in positioning accuracy, integrity, and availability. Positioning performance of currently available and expected future positioning solutions is assessed against their cost. There are currently available automotive-grade and ITS suitable positioning systems that achieve lane-level accuracy, conditions-dependent, with some uncertainty. More advanced systems are expected to provide within-lane positioning with tight integrity measures.

Human Machine Interface

Every device that is meant for people to use, cars included, should provide means that enable successful interaction. This is what Human Computer Interaction (HMI) is all about: how to design an interface that enables intuitive, simple and timely interaction with a machine. Depending on the nature of the task some of these aspects may have higher priority compared to others. However, all three are extremely important in vehicles, because driving is a complex hands-busy, eyes-busy activity that poses both physical and cognitive load on drivers. In a situation like this, it is necessary for an HMI to provide adequate information to drivers without negatively affecting their primary task of driving. Information presented to drivers can be roughly divided in two categories: infotainment and safety. Infotainment is mostly concerned with convenience features in vehicles, such as navigation, music, climate control, phone, etc. V2X communication enables a completely new horizon of sensing that is not achievable with any of the currently available vehicle sensors, such as radar, lidar, camera, etc.. This makes it possible to design completely new safety-related and Advanced Driver Assistance Systems (ADAS) compared to what was possible before. In any case, the corresponding HMI should effectively explain the situation on the road and stimulate drivers to perform adequate actions (such as avoiding an obstacle or preemptive braking). This can be achieved by using any kinds of modalities (and their combinations) that influence people's basic senses: sight, hearing, touch, smell and taste.

V2V Vehicle Safety Communication

National Highway Traffic Safety Administration (NTHSA) has been interested in V2V communication as the next step in addressing grooving rates of fatalities from vehicle related crashes. Today's crash avoidance technologies depend on on-board sensors like camera and radar to provide awareness input to the safety applications. These applications are warning the driver of imminent danger or sometimes even act on the driver's behalf. However, even technologies like those cannot predict a crash that might happen because of a vehicle which is not very close or not in the line of sight to the host vehicle. A technology that can "see" through another vehicle or obstacles like buildings and predict a danger can fill these gaps and reduce crashes drastically. V2V communications can provide vehicles the ability to talk to each other and therefore see around

UNIT 20 CONNECTED VEHICLES

corners and through the obstacles over a longer distance compared to the current on-board sensors. It is estimated that V2X communications address up to 80% of the unimpaired crashes. By means of Notice of Proposed Rulemaking (NPRM), NHTSA is working towards standardization of V2V communications and potentially mandating the broadcast of vehicle data (e. g. GPS coordinates, speed, acceleration) over DSRC through V2V. A vehicle needs an On-Board Unit (OBU) to establish the V2V communication with other vehicles also equipped with OBUs or V2I communication with the traffic infrastructure equipped with Road-Side Units (RSUs). In general, an OBU has a DSRC radio for transmission and reception, GNSS receiver, a processor, and several interfaces (e. g. CAN, Ethernet, GPS) for obtaining the vehicle data. BSM is a broadcast message typically transmitted frequently up to 10 times a second. Content of BSM includes vehicle information such as vehicle speed, location, and brake status. Safety applications use the remote vehicles (RVs) data from BSM and Host Vehicle (HV) data from the OBU interfaces like CAN and GNSS to predict a potential crash and alert the driver. V2V messages could also potentially be fused with onboard sensors like Radar, LiDAR, and Camera to improve the confidence level of vehicle detection for safety applications or even for autonomous driving to some extent. Majority of the crash scenarios can be addressed by the following safety applications: Forward Collision Warning (FCW), Electronic Emergency Brake Light (EEBL), Intersection Move Assist (IMA), Left Turn Assist (LTA), Do Not Pass Warning (DNPW), and Blind Spot Warning/Lane Change Warning (BSW/LCW).

NEW WORDS

1. prevail [pri'veil] v. 流行,盛行,被接受,战胜
2. latency ['leitənsi] n. 延迟,时延
3. amendment [ə'mendmənt] n. 修改,修订,修正案
4. allocate ['æləkeit] v. 分配,分派,划拨
5. Infrastructure ['infrəstrʌktʃə(r)] n. 基础设施,基础建设
6. Pedestrian [pə'destriən] n. 行人,步行者
7. cyclist ['saiklist] n. 骑自行车的人
8. Pothole ['pɒthəʊl] n. 壶穴,坑洼,坑槽
9. leverage ['liːvəridʒ] v. 发挥杠杆作用,利用
10. inertial [i'nɜːʃl] adj. 不活泼的,惯性的
11. robustness [rəʊ'bʌstnəs] n. 鲁棒性
12. diverse [dai'vɜːs] adj. 形形色色的,不同的
13. intuitive [in'tjuːitiv] adj. 直觉的,直观的

PHRASES AND EXPRESSIONS

1. connected vehicles   联网车辆,网联汽车
2. hinge on   取决于……,以……为转移
3. Dedicated Short-Range Communication (DSRC)   专用短程通信
4. site situations   现场情况

5. nonline of sight 非视距,非直视
6. Human Machine Interface 人机界面
7. Advanced Driver Assistance Systems (ADAS) 高级驾驶人辅助系统

NOTES TO THE TEXT

1. Integration of other positioning-relevant data through sensor fusion, such as that from inertial, ranging, and vision sensors, but also from maps, improves positioning robustness across diverse environments.

通过传感器融合集成其他与位置相关的数据,例如来自惯性、测距和视觉传感器的数据,以及来自地图的数据,可以提高不同环境下的定位鲁棒性。

2. A technology that can "see" through another vehicle or obstacles like buildings and predict a danger can fill these gaps and reduce crashes drastically.

一种能够透过另一辆汽车或建筑物等障碍物"看到"并预测危险的技术可以填补这些空白,并大幅减少碰撞。

EXERCISES

Ⅰ. Answer the following questions

1. What is the most important message in V2V communication?
2. What are the benefits of V2V communication?
3. What is the feature of the V2X technology?
4. How to improve positioning accurate of a connected vehicle across diverse environments?
5. What are the design requirements of HMI of connected vehicles?

Ⅱ. Translate the following into Chinese

1. The connected vehicles are important components of intelligent transportation systems (ITS) in which vehicles communicate with each other and with communications infrastructure to exchange safety messages and other critical information (e.g., traffic and road conditions).

2. As the autonomous vehicles are being equipped with many sensors such as cameras, RADAR, LIDAR, and mechanical control units, etc. These sensors share critical sensor information with onboard devices through CAN bus and with other nearby vehicles as well.

3. There are three modes of communications in vehicular networks: vehicle-to-vehicle (V2V), infrastructure-to-infrastructure (I2I), and vehicle-to infrastructure (V2I). Besides these, there are two more types of communication — vehicle to pedestrian (V2P) and vehicle to anything (V2X) — that are expected to become part of the future connected vehicular ecosystem.

Reading Material: Vehicle to Infrastructure Communications

Vehicle to Infrastructure communications (V2I) is an attractive solution for many connected vehicles problems. As such, V2I technology has been a focal point for extensive Intelligent Transportation Systems (ITS) research and deployment efforts in the recent few years. This activity has led to a leap in the technology readiness for mass deployment and adoption. Examples of V2I technology advantages are provided in the following:

(1) Early benefit. Benefit to early connected vehicle adopters is probably the main driver behind the recent push for V2I research and deployment in the United States. Projecting into the future, it may take up to 10 years from a specific date to realize a 50% market penetration rate for DSRC equipped vehicles assuming all new vehicles are equipped starting from this date. Customer purchasing vehicles that are equipped with V2V technology will suffer from limited benefit resulting from rare encounters between V2V vehicles during that time. V2I technology can address this issue by providing benefit to early V2V adopters resulting from interaction with infrastructure instead of other equipped vehicles.

(2) Interface to road infrastructure. Vehicles interact with different type of roadway infrastructure during their everyday commute. This ranges from traffic lights and road signs all the way to the pavement markings. Improving this interaction by adding a communication link between vehicles and roadway infrastructure allows for more information, at higher distances, to be conveyed to vehicles from the infrastructure and the vice versa leading to safety and mobility benefits among others.

(3) Expanding connected vehicle benefits to sparsely populated areas. V2I can be used to convey safety information (e.g. spot weather information) in a suburban and rural area where V2V communication may not be an option. Infrastructure may have its own information to be shared with vehicles, such as traffic light controller data or data collected from weather sensor. Alternatively, infrastructure may relay information transmitted from other vehicles that passed through an area in the recent past (e.g. Traction Control System activation inferring a slippery road).

(4) Assist future autonomous vehicle functionality. Adding future automated vehicles into the equation. V2I connectivity extends from just providing safety and mobility value to becoming a necessity. Automated vehicles operation requires certain information about the roadway, such as up to date HD maps, which can be provided by the infrastructure.

Several wireless communication technologies are being investigated in the industry and research community to support V2I communications. Examples of these technologies include DSRC, cellular communications, satellite communication and infrared communications. Each of these technologies has their advantages and disadvantages in terms of cost, availability and technical performance. However, it may be concluded that DSRC is currently the front-runner judging from the ongoing deployment effort across the United States. Notably, 5G cellular communication has been gaining momentum recently as a promising future technology that may compete with DSRC.

MapData (MAP)

This message offers the receiving side with a full description of an intersection, or multiple intersections, geometry. Such information enables roadway users, such as cars, motorcycles or pedestrians, to localize themselves at a lane-level accuracy within the intersection area. Lane level localization within an intersection or a corridor enable several applications, such as Red-Light Violation Warning.

Message Structure

An overview of MAP message architecture including some of the essential elements structure can be seen in Figure 20-1. The standard defines additional optional and "placeholder" data frames and elements which the reader can explore further in the SAE J2735 document if interested.

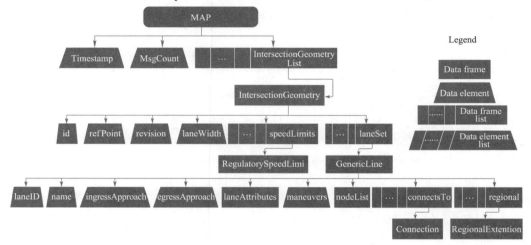

Figure 20-1   MAP message architecture

MAP message can describe multiple intersections through DF_IntersectionGeometry data frame, each with a regionally unique identifier (DE_IntersectionID). An RSU transmitting MAP is also required to send the message revision number using DE_MsgCount. Going to further lower layers in DF_IntersectionGeometry we find the following fields that are used for lanes geometry description:

(1) refPoint: a WGS-84 coordinate system location that includes longitude, latitude and optionally altitude. This location serves as a reference point using which, any point in the intersection geometry can be described by taking offsets to the reference point instead of using the full coordinates of that point. This method of using offsets to a reference point to represent geometry improves efficient by reducing the size of the MAP message.

(2) laneWidth: an optional field used to provide the width for all lanes in the intersection in centimeters unless otherwise specified in the following data frames/elements.

(3) speedLimits: an optional list providing regulatory speeds for all lanes in the intersection unless otherwise specified in the lane description.

(4) laneSet: this a mandatory list that contains all of the details regarding all lanes geometry in the intersection. laneSet is represented by DF_LaneList in the stan-dard, which is a sequence of up to 255 DF_GenericLane. Each DF_GenericLane contains information about a single lane in the intersection:

(a) laneID: a unique ID assigned to the corresponding lane in the intersection.

(b) name: an optional descriptive name that can be used for debugging purposes.

(c) ingressApproach and egressApproach: optional unique indexes for different approaches in the intersection roads for both ingress and egress direction to the intersection respectively.

(d) laneAttributes: a field containing attributes for a lane including lane angles and speed limits.

(e) maneuvers: optional field that specifies the allowed maneuvers on a lane including straight, right, left, left or right turn on red, lane change, no stop, yield, move after a full a stop and proceed with caution.

(f) nodeList: a list of nodes, each including a lateral offset, longitudinal offset and optional altitude offset and lane width, representing the lane geometry. This is the key field in MAP message that vehicles would use to map match themselves to a particular lane, and location within a lane. Such localization information can then be used for a variety of applications including Red Light Violation Warning.

(g) connectsTo: an optional field comprising a list of lanes that connect to this particular lane beyond the stop bar.

(h) overlays: a list of lanes that have overlapping paths with the current lane.

(i) regional: this an additional optional field reserved for regions that may require certain additions to the message.

NEW WORDS

1. deployment   [di'plɔimənt]   n. 部署, 调集
2. commute   [kə'mju:t]   v. 通勤; n. 上下班路程
3. field   [fi:ld]   n. 〈计〉字段

PHRASES AND EXPRESSIONS

1. pavement markings   路面标线
2. unique identifier   唯一标识符
3. reference point   参考点
4. unless otherwise specified   除另有说明者外, 除非另有说明
5. lane width   车道宽度
6. ingress Approach and egress Approach   入口通道和出口通道

NOTES

Improving this interaction by adding a communication link between vehicles and roadway infrastructure allows for more information, at higher distances, to be conveyed to vehicles from the infrastructure and the vice versa leading to safety and mobility benefits among others.

通过在车辆和道路基础设施之间添加通信链路来改善交互, 可以实现在更远距离将更多信息从基础设施传输到车辆, 反之亦然, 从而提高安全性和机动性。

APPENDIX A ABBREVIATIONS OF AUTOMOTIVE ENGLISH

ABS	anti-lock brake system	防抱死制动系统
AC	alternating current	交流电
A/C	air conditioner 或 air conditioning	空调器,空调
ACC	adaptive cruise control	自适应巡航控制
ACL	air cleaner	空气滤清器
ACT	air charge temperature	进气温度
ADAS	advanced driver assistance systems	高级驾驶人辅助系统
AEB	automatic emergency braking	自动紧急制动
A/F	air fuel ratio	空燃比
AH 或 a-h	ampere-hour	安·时
ANT	antenna	天线
AP	accelerator pedal	加速踏板
API	American Petroleum Institute	美国石油协会
APP	accelerator pedal position	加速踏板位置
APV	all purpose vehicle	多用途车辆
ASE	Automotive Service Excellence	(美国)汽车维修技能鉴定协会
ASM	assembly	总成
ASR	anti-slip regulation	防滑调节,牵引力控制
A/T 或 AT	automatic transmission[transaxle]	自动变速器[变速驱动桥]
ATDC	after top dead center	上止点后
ATF	automatic transmission fluid	自动变速器液
ATM	automatic transmission	自动变速器
AUTO	automatic	自动的
AVG	average	平均值
AWD	all wheel drive	全轮驱动
BA	brake assist	辅助制动装置
BARO	barometric pressure	气压,大气压力
BAT	battery	蓄电池

APPENDIX A ABBREVIATIONS OF AUTOMOTIVE ENGLISH

Continued

BEV	battery electric vehicle	纯电动汽车
BCU	battery control unit	蓄电池控制单元
BDC	bottom dead center	下止点
BHP 或 b. h. p	brake horsepower	制动功率
B/L	bi-level	(空调出风)分层通风,双向
BMS	battery management system	蓄电池管理系统
BMW	Bayerische Motoren Werke	宝马汽车公司
BP	brake pressure	制动压力
BSD	blind spot detection	盲点侦测系统,盲区检测
BSM	basic safety message	基本安全信息
BTDC	before top dead center	上止点前
CAFE	corporate average fuel economy	全公司平均油耗
CAN	controller area network	控制器局域网
CANP	canister purge	炭罐脱附
CB	circuit breaker	电路断路器
CBE	cab-behind-engine	发动机前置
CCC	converter clutch control	变矩器锁止离合器控制
CD	coefficient of drag	空气阻力系数
CDI	capacitive discharge ignition	电容放电点火
CFI	continuous fuel injection	连续燃油喷射
CFI	central fuel injection	节气门体燃油喷射
CG	center of gravity	重心
CHG	charging	充电
CHK ENG	check engine	(警告灯)检查发动机
CHMSL	center high mount stop lamp	中置高位制动灯
CI	①central injection ②compression ignition	①节气门体燃油喷射 ②压燃
CIS	continuous injection system	连续燃油喷射系统
CIS-E	continuous injection system-electronic	电控连续燃油喷射系统
CKD	completely knocked down kits	全散件组装
CKT	circuit	电路
CKP	crankshaft position	曲轴位置
CKPS	crankshaft position sensor	曲轴位置传感器
CL	①closed loop ②clutch	①闭环 ②离合器
CNG	compressed natural gas	压缩天然气
COE	cab over engine	平头驾驶室

		Continued
CP	crankshaft position	曲轴位置
CPE	coupe	双门乘用车
CPU	central processing unit	中央处理器
CPS	crankshaft position sensor	曲轴位置传感器
CTO 或 CTOX	continuous trap oxidizer	连续捕集式氧化器
CV	①commercial vehicle ②constant velocity	①商用车 ②等速
CVJ 或 CV joint	constant velocity joint	等速万向节
CVT	continuously variable transmission	无级变速器
CW	curb weight	整备质量
CYL 或 cyl	cylinder	汽缸
DC	①direct current ②drag coefficient	①直流电 ②空气阻力系数
DEF	defogger	除雾器
DFI	direct fuel injection	（柴油机）直接燃油喷射
DFI	digital fuel injection	数字燃油喷射,多点燃油喷射
DFL	deflector	导流板
DI	direct ignition	直接点火,无分电器点火
DI	direct injection	直接燃油喷射,直喷
DID	direct injection diesel	直喷式柴油机
DIFF	differential	差速器
DIN		德国工业标准
DIS	direct ignition system	直接点火系统
DLC	data link connector	数据(通信)链路连接器
DLX 或 DX	deluxe	豪华的,高级的
DMCM	drive motor control module	驱动电动机控制模块
DNPW	do not pass warning	禁止超车警告
DOHC 或 dohc	double overhead camshafts	双顶置凸轮轴
DOT	Department of Transportation	(美)交通部
DRL	daytime running lamps	日间行车灯
DSRC	dedicated short-range communication	专用短程通信
DTC	diagnostic trouble code	诊断故障码
DTM	diagnostic test mode	诊断测试模块
EATX	electronic automatic transaxle	电控自动变速驱动桥
EBD	electric brake force distribution	电控制动力分配
EC	engine control	发动机控制
ECCS	electronic concentrated engine control system	发动机电子集中控制系统

APPENDIX A ABBREVIATIONS OF AUTOMOTIVE ENGLISH

Continued

ECD	electronic control diesel	电子控制柴油机
ECI-MULTI	electronically controlled injection multiport	电控多点燃油喷射
ECL	engine coolant level	发动机冷却液面
ECM	electronic control module	电子控制模块
	engine control module	发动机控制模块
ECON	economy	经济,节约
ECT	electronic controlled transmission	电子控制(自动)变速器
	electronic controlled transaxle	电子控制(自动)变速驱动桥
	engine coolant temperature	发动机冷却液温度
ECU	electronic control unit	电子控制单元
EDF	electro-drive fan	电动风扇
EEBL	electronic emergency brake light	电子紧急制动灯
EEC	electronic engine control	发动机电子控制
EECS	evaporative emission control system	蒸发排放物控制系统
EFI	electronic fuel injection	电子控制燃油喷射
EGR	exhaust gas recirculation	废气再循环
EHC	electrically heated catalyst	电加热催化器
EI	electronic ignition	电子点火
ELB	electrically controlled braking system	电控制动系统
ELR	emergency locking retractor	(安全带)紧急锁止式卷收器
EM	engine modification	发动机修正
EMC	electromagnetic compatibility	电磁兼容性
EMR	engine maintenance reminder	发动机维护提醒器
ENG	engine	发动机
EPA	Environmental Protection Agency	(美)环保署[局]
EPS	electric power steering	电子助力转向
ESA	electronic spark advance	电子(控制)点火提前
ESP	electronic stability program	电子稳定程序
ESC	electronic stability control	电子稳定控制
ESS	energy storage system	储能系统
ETC	electronic throttle control	电子节气门控制(装置)
ETCS-i	electronic throttle control system intelligent	智能型电子节气门控制装置
EV	①electric vehicle ②exhaust valve	①电动汽车 ②排气门
EVAP	evaporative emission	蒸发排放物
EVP	exhaust gas recirculation valve position	废气再循环阀位置

Continued

EVR	exhaust gas recirculation vacuum regulator	废气再循环真空调节器
FBC	feed back control	反馈控制
FC	①fan control ② fuel cell(s)	①风扇控制 ②燃料电池
FCEV	fuel cellelectric vehicle	燃料电池电动汽车
FCHEV	fuel cell hybridelectric vehicle	燃料电池混合动力电动汽车
FCW	forward collision warning	前向碰撞警告
FE	fuel economy	燃油经济性
FF	front-engine front-wheel-drive	前置发动机前轮驱动
FI	fuel injections	燃油喷射
FMVSS	Federal Motor Vehicle Safety Standard	(美)联邦汽车安全标准
FP F/P	fuel pump	燃油泵
Fr	front	前
f/r	front/rear	前/后
FR	front-engine rear-wheel-drive	发动机前置后轮驱动
FRP	fuel rail pressure	燃油轨油压
FRZF	freeze frame	(显示器用字符)保持帧
FTP	fuel tank pressure	燃油箱压力
FUEL PRES	fuel pressure	(显示器用字符)燃油压力
FUEL SYS	fuel system status	(显示器用字符)燃油系状况
FWD	①front wheel drive ② four wheel drive	①前轮驱动 ②四轮驱动
fwd	forward	向前的,(变速器)前进挡
F4WD	full time four wheel drive	全时四轮驱动
GAS	gasoline	汽油
GAWR	gross axle weight rating	轴额定总质量,额定轴载荷
GDI	gasoline direct injection	汽油直接喷射
GDL	gaseous-discharge lamp	气体放电灯
GEN	generator	发电机
GL	①gear lubricant ② grand luxury	①齿轮油 ②特豪华的
GM	General Motors Corporation	(美)通用汽车公司
GND 或 GRD	ground	搭铁
GPM 或 gpm	gallons per mile	加仑数每英里
GPS	global positioning system	全球卫星定位系统
GT	grand touring car	高性能轿车
GVW	gross vehicle weight	车辆(最大)总质量
HAC	high altitude compensator	高海拔补偿器

APPENDIX A ABBREVIATIONS OF AUTOMOTIVE ENGLISH

Continued

HB	high beam	远光
H/B 或 HB	hand back	舱背式(车身)
HC	hydrocarbon	碳氢化合物
HDC	hill descent control	陡坡缓降(控制)
HEI	high energy ignition	高能点火
HEV	hybrid electric vehicle	混合动力电动汽车
H-fuse	high current fuse	大电流熔断器
HID	high-intensity discharge	高强度放电
HMI	Human Machine Interface	人机界面
HOS	heated oxygen sensor	加热型氧传感器
HT	hard top	(轿车)硬顶
HV	hybrid vehicle	混合动力车
HVAC	heating, ventilation, air conditioning	供暖、通风和空调
IA	intake air	进气
IAC	idle air control	怠速(空气)控制
IAT	intake air temperature	进气温度
IATS	intake air temperature sensor	进气温度传感器
IC	①ignition control ②integrated circuit	①点火控制 ②集成电路
ICE	internal combustion engine	内燃机
I/C	intercooler	中冷器
ICP	injection control pressure	喷射控制压力
ICM	ignition control module	点火控制模块
IDI	integrated direct ignition	整体式直接点火
	indirect (diesel) injection	柴油机间接喷射
IFI	indirect fuel injection	(柴油机)间接燃油喷射
IG	ignition	点火
I/M 或 IM	inspection and maintenance	检查和维护
IMA	Intersection Movement Assist	交叉路口移动辅助系统
I/P	instrument panel	仪表板
i-VTEC	intelligent VTEC	智能型可变配气正时和气门升程控制装置
ISC	idle speed control	怠速控制
ISO	International Standardization Organization	国际标准化组织
ITS	Intelligent Transportation Systems	智能交通系统
KD	knock down	散件就地装配
KS	knock sensor	爆震传感器

Continued

L	①liter ②low ③luxe 或 luxury	①升 ②低的 ③豪华的
LAN	local area network	局域网
LB	①lift back ②low beam	①(车身)翘尾式 ②(前照灯)近光
lb	pound	磅
LCD	liquid crystal display	液晶显示器
LED	light emitting diode	发光二极管
LEV	low emission vehicle	低排放汽车
LF	left front	左前
LHD	left hand drive	左方驾驶
LIDAR	laser intensity direction and ranging	激光强度定向与测距,激光雷达
LLC	long-life coolant	长效冷却液
LNG	liquefied natural gas	液化天然气
LPG	liquified petroleum gas	液化石油气
LR	left rear	左后
LSD	limited slip differential	防滑式差速器
LSPV	load sensing proportioning valve	感载比例阀
LUS	lock up solenoid valve	锁止电磁阀
LX	luxury	豪华
MAF	mass air flow	空气质量流量,质量型空气流量
MF	maintenance free	免维护
MFI	multiport fuel injection	多点燃油喷射
MIL	malfunction indicator lamp	故障指示灯
MLPS	manual lever position sensor	手动变速杆位置传感器
MON	motor octane number	马达法辛烷值
MPG 或 mpg	miles per gallon	英里数每加仑
MPH	miles per hour	英里数每时
MPI	①multipoint injection ②multiport injection	多点燃油喷射
MPV	multipurpose vehicle	多用途(汽)车
MS	mud and snow	(轮胎)泥雪地,全天候
MT	manual transmission	手动变速器
N	①neutral ②Newton ③nitrogen	①(变速器)空挡 ②牛顿 ③氮
NA	not available	不提供
NC	normally closed	常闭
NDS	neutral drive switch	空挡起动开关
NHTSA	National Highway Traffic Safety Administration	(美)国家公路交通安全署

APPENDIX A ABBREVIATIONS OF AUTOMOTIVE ENGLISH

Continued

NLGI	National Lubricating Grease Institute	全美润滑脂学会
NO	normally open	常开(的)
NORM	normal position	通常位置
NOX	nitrogen oxide	氮氧化物
NTC	negative temperature coefficient	负温度系数
OBD	on board diagnostic	车载诊断装置
OC	oxidation catalytic converter	氧化催化转换器
oct	octane number	辛烷值
OCV	oil control valve	机油控制阀
OD	outer diameter	外径
O/D	overdrive	(变速器)超速挡
OEM	original equipment manufacturer	原装设备制造商[厂]
OH 或 O/H	overhaul	大修
OHC	overhead camshaft	顶置凸轮轴
OHV	overhead valve	顶置气门
OL 或 OP	open loop	开环
OPT	option	选装件
OS 或 O2S	oxygen sensor	氧传感器
O/S	oversize	加大尺寸
PAIR	pulsed secondary air injection	脉冲二次空气喷射
PC	passenger car	乘用车,小客车
PCM	powertrain control module	动力系统控制模块
PCV	positive crankcase ventilation	曲轴箱强制通风
PFI	port fuel injection	进气口燃油喷射
PGM-FI	programmed fuel injection	程控燃油喷射
PIP	position indicator pulse	(曲轴)位置指示器脉冲
PKB	parking brake	驻车制动器
PM	particulate matter	微粒
PN 或 P/N	①park/neutral ②part/number	①驻车挡/空挡 ②零件号
PNP	park/neutral position	驻车挡空挡位置
PROM	programmable read only memory	可编程序只读存储器
PS	power steering	动力转向
PSA	Peugeot/Citroen SA	标致/雪铁龙公司
PSC	power steering control	动力转向控制
PSI/psi	pound per square inch	磅每平方英寸

Continued

PSP	power steering pressure	动力转向液压
PTC	positive temperature coefficient	正温度系数
PTO	power take-off	取力器,动力输出轴
PTOX	periodic trap oxidizer	间歇捕集式氧化器
PU	pickup	轻型客货两用车,皮卡
PV	proportioning valve	比例阀
PWR	①power ②power position	①电源 ②(自动变速器)强力位置
QA	quality assurance	质量保证
RAM	random access memory	随机存储器
R&D	research and development	研究与开发
R&I	remove and install	拆卸和安装
R&R	remove and repair	拆卸并修理
RAV4	recreational active vehicle 4WD	四轮驱动灵巧型休闲车
R/B	relay block	继电器盒
REEV	Range extended electric vehicle	增程式电动汽车
REF	reference	参照,基准
REV	reverse	(变速器)倒挡
RHD	right-hand drive	右侧驾驶
RKE	remote keyless entry	无线遥控门锁
RM	relay module	继电器模件
r/min	revolutions per minute	转/分
ROM	read only memory	只读存储器
RON	research octane number	研究法辛烷值
RPM 或 rpm	revolutions per minute	发动机转速
RR	right rear	右后
RU	running	运转,运行
RV	recreational vehicle	休闲车
RWD	rear wheel drive	后轮驱动
SAE	Society of Automotive Engineers	美国汽车工程师学会
SASV	secondary air switching valve	二次空气转换阀
SBS	supercharger bypass solenoid	增压器废气旁通电磁阀
SC	supercharger	增压器
SCB	supercharger bypass	增压器废气旁通
SCV	swirl control valve	湍流控制阀
SDN	sedan	轿车

APPENDIX A ABBREVIATIONS OF AUTOMOTIVE ENGLISH

Continued

sec	secondary	第二的,从属的,副的
SEFI 或 SFI	sequential electronic fuel injection	电子顺序燃油喷射
sfc	specific fuel consumption	功率时间质量油耗,比油耗
SGL	super grand luxurious	超豪华
SI	spark ignition	火花点火
SKD	semi knock down	半散件组装
SLA	short long arm	(悬架)长短(横摆)臂
SLP	selection lever position	变速杆位置
SOHC	single overhead camshaft	单顶置凸轮轴
SOL	solenoid	电磁阀,带活动衔铁的电磁线圈
SPD	speed	转速,车速
SPEC	specification	规格,技术参数
SPI	single point injection	单点燃油喷射
SPL	smoke puff limiter	烟雾限止器
SPV	special purpose vehicle	专用汽车
SRI	service reminder indicator	维护指示灯
SRS	supplemental restraint system	辅助约束系统
SRT	system readiness test	系统准备状态测试
SS	shift solenoid	换挡电磁阀
SST	special service tools	专用维修工具
ST	scan tool	故障诊断仪
STC	stability & traction control	稳定性和牵引力控制(装置)
STD	standard	标准
STLR 或 stlr	semitrailer	半挂车
SUV	sport utility vehicle	运动型多用途车,多用途跑车
SW 或 S/W	switch	开关
SYS	system	系统
T/A	transaxle	变速驱动桥
TAC	①tachometer ②throttle actuator control	①转速表 ②节气门执行器控制
TACH	tachometer	转速表
TB	throttle body	节气门体
TBI	throttle body (fuel) injection	节气门体燃油喷射
TBT	throttle body temperature	节气门体温度
TC 或 T/C	①traction control ②turbocharger	①牵引力控制 ②(废气)涡轮增压器
TCC	torque converter clutch	变矩器锁止离合器

Continued

TCCP	torque converter clutch pressure	变矩器锁止离合器液压
TCM	transmission control module	变速器控制模块
TCS	traction control system	牵引力控制装置
TCV	timing control valve	正时控制阀
TD	turbo diesel	涡轮增压柴油机
TDC	top dead center	上止点
TDI	turbo direct injection	涡轮增压直接喷射
TFI	thick film ignition	厚膜点火
TEP	transmission fluid pressure	变速器液压
TL	tubeless tire	无内胎轮胎
T/M	transmission	变速器
TOHC 或 tohc	twin overhead camshaft	顶置双凸轮轴
TP	throttle position	节气门位置
TRC	traction control system	牵引力控制系统
TRK 或 trk	truck	货车,卡车
TRS	transmission range selection	变速器挡位选择
TURBO 或 turbo	turbocharge	涡轮增压
TVS	thermal vacuum switch	温控真空开关
TVV	thermal vacuum valve	温控真空阀
TWC	three way catalytic converter	三效催化转换器
TWC + OC	three way oxidation catalytic converter	三效氧化催化转换器
UI	unit injector	泵—喷油器
UIS	unit injector system	泵—喷油器装置
UJ 或 U-joint	universal joint	万向节
ULEV	ultra-low emission vehicle	超低排放车辆
UP	unit pump	(柴油机)单体泵
UPS	unit pump system	单体泵装置
U/S	undersize	缩小尺寸
V2I	vehicle to infrastructure	车—路
V2P	vehicle to pedestrian	车—行人
V2V	vehicle to vehicle	车—车
V2X	vehicle to everything	车——切(车、路、人等)
VAC	vacuum	真空
VAF	volume air flow	体积型空气流量
VAT	vane air temperature	叶片(式空气流量计中)空气温度

APPENDIX A ABBREVIATIONS OF AUTOMOTIVE ENGLISH

Continued

VC	viscous clutch [coupling]	黏液离合器
VCM	vehicle control module	车辆控制模块
VCRM	variable control relay module	可调控继电器模块
VCV	vacuum control valve	真空控制阀
VIN	vehicle identification number	车辆识别代号
VIS	variable geometry intake system	可变几何形状进气系统
VR	voltage regulator	电压调节器
VSA	vehicle stability auxiliary control	车辆稳定性辅助控制
VSC	vehicle stability control	车辆稳定性控制装置
VSS	vehicle speed sensor	车速传感器
VSV	vacuum solenoid valve	真空电磁阀
VSV	vacuum switching valve	真空开关阀
VTEC	variable timing and lift electronic control	可变配气正时和气门升程电子控制装置
VTV	vacuum transmitting valve	真空传输阀
w/b 或 wb	wheel base	轴距
WG 或 WGN	wagon	旅行车
WOT	wide open throttle	节气门全开
WOTS	wide open throttle switch	节气门全开开关
WSS	wheel speed sensor	轮速传感器
WU-OC	warm up oxidation catalytic converter	暖机氧化催化转换器
WU-TEC	warm up three way catalytic converter	暖机三效催化转换器
ZEV	zero emission vehicle	零排放车辆
2WD	two wheel drive	两轮驱动
4WD	four wheel drive	四轮驱动
4GR	fourth gear	第四挡
4WS	four wheel steering	四轮转向

APPENDIX B MAIN CONSTANT AUTOMOBILE PARTS

Engine	发动机
engine block	汽缸体
cylinder line	汽缸套
cylinder head	汽缸盖
cylinder head cover	气门室盖
cylinder head gasket	汽缸垫
rear main bearing cover	后主轴承盖
main bearing cap	主轴承盖
oil pan	油底壳
piston	活塞
piston ring	活塞环
piston pin	活塞销
connecting rod	连杆
connecting rod cap	连杆盖
flywheel	飞轮
crankshaft	曲轴
crankshaft timing gear	曲轴正时齿轮
crankshaft sprocket	曲轴正时链轮
camshaft	凸轮轴
camshaft timing gear	凸轮轴正时齿轮
camshaft sprocket	凸轮轴正时链轮
camshaft bearing bush	凸轮轴衬套
valve	气门
valve rocker arm	气门摇臂
valve spring	气门弹簧
valve guide	气门导管
rocker shaft bracket	摇臂轴承座
oil pipe	油管

APPENDIX B MAIN CONSTANT AUTOMOBILE PARTS

Continued

oil flexible hose	机油软管
oil filler cap	机油盖
dipstick	机油标
oil pump	机油泵
oil pump gears	油泵齿轮
oil suction pipe joint	进油管接头
oil filter	机油滤清器
radiator	散热器
radiator shutter	散热器百叶窗
fan	风扇
water pump	水泵
water tube	水管
engine water jacket	发动机水套
fuel pump	汽油泵
fuel pump bracket	汽油泵支架
fuel filer	燃油滤清器
fuel tank	燃油箱
air cleaner	空气滤清器
fuel injector	喷油嘴
needle valve	针阀
Chassis	**底盘**
transmission	变速器
gearbox housing	变速器壳
shift lever	变速杆
shift lever handle	变速杆手柄
input shaft	输入轴
planet pinion	行星齿轮
first driven gear	一挡从动齿轮
reverse driving gear	倒挡驱动齿轮
synchromesh	同步器
accelerator pedal	油门踏板
clutch	离合器
clutch plate	离合器片
clutch pedal pad	离合器踏板
clutch pedal lever	离合器踏板臂
(clutch) main cylinder	(离合器)主缸

Continued

main cylinder piston	主缸活塞
coupling	耦合器
turbine	涡轮
turbine bearing	涡轮轴承
drive shaft	传动轴
universal joint	万向节
spider	十字轴
shaft tube yoke	万向节叉
yoke shaft	传动轴管
differential	差速器
differential case	差速器壳
final drive housing	主传动器壳
chassis frame	车架
front beam axle	前桥
steering knuckle	转向节
steering knuckle pivot	转向节销
leaf spring	钢板弹簧
coil spring	螺旋弹簧
torsion bar	扭杆弹簧
shock absorber	减振器
tired wheel	轮辋
tire	轮胎
inner tube	内胎
inner tube valve	内胎气门嘴
tube air valve	气门芯
steering gear	转向器
steering wheel	转向盘
steering shaft	转向轴
service brake pedal	制动踏板
parking brake handle	手制动杆
parking brake cable	停车制动绳
brake cylinder	制动轮缸
brake band	制动带
friction lining	制动蹄摩擦衬片
brake drum	制动鼓
floating shoe	浮动蹄

APPENDIX B MAIN CONSTANT AUTOMOBILE PARTS

Continued

brake disk	制动盘
friction pad	摩擦块
floating caliper	浮动钳
friction disk	摩擦盘
Body	**车身**
front wheel valance	前轮挡泥板
roof front top rail	车身前横梁
front bumper	前保险杠
hood	发动机舱盖
floor panel	地板,底板
trunk lid	行李舱盖
fender	翼子板
front door	前车门
front panel	前护板
sun visor	遮阳板
mirror	后视镜
grad handle	把手
ash tray	烟灰盒
arm-rest	扶手
inside door handle	车门内手柄
outside door handle	车门外手柄
door lock knob	门内锁止按钮
instrument panel	仪表板
air bag	安全气囊
seat	座椅
seat cushion	座椅垫
seat back	座椅靠背
safety belt	安全带
Electrical Equipment	**电气设备**
windscreen washer	风窗清洗器
windscreen wiper	刮水器
battery	蓄电池
generator	发电机
generator regulator	发电机调节器
starter	起动器

Continued

spark plug	火花塞
ignition coil	点火线圈
ignition distributor	点火分电器
magneto	磁电机
headlamp	前照灯
turn signal	转向指示灯
Electric Vehicle	**电动汽车**
on-board energy source	车载能源
propulsion system	驱动系统
electric drive	电驱动系统
electric power train	电动动力系统
hybrid power train	混合动力系统
drive motor	驱动电机
regenerative braking	制动能量回收系统
power battery system	动力蓄电池系统
battery carrier	电池托架
electric chassis	电平台
charging inlet	充电插孔
power cable	动力电缆
battery overheat warning device	电池过热报警装置
residual capacity gauge	剩余电量显示器
motor over current warning device	电机过流报警装置
motor over revolution warning device	电机超速报警装置
convertor	变换器
inventor	逆变器
rectifier	整流器
chopper	斩波器
secondary cell	单体蓄电池
cell block	蓄电池电芯组
traction battery enclosure	动力蓄电池箱
swapping traction battery enclosure	快换动力蓄电池箱
battery pack	蓄电池包
ventilation device	排气装置
high voltage fuse	高压熔断器
high voltage relay	高压继电器

REFERENCES

[1] J. Y. Wong. *Theory of Ground Vehicle* [M]. Fourth Edition. Hoboken, New Jersey: John Wiley & Sons, Inc., 2008.

[2] A. E. Schaller. *Total Automotive Technology* [M]. Delmar Learning, a division of Thomson Learning, Inc., 2004.

[3] Rajesh Rajamani. *Vehicle Dynamics and Control* [M]. New York: Springer Science Business Media, Inc., 2012.

[4] 黄汽驰. 汽车专业英语[M]. 北京:机械工业出版社,2017.

[5] 宋进桂,徐永亮. 新能源汽车专业英语[M]. 北京:机械工业出版社,2020.

[6] M. Ehsani, Y. Gao, et al. *Modern Electric, Hybrid Electric, and Fuel Cell Vehicles* [M]. Third Edition. Florida: Taylor & Francis Group, 2018.

[7] 闫建来. 智能网联汽车导论[M]. 北京:机械工业出版社,2019.

[8] Henning Wallentowitz. 汽车工程学 III:汽车安全系统(英文版)[M]. 北京:机械工业出版社,2009.

[9] V. K. Kukkala, J. Tunnell, et al. *Advanced Driver-Assistance Systems* [J]. IEEE Consumer Electronics Magazine, August 2018:18-25.

[10] Radovan Miucic. Connected Vehicles-Intelligent Transportation Systems[M]. Springer Nature Switzerland AG., 2019.